T0034108

Coin of the Realm

Other Books by Carl Phillips

POETRY

The Rest of Love
Rock Harbor
The Tether
Pastoral
From the Devotions
Cortège
In the Blood

TRANSLATION

Sophocles' *Philoctetes*

Coin of the Realm

Essays on the Life and Art of Poetry

CARL PHILLIPS

Graywolf Press
SAINT PAUL, MINNESOTA

Publication of this volume is made possible in part by a grant provided by the
Minnesota State Arts Board, through an appropriation by the Minnesota State
Legislature; a grant from the Wells Fargo Foundation Minnesota; and a grant from
the National Endowment for the Arts, which believes that a great nation deserves
great art. Significant support has also been provided by the Bush Foundation;
Target, Marshall Field's and Mervyn's with support from the Target Foundation;
the McKnight Foundation; and other generous contributions from foundations,
corporations, and individuals. To these organizations and individuals we offer our
heartfelt thanks.

Published by Graywolf Press
2402 University Avenue, Suite 203
Saint Paul, Minnesota 55114
All rights reserved.

www.graywolfpress.org

Published in the United States of America
Printed in Canada

ISBN 1-55597-401-5

2 4 6 8 9 7 5 3 1
First Graywolf Printing, 2004

Library of Congress Control Number: 2003112163

Cover design: Scott Sorenson
Cover photo: Jeffrey Coolidge, Iconica

Reprint Acknowledgments

Contents

I

II

III

I

The Case for Beauty

Beauty, at least when it is referred to by that name—suffers the same treatment by too many contemporary poets (and students of poetry) as does authority in poetry. It gets dismissed as naïve, or irrelevant, or somehow on the wrong side of the field on whose *other* side we are all assumed to have happily set up camp together. But to hold that assumption is to exercise the very sort of authority that the mysterious "they" hold suspect. It also suggests that beauty is monolithic, one-dimensional, and finally inorganic—without the capacity for evolution, without susceptibility to time.

It is easy enough to trace this attitude in terms of history, but in the end as uninteresting as is anything that's easy. Curious only; unseductive.

About beauty, as about all other versions of abstraction (which includes the abstraction of history), there is a general nervousness that I see as symptomatic of an ever-increasing unwillingness to think athletically—that is, *without* (as opposed to *in concert with*) the safer (*easier*) toeholds of the concrete. And that unwillingness looks sometimes sore in danger of becoming an inability, even as the merely vestigial must eventually disappear.

Equally on the rise: an unwillingness to be held accountable—to take responsibility, which is what authority requires; it forces the artist to take a stand and to reckon with such issues as intention, meaning, self, and their relationship to what Marianne Moore calls "the genuine." And since abstraction is generally conflated with authority—as, erroneously, the concrete is not—what hope for beauty?

The authority of a plum is different from that of, say, beauty, but no less complex.

There is also the general conviction about beauty that all has been said about it; in that respect, it apparently resembles light and shadow, the body (which is becoming more and more categorized as an abstraction itself, has anyone noticed?), water, and—in sudden flight—the dead: low, across it. . . . The point about beauty is to see it. The point of the poem is not to say anything about beauty, but to enact the vision of it. As for statements, in a poem about beauty: that's precisely where, if it has been successfully enacted on the page, the vision's work begins.

As the philosopher once said, "Oh well—all's either lost or it is not," and returned to that from which he'd been distracted:

A star

A sky

A snowfield

The fish,

the vine—twisted,
bloomless—

whose ugliness gets
outvoted by its having
alone of its kind
survived

The victory that
knows to blush,

and the one that can't

⸻

Not *as if* fine distinctions mattered,
but *because* they do

Back home,
they baled the hay, they
roll it, here

⸻

Magdalene,
Magdalene—

in equal parts,

"The Craven"

"She-Who-Kisses-the-Bloody-Wounds"

⸻

One of those perhaps

silos through which by
day the smaller carrion-birds

pass,
wanting and unimpeded

This is my case for Beauty.

Myth and Fable: Their Place in Poetry

The difference between myth and fable? Myth is a verbal mapping out of what is known but not understood—or wasn't understood, anyway, at the time of the myth's origin: the facts of eclipse, drought, incest, sudden rage, why the hyacinth's petals have the markings that they do, why the Nile flows upward, why the reeds along the Nile's banks make the sounds they make when the wind is upon them, what happens after death, what is death—these are some examples. Myth, as Randall Jarrell says, is "the story / We make of life." The human instinct is toward rationalization; words are the agents of rationalization that precede science, and they remain what we hold onto in those areas—the metaphysical—where science remains, thus far, inadequate. Cardiology cannot yet account entirely for the broken heart.

But if myth is our means of explaining, to ourselves, what we know but don't understand, then fable is how we convey what we have come to understand to those who are less experienced and are in need of instruction. I think of Aesop, whose fables inevitably end with an instructive moral. There is also that category of fables known as the fairy tale—those stories that portray childhood as the murky place it mostly is, in which to trust can be as treacherous as to disobey, and authority is no more stable than appearance—no more, no less. With the exception of the odd fairy godmother, the rescuing gods are absent from fable, and replaced by adult human beings or—back to Aesop— by thinly disguised, much-anthropomorphized talking animals whose story is narrated by an invisible, omniscient, and human teller of tales.

In his book *The Hero with a Thousand Faces,* Joseph Campbell puts forward the theory that there is finally a single collection of myths, an ur-mythology that all humans somehow inherit. Every culture, for example, seems to have a myth that addresses death and the afterlife. Given that mortality and a consciousness of it are among the defining characteristics of being human, it makes sense that every culture will attempt to explain the inexplicable. But then this ur-mythology gets filtered through the varying lenses of particular cultural experience. A coastal culture might reasonably think in terms of an afterlife that involves sailing past the visible horizon where, presumably, the world must end. A land-bound culture might not know of the sea—any afterlife will have to be relegated to the earth below or to what lies beyond what we can see of the sky. Even as climate is said to have generated not only distinctive architectures but entire sensibilities—compare Scandinavian culture with that of the Mediterranean—so, too, the way in which we account for the irrational will be via the compass points of what we do know and understand. It is very much as Xenophanes, the fifth-century BC Greek lyric poet, once said—that if cows could write, their gods would have hooves, and if fish could write, their gods would have scales and gills.

We can only know anything through the lenses of our own experience, and we will tend to explain what we don't understand through what we do. In this sense, mythology is a comforter of sorts, putting the seemingly meaningless within the context of meaning—that is, of nameability as a form of possession. Part of the pleasure of mythology has to do with ownership, with establishing superiority over that which threatens, psychologically, to overwhelm the part of us that is empirical.

Fable—especially in the context of the fairy tale—takes particular advantage of the empirical instinct in humans, that need to prove a thing through sensory experience, and becomes a means of pointing out the dangers of empiricism. More often than not, it is designed for children—designed by adults who have learned by trial and error, and conveyed in such a way as to instill fear. To some degree, fable would appear to be a means of helping children to do the impossible, namely, to ignore the empirical instinct. Part of the tale's purpose is to show the near-disasters that can result from undisciplined or unthinking behavior: running away from home, spending too much time listening to strangers. But the tale achieves its effect by means of seduction, by the spinning of words in such a way as to make the listener a participant of sorts in the very behavior that could destroy. We *want* to listen, we want to follow, we want to touch, and taste. And the adult tale-teller knows that we want these, and manipulates our desire in the name of instruction.

But there are also fables whose point is to demonstrate the merits of a patient goodness—Cinderella is an example, as is Snow White. And yet, part of the eventual triumph of these two characters lies in a ready trust and belief in strangers—be they fairy godmothers or the seven dwarves. This kind of trust is exactly what we are told to avoid, in such tales as that of Little Red Riding Hood. A conundrum—behind which, possibly, is a lesson about discernment: that it is necessary and also unreliable; that all of our attempts to rationalize are finally themselves bounded by something like chance or fate or what can never be known exactly; that our knowledge is finite—there is a certain mortality to it that makes sense. Isn't mortality one of those human lenses through which, necessarily, we assign meaning to our individual experience?

Myth can incorporate fable, though I can think of no instances in the opposite direction. A good example of myth incorporating fable is the story of Daedalus and Icarus. The part that is myth is that which seeks to explain the conundrum that freedom should be the conduit for destruction—remember that the father and son have been imprisoned and that they have only escaped because of the artistic gifts of Daedalus, who has managed to craft wings from feathers and wax and reeds. Somewhere in the myth lies, as well, the human need to account for why art should be a conveyer of beauty and disaster and irreparable loss. But there is also moral instruction in the story—and this is where fable is concerned. Part of the lesson is that a child should obey a parent. As Ovid tells the story in his *Metamorphoses,* another implied lesson is that humans should not attempt to surpass their inherent nature—by rivaling the gods, which is what Daedalus ostensibly (unwittingly?) does when he transforms his son and himself into humans with the ability to fly—super-humans, one step closer, therefore, to the state of the gods.

Fable tends to offer us a set of archetypes. What is fable without, eventually, the wicked stepmother, the variously indifferent or abusive father, the rescuing soulmate in the form of Prince Charming, the ostracized—whether as the troll under the bridge, or the wart-marked witch, or the plainly ugly duckling, or the talking frog whose greatest wish is to be kissed? Myth, on the other hand, tends to suggest an instability to the apparently archetypal. Ares may be the god of war, the model of courage and violence that does not flinch, but at one point in Homer's *Iliad*, he runs howling and complaining from the battlefield after being wounded by Diomedes. Penelope is the model of the faithful, patient wife, stalling her suitors through a ten-year deception, in the belief that her husband Odysseus will return. But she is actually at the point of relenting, of agreeing to marry another, when Odysseus does walk in the door. And Orpheus, the archetypal lover who literally goes through hell to win his wife back from the dead, is finally unable to obey a simple command, to avoid turning back and looking at his wife as they exit hell—thus, he loses her all over again. Of course, Orpheus was an artist—a poet—and perhaps the myth means to say something about the artist's tendency to favor his own concerns over a love for others—a whole other archetype, altogether.

It is precisely because of their coming together around commonalities of human experience that myth and fable have such universal appeal. When the point of a myth is, say, to explain death, it doesn't matter whether the context is Babylonian—as in the *Gilgamesh* epic—or Roman, as in Book VI of Virgil's *Aeneid*, or Egyptian, or Native American. We understand the human fact of loss and the instinct to grieve and to understand loss, and it doesn't matter where that story takes place or in what time period, so long as we can see clearly the landmarks of loss, grief, and knowing, regardless of our own cultural background. Nor do we balk at the notion of a race between a tortoise and a hare, since the point is less about the identities of the participants—they could easily, for example, have been the snail and the cheetah—and more about idle boasting and about consistency and patience. And it is this that makes mythology and fable ideal teaching tools—their ability to be relevant in a classroom to students of all colors, all ages, all nationalities, both sexes.

We have another role with respect to myth and fable, other than that of inheritors. We are also the living version of the written, we give flesh to word, and in that sense are custodians of myth, responsible not just for the fact of its survival but for how—in what version—it will survive. We can retell, word for word, an ancient Greek myth, which is one way to keep it alive—by remembering. But every time we write of human experience through (necessarily) the lens of our own experience, we are in essence giving an updated variation of the myth: a simultaneous keeping alive and pushing forward of an inherited tradition of what it is to be human. This is also what poetry does. A love poem has as its subject one of the oldest aspects of human experience; it participates, from the start, in an inherited tradition of experience. As well, it inherits a long tradition of poems about love. What makes a love poem necessary anymore is that contexts of time, place, and history are in constant shift, and love's definition will shift in accordance with context. What makes for an original love poem is its ability to show us something new about a subject we may well think we've figured out. What makes it possible to write an original love poem is that we are, again, each in possession of our own lens of experience—no one can ever know the world precisely as each of us uniquely does. This is what is being referred to when Eliot speaks of the relationship between tradition and the individual talent, this latter being what I mean by my term "lens of experience." It is the reason why the fact of Homer does not obviate the need for Shakespeare, nor does Shakespeare obviate the need for Emily Dickinson or Langston Hughes.

Poetry shares, then, with myth and fable the strategy of building story around human experience, as a means of explaining that experience, or attempting to, and as a means of (sometimes) offering instruction regarding that experience. Also shared is a motivation. The reason I began writing—and continue to write—springs from a desire to understand in my own terms what is insufficiently understandable in the terms made available to me. But a shared strategy and motivation will not make myth out of poetry. Myth and fable are distinguishable by their applicability across time and cultural differences. When poetry has this quality, it is called—or I call it—resonant. This resonance gives poetry the valence and stamina of myth, at which point it can fairly be called great poetry. Some poetry takes on the mythic subject—love, death, loss, fear—but grounds that subject in such specifically autobiographical detail that we learn little more from reading the poem than that poet X has had such-and-such experience. The poem then has more the qualities of the journal or diary, its effect may be more cathartic than instructive (both for reader and writer), more therapy than education, more history than myth, less resonant than reportorial. Which is not for a moment to say that such writing is not poetry, of which there are many different orders.

Part of the appeal of myth and fable to our imaginations is that these archetypal stories are and are not our stories. To read them is to see immediately our relationship to and divergence from those stories—and something almost kinetic occurs upon such a realization. Two new narratives are set into motion—the narratives of our distance *from* and approximation *to* the mythic. I would say that the majority of poems that revisit myth and fable fall into this category, as opposed to the category in which we choose simply to retell the myth/fable, without any updating or otherwise altering of context—in those cases, the myth gets retold, it does not get re-seen, seen in a new light. But to revisit myth from our own more recent experience can often yield precisely this re-visioning effect.

The ways of revisiting myth are numerous. A popular one is the questioning-of-authority method: the myth itself being the authority under interrogation. The usual strategy here is to take a different point of view within the myth or fable—that is, the poet becomes the speaker for someone who usually is assigned no voice in the narrative. This can be an ideal way to discuss a particular genre of poetry—that of the persona poem, and the various reasons for writing from one point of view over another, beginning with the fact that persona means "mask." What is the relationship between speaker and poet? Given that a mask's uses are many—hiding, deceiving, protecting—what is the reason for masks in a given poem? Consider the effects of two rather different treatments of the Little Red Riding Hood story, in the poems of Agha Shahid Ali and Martha Collins:

The Wolf's Postscript to "Little Red Riding Hood"

First, grant me my sense of history:
I did it for posterity,
for kindergarten teachers
and a clear moral:

Little girls shouldn't wander off
in search of strange flowers,
and they mustn't speak to strangers.

And then grant me my generous sense of plot:
Couldn't I have gobbled her up
right there in the jungle?
Why did I ask her where her grandma lived?
As if I, a forest-dweller,
didn't know of the cottage
under the three oak trees
and the old woman who lived there
all alone?
As if I couldn't have swallowed her years before?

And you may call me the Big Bad Wolf,
now my only reputation.
But I was no child-molester
though you'll agree she was pretty.

And the huntsman:
Was I sleeping while he snipped
my thick black fur
and filled me with garbage and stones?
I ran with that weight and fell down,
simply so children could laugh
at the noise of the stones
cutting through my belly,
at the garbage spilling out
with a perfect sense of timing,
just when the tale
should have come to an end.

━AGHA SHAHID ALI

The Good Gray Wolf

Wanted that red, wanted everything tucked inside
that red, that body, it seemed, turned inside out,
that walking flower, petals furled, leaved
by the trees by the forest path, the yellow basket
marking the center—

                    wanted to raise that rose
petal skin to my gray face, barely to brush
that warmth with my cold nose, but I knew she'd cry
for mercy, help, the mother who'd filled the basket
that morning, Wolf, she'd cry, Wolf, and she'd
be right, why should she try to see beyond
the fur, the teeth, the cartoon tongue wet
with anticipation?

             And so I hid behind
a tree as she passed on the path, then ran, as you know,
to her grandmother's house, but not as they say, I knocked
and when she answered I asked politely for her
advice. And then, I swear, she offered me tea,
her bonnet, an extra gown, she gave me more
than advice, she tucked me into a readied bed,
she smoothed my rough fur, I felt light
as a flower, myself, stamened and stemmed in her
sweet sheets.

              Not ate her, you see, but rather became
her, flannel chest for the red head, hood
that hid the pearl that when I touched it flushed
and shone. What big eyes! and she opened the cape,
What ears! and she took my head to her heart, teeth,
tongue, mouth to her mouth, and opened everything,
opened me, Woof-woof, she cried, Sweet rose,
I crooned, crawling inside, wolf to flower,

gray to rose, grandmother into child
again, howl to whisper, dagger to cloak,
my mother father animal arms, disarmed
by love, were all she ever dreamed of.

↞ MARTHA COLLINS

Clearly it is possible to look at the same fable, from the same point of view—the wolf's, in this case—and still come up with poems with two distinctly different intentions and possibilities for interpretation. On one hand, Ali's wolf is, stanza by stanza, half justifying his behavior and half correcting the common conclusions about his motivations. But he does this in terms that lead me to believe that Ali's point is less about the wolf than about art itself—of theater, in particular—about the intentions of art vs. its actual achievements, about the audience and the artist's relationship to it. Note how of the four stanzas, three make specific mention of artistic concerns: a desire for posterity and an intention to instruct are announced in stanza one, stanza two concerns plot, three the problem of typecasting, and stanza four the need for a sense of timing, as well as the notion that the artist should be willing to suffer in the *service* of art, given the wolf's suggestion that he wasn't sleeping when he was cut open, but that he was willingly cut open so as to be able to entertain, even at the end—in a sort of musical comedy ("I ran with that weight and fell down, / simply so children could laugh / at the noise of the stones / cutting through my belly"). In the end, Ali's poem isn't very much about the story of Little Red Riding Hood at all, but about story itself, and the telling of it.

Collins's poem takes as its start what Ali's poem mentions only fleetingly, the notion that the wolf could be considered a child-molester. But it goes beyond that, past the first stanza's announcement of the wolf's desire for Little Red Riding Hood (a sexual desire for deflowering the virgin, as the botanical imagery makes clear), beyond the wolf's realization that deception will be necessary, to the news that puts the wolf's lust in a comparatively benign light: the grandmother, who we are usually told gets eaten by the wolf, serves as a kind of pimp, as she provides the means of deception by which the wolf will finally have Little Red Riding Hood for his own—which he does, by poem's end, in a scene that suggests Little Red Riding Hood's willingness to have sex—blurring our notions of force and consent in the area of sex—even as identity gets increasingly blurred: who exactly is having sex with the girl—her grandmother, her parents, human or animal, and what is so terrible if it amounts to love?

There is something vaguely sadistic about many fables—those that seek to instruct children, by means of fear, away from the very seduction that is the fable's strategy (seduction via storytelling itself). Collins's poem speaks in part to this complicated aspect of the storyteller, by questioning the authority of the adult world; the poem suggests that if instruction is a part of fable, then that instruction might well be against the instructors themselves, or should be. And, at the same time, Collins's poem questions the moral assumptions of the fairy tale—what makes the wolf so bad? How innocent *is* the little girl? Who is above or beyond desire?

Similar questions are raised in Louise Glück's "Gretel in Darkness."

This is the world we wanted.
All who would have seen us dead
are dead. I hear the witch's cry
break in the moonlight through a sheet
of sugar: God rewards.
Her tongue shrivels into gas. . . .

       Now, far from women's arms
and memory of women, in our father's hut
we sleep, are never hungry.
Why do I not forget?
My father bars the door, bars harm
from this house, and it is years.

No one remembers. Even you, my brother,
summer afternoons you look at me as though
you meant to leave,
as though it never happened.
But I killed for you. I see armed firs,
the spires of that gleaming kiln—

Nights I turn to you to hold me
but you are not there.
Am I alone? Spies
hiss in the stillness, Hansel,
we are there still and it is real, real,
that black forest and the fire in earnest.

What gets upended here is the assumption—or the many assumptions—of
fairy tale itself: that the parental world is safe, that the strange and foreign
is dangerous, that the dangerous is by definition a bad thing. But note
how, in the second stanza of Glück's poem, there is an emphasis on the
word "bars"—as verb, in the sense of protecting, but the phrasing reminds
us that to bar a thing out is to bar something else in. Also in that stanza,
we are told that "harm" is what has been barred out—we are also told we
are now "far from women's arms / and memory of women"—it is hard
not to put the two together, as if harm and women have become somehow synonymous—which may once have been true in the person of the
witch, but Gretel, our speaker, is now a woman herself, barred in with her
brother and her father, both idle in "the world we wanted." Gretel—who
has killed for her brother, is no idler by nature—is barred from her own
kind, by which we begin to understand she means not just women, but
individuals with a taste for life's edge. The authority questioned here is
the one that suggests there are limited places for a woman, that the best
place is under the guardianship of her male family, and that this place is
necessarily a place of joy. More than retelling a fairy tale, Glück manages
here to make what we might call a feminist statement, at the very least
a statement regarding societal assumptions about freedom, and society's
confining definitions for the roles of men and women—and of children
and adults. Her strategy (employed, as well, by Tennyson in his "Ulysses")
is to look past the time period of the story itself, and then to ask what
happens after the end—what are the details contained in the phrase "and
they lived happily ever after?"

Another way to question a myth's authority is from outside the myth,
within the context of later experience. W. H. Auden's "Musée des Beaux
Arts" suggests that, yes, myth may be archetypal, but the archetypal has no

power to stop the world—its resonance does not extend to the worlds of commerce, agriculture, daily life essentially.

> About suffering they were never wrong,
> The Old Masters: how well they understood
> Its human position; how it takes place
> While someone else is eating or opening a window or just walking
>   dully along;
> How, when the aged are reverently, passionately waiting
> For the miraculous birth, there always must be
> Children who did not specially want it to happen, skating
> On a pond at the edge of the wood:
> They never forgot
> That even the dreadful martyrdom must run its course
> Anyhow in a corner, some untidy spot
> Where the dogs go on with their doggy life and the torturer's horse
> Scratches its innocent behind on a tree.
>
> In Brueghel's *Icarus,* for instance: how everything turns away
> Quite leisurely from the disaster; the ploughman may
> Have heard the splash, the forsaken cry,
> But for him it was not an important failure; the sun shone
> As it had to on the white legs disappearing into the green
> Water; and the expensive delicate ship that must have seen
> Something amazing, a boy falling out of the sky,
> Had somewhere to get to and sailed calmly on.

Suffering, then, is seen in perspective by everyone but the sufferer himself, says Auden. This doesn't alter the lessons to be gleaned from and the philosophical trajectory initiated by our reading the myth of Daedalus and Icarus—but neither do those trajectories and lessons outweigh or negate a world response that is perhaps worse than indifference—it is a not-knowing, an ignorance of there being any suffering to which to *be* indifferent.

Anne Sexton's revisiting of this same myth takes a slightly different perspective—about suffering, she is not indifferent, nor does she see suffering as the point of focus. Rather, suffering becomes a part of the price to be paid for triumph, and the price is apparently worth paying.

To a Friend Whose Work Has Come to Triumph

Consider Icarus, pasting those sticky wings on,
testing that strange little tug at his shoulder blade,
and think of that first flawless moment over the lawn
of the labyrinth. Think of the difference it made!
There below are the trees, as awkward as camels;
and here are the shocked starlings pumping past
and think of innocent Icarus who is doing quite well:
larger than a sail, over the fog and the blast
of the plushy ocean, he goes. Admire his wings!
Feel the fire at his neck and see how casually
he glances up and is caught, wondrously tunneling
into that hot eye. Who cares that he fell back to the sea?
See him acclaiming the sun and come plunging down
while his sensible daddy goes straight into town.

Note the tone of that final line—she could hardly be more clear about how *ordinary,* unappealing is the life of Daedalus, and how wonderful the life of the boy whose fault lay in *hubris,* his refusal to accept the limits laid out by his father, his trying to approach (as if to rival?) the sun itself. Sexton's revisiting of this myth ends up as a question of ethics, moral code, and who established it, or should. Note, by the way, how she does this within one of the oldest literary traditions, that of the English sonnet—this poem is also one where the moral argument is conducted by the relationship between content and form—the content itself defying the usual content deemed appropriate to the sonnet.

This relationship between form and content, and its role in how we interpret the poem's meaning, can be seen all the more when we contrast the formal strategies two poets employ when handling the same content—the same myth, in this instance. Compare, for example, William Carlos Williams's "Landscape with the Fall of Icarus."

According to Brueghel
when Icarus fell
it was spring

a farmer was ploughing
his field
the whole pageantry

of the year was
awake tingling
near

the edge of the sea
concerned
with itself

sweating in the sun
that melted
the wings' wax

unsignificantly
off the coast
there was

a splash quite unnoticed
this was
Icarus drowning

Williams has come up with a form that is mimetic not only of the order of events but of the various distribution of attention to those events in the Brueghel painting upon which the poem is based. In Sexton's poem, the form/content relationship conveys less about the details of the narrative than about how we are encouraged to *interpret* those details. Which is not to say, however, that Williams has no interest in interpretation; rather, he manages a sly ambiguity, by having Icarus on one hand be the point to which everything else in the poem (as well as our attention) emphatically leads; and on the other hand, Icarus is the last and the potentially least significant figure in the poem, certainly the one given the least amount of description. Where the two poems come together is in their stance that suffering is more incidental than the myth itself suggests; but see how differently this gets conveyed within the two poems? Again, this is evidence of how the same myth can be returned to repeatedly, each time with different results—not just from different writers, but even from the same writer: each time we return to a myth or fable, we see it different necessarily, because we return with deepened and broadened experience as readers and as writers.

~⁊∾

Robert Hayden's treatment of the Daedalus and Icarus myth has a different purpose altogether—authority isn't being questioned. Rather, this poem is an example of another category of poem, in which the existing myth is used as scaffolding across which a larger argument is laid out. I have mentioned that part of the point of the Daedalus and Icarus myth concerns freedom, and the ambiguity surrounding it as we learn that freedom can lead to disaster. In "O Daedalus, Fly Away Home," Hayden returns to this conundrum within the particular context of African American experience.

> Drifting night in the Georgia pines,
> coonskin drum and jubilee banjo.
> > Pretty Malinda, dance with me.
>
> Night is juba, night is conjo.
> > Pretty Malinda, dance with me.
>
> Night is an African juju man
> weaving a wish and a weariness together
> > to make two wings.
>
> > *O fly away home fly away*
>
> Do you remember Africa?
>
> > *O cleave the air fly away home*

My gran, he flew back to Africa,
just spread his arms and
      flew away home.

Drifting night in the windy pines;
night is a laughing, night is a longing.
      Pretty Malinda, come to me.

Night is a mourning juju man
weaving a wish and a weariness together
      to make two wings.

    O fly away home fly away

The title tells us to think of Daedalus—but the poem opens "in the Georgia pines," to immediately disorienting effect. How does this relate to the sorrows of Daedalus? Further, the scene laid out by the first two stanzas seems a pleasing one, of music, dance, and attractive dance partners. But once we know that juba is not only an African work-dance or dance for the dead, but also a dance performed by Southern plantation Negroes, the possibility opens that this poem takes place during the time of slavery in America, or in a period shortly thereafter. This would explain, too, why the juju man (medicine man, spirit worker) is trying to fashion a set of wings for escape; though, given that his work materials are "a wish and a weariness," success seems anything but certain. No wonder the juju man, by poem's end, is in mourning. But this poem is more than about a lack of ability to return home, which is the part that hearkens back to the original myth. Hayden brings a new dimension to the original myth—to the notion of freedom—by reminding us about the loss of memory of home that can quickly take hold of a displaced people. To remember is a kind of knowing—to be stripped of that knowledge is to be denied a measure of freedom, both intellectually and psychologically. There is a way, then, in which Hayden is making use of the Daedalus and Icarus myth to deepen the discussion about freedom, and to generate further examination of the history of African Americans in this country—in the course of which, he gives us a window onto the African American psyche—which, in turn, can resonate beyond that particular race of people to be an examination of the psychology of the exiled, the displaced, the alienated. As well, by aligning African American experience with Greek mythology, there's an implicit statement being made about the experience of a historically outcast people—namely, that their experience, their history, is of mythic proportions, is no less resonant, *and* instructive.

~~

I mentioned earlier how myth in particular is a means of comforting ourselves with an explanation for what seems to defy explanation. It presents in orderly form—that of narrative—what lacks order, and makes of the abstract something more concrete. There's a sense of completeness that recalls the effect of rhyme when it occurs in an otherwise unrhymed poem, namely, closure and the chance of harmony within the dissonant, to name a couple of possible effects.

What also occurs, though, is that the story that gets told tells something of the teller (which, again, is what Xenophanes was suggesting in the poem cited earlier). Even as the psychiatrist listens to the client's narrative not for the narrative alone but for another narrative implied by the more immediate one, so, too, I have often thought of poems as advance bulletins from the interior. Part of the urge toward fabulation—and poetry is a kind of fabulating—has to do with mapping consciousness itself. It sorts in the way that dream does—it is not coincidental at all that so many poems use dream as their initial framework. One such poem is Randall Jarrell's "The House in the Wood"—at one point, it is identified as "only a nightmare," one from which "No one wakes up, nothing happens." What the poem suggests is an urge toward ordering of a particular kind, to reduce psychic disjunction and anxiety.

> At the back of the houses there is the wood.
> While there is a leaf of summer left, the wood
>
> Makes sounds I can put somewhere in my song,
> Has paths I can walk, when I wake, to good
>
> Or evil: to the cage, to the oven, to the House
> In the Wood. It is a part of life, or of the story
>
> We make of life. But after the last leaf,
> The last light—for each year is leafless,

Each day is lightless, at the last—the wood begins
Its serious existence: it has no path,

No house, no story; it resists comparison . . .
One clear, repeated, lapping gurgle, like a spoon

Or a glass breathing, is the brook,
The wood's fouled midnight water. If I walk into the wood

As far as I can walk, I come to my own door,
The door of the House in the Wood. It opens silently:

On the bed is something covered, something humped
Asleep there, awake there—but what? I do not know.

I look, I lie there, and yet I do not know.
How far out my great echoing clumsy limbs

Stretch, surrounded only by space! For time has struck,
All the clocks are stuck now, for how many lives,

On the same second. Numbed, wooden, motionless,
We are far under the surface of the night.

Nothing comes down so deep but sound: a car, freight cars,
A high soft droning, drawn out like a wire

Forever and ever—is this the sound that Bunyan heard
So that he thought his bowels would burst within him?—

Drift on, on, into nothing. Then someone screams
A scream like an old knife sharpened into nothing.

It is only a nightmare. No one wakes up, nothing happens,
Except there is gooseflesh over my whole body—

And that too, after a little while, is gone.
I lie here like a cut-off limb, the stump the limb has left . . .

Here at the bottom of the world, what was before the world
And will be after, holds me to its black

Breasts and rocks me: the oven is cold, the cage is empty,
In the House in the Wood, the witch and her child sleep.

The poem's reference, of course, is to the same Hansel and Gretel story that was referred to by Louise Glück in "Gretel in Darkness." Unlike the Glück poem, however, we aren't entirely inside the fairy tale. Stanza three offers us the clues of the cage, the oven, and the House in the Wood—straightforward enough—but we are later told of such anachronisms as cars and freight cars. Where we are, precisely, is inside a wood, which is inside a tale, which is inside a nightmare, which is inside the consciousness of the dreamer—the speaker of the poem—who describes himself as clearly alienated from what we might think of as normal sensory experience: "I lie here like a cut-off limb, the stump the limb has left . . ." Rather than revisiting the fairy tale, the poem seeks a calmer space, prior to that in which will be delivered the story's less calming elements—murder, deception, loss, terror. The witch is a mother, at poem's end, peacefully asleep with her child. How she became the more terrifying figure in the Hansel and Gretel story isn't the point, apparently. One way to read Jarrell's poem is as a map of the shattered psyche, a poem in which the psyche names what it would return to, without being *able* to return to it. The urge is toward the lost mother figure—toward, particularly, the figure of unseparated mother and child. The poem itself reminds us that our urge toward fabulation arises from our need to rationalize both the *exterior* and *interior* aspects of our experience.

Another purpose that myth and fable serve in poetry is to offer the poet a means of putting forward his or her *ars poetica*—if we can call the Jarrell poem an instance of mapping out consciousness, we might consider as maps of aesthetic consciousness the different handlings of the Orpheus and Eurydice story in the poems of Jorie Graham and John Ashbery:

Orpheus and Eurydice

Up ahead, I know, he felt it stirring in himself already, the glance,
the darting thing in the pile of rocks,

already in him, there, shiny in the rubble, hissing Did you want to
                                                                    remain
completely unharmed?—

the point-of-view darting in him, shiny head in the ash-heap,

hissing Once upon a time, and then Turn now darling give me
                                                            that look

that perfect shot, give me that place where I'm erased. . . .

The thing, he must have wondered, could it be put to rest, there, in
                                                            the glance,
could it lie back down into the dustyness, giving its outline up?

When we turn to them—limbs, fields, expanses of dust called
                                            meadow and avenue—
will they be freed then to slip back in?

Because you see he could not be married to it anymore, this field with
                                                            minutes in it
called woman, its presence in him the thing called

future—could not be married to it anymore, expanse tugging his
                                                mind out into it,
tugging the wanting-to-finish out.

What he dreamed of was this road (as he walked on it), this
                                            dustyness,
but without their steps on it, their prints, without
song—

What she dreamed, as she watched him turning with the bend
in the road (can you
understand this?)—what she dreamed

was of disappearing into the seen

not of disappearing, lord, into the real—

And yes she could feel it in him already, up ahead, that
wanting-to-turn-and-
cast-the-outline-over-her

by his glance,

sealing the edges down,

saying I know you from somewhere darling, don't I,
saying You're the kind of woman who etcetera—

(Now the cypress are swaying) (Now the lake in the distance)
(Now the view-from-above, the aerial attack of *do you
remember?*)—

now the glance reaching her shoreline wanting only to be recalled,
now the glance reaching her shoreline wanting only to be taken in,

(somewhere the castle above the river)

(somewhere you holding this piece of paper)

(what will you do next?) (—feel it beginning?)

now she's raising her eyes, as if pulled from above,

now she's looking back into it, into the poison the beginning, giving herself to it, looking back into the eyes,

feeling the dry soft grass beneath her feet for the first time now the
                                                                    mind

looking into that which sets the _____ in motion and
                                                    seeing in there

a doorway open nothing on either side
(a slight wind now around them, three notes from up the hill)

through which morning creeps and the first true notes—

For they were deep in the earth and what is possible swiftly took hold.

☛ JORIE GRAHAM

And here is the Ashbery:

Syringa

Orpheus liked the glad personal quality
Of the things beneath the sky. Of course, Eurydice was a part
Of this. Then one day, everything changed. He rends
Rocks into fissures with lament. Gullies, hummocks
Can't withstand it. The sky shudders from one horizon
To the other, almost ready to give up wholeness.
Then Apollo quietly told him: "Leave it all on earth.
Your lute, what point? Why pick at a dull pavan few care to
Follow, except a few birds of dusty feather,
Not vivid performances of the past." But why not?
All other things must change too.
The seasons are no longer what they once were,
But it is the nature of things to be seen only once,
As they happen along, bumping into other things, getting along

Somehow. That's where Orpheus made his mistake.
Of course Eurydice vanished into the shade;
She would have even if he hadn't turned around.
No use standing there like a gray stone toga as the whole wheel
Of recorded history flashes past, struck dumb, unable to utter an
                                                        intelligent
Comment on the most thought-provoking element in its train.
Only love stays on the brain, and something these people,
These other ones, call life. Singing accurately
So that the notes mount straight up out of the well of
Dim noon and rival the tiny, sparkling yellow flowers
Growing around the brink of the quarry, encapsulizes
The different weights of the things.
                            But it isn't enough
To just go on singing. Orpheus realized this
And didn't mind so much about his reward being in heaven
After the Bacchantes had torn him apart, driven
Half out of their minds by his music, what it was doing to them.
Some say it was for his treatment of Eurydice.
But probably the music had more to do with it, and
The way music passes, emblematic
Of life and how you cannot isolate a note of it
And say it is good or bad. You must
Wait till it's over. "The end crowns all,"
Meaning also that the "tableau"
Is wrong. For although memories, of a season, for example,
Melt into a single snapshot, one cannot guard, treasure
That stalled moment. It too is flowing, fleeting;
It is a picture of flowing, scenery, though living, mortal,
Over which an abstract action is laid out in blunt,
Harsh strokes. And to ask more than this
Is to become the tossing reeds of that slow,
Powerful stream, the trailing grasses
Playfully tugged at, but to participate in the action
No more than this. Then in the lowering gentian sky
Electric twitches are faintly apparent first, then burst forth

Into a shower of fixed, cream-colored flares. The horses
Have each seen a share of the truth, though each thinks,
"I'm a maverick. Nothing of this is happening to me,
Though I can understand the language of birds, and
The itinerary of the lights caught in the storm is fully apparent to me.
Their jousting ends in music much
As trees move more easily in the wind after a summer storm
And is happening in lacy shadows of shore-trees, now, day after day."

But how late to be regretting all this, even
Bearing in mind that regrets are always late, too late!
To which Orpheus, a bluish cloud with white contours,
Replies that these are of course not regrets at all,
Merely a careful, scholarly setting down of
Unquestioned facts, a record of pebbles along the way.
And no matter how all this disappeared,
Or got where it was going, it is no longer
Material for a poem. Its subject
Matters too much, and not enough, standing there helplessly
While the poem streaked by, its tail afire, a bad
Comet screaming hate and disaster, but so turned inward
That the meaning, good or other, can never
Become known. The singer thinks
Constructively, builds up his chant in progressive stages
Like a skyscraper, but at the last minute turns away.
The song is engulfed in an instant in blackness
Which must in turn flood the whole continent
With blackness, for it cannot see. The singer
Must then pass out of sight, not even relieved
Of the evil burthen of the words. Stellification
Is for the few, and comes about much later
When all record of these people and their lives
Has disappeared into libraries, onto microfilm.
A few are still interested in them. "But what about
So-and-so?" is still asked on occasion. But they lie
Frozen and out of touch until an arbitrary chorus

Speaks of a totally different incident with a similar name
In whose tale are hidden syllables
Of what happened so long before that
In some small town, one indifferent summer.

↰John Ashbery

Graham's poem offers us many clues that we are meant to think about art itself while reading the poem. Orpheus, of course, *is* an artist, first of all. But Graham attaches to him such lines as "the point-of-view darting in him . . . hissing Once upon a time, and then Turn now . . . ," lines that give three terms from narrative: "point of view," "Once upon a time" (indicating the convention of how a narrative begins), and "Turn now," which could refer to the point at which a narrative's trajectory turns, or the volta in a sonnet, or the place at which the line of a poem turns or breaks. Clearly, we are meant to see Orpheus as symbolic not just of the artist but of the artist caught up just now in the very act of thinking how he should proceed *as* an artist. The seeming catalyst for this artistic "crisis," is the fact of Eurydice, who is threatening because she represents time, mortality, the notion of ending. Hence, his thinking of her as a "field with minutes in it," a "thing called // future," this thing that brings out the "wanting-to-finish;" hence, too, his dream, which more or less equals a retreat from the idea of finished event. As it turns out, Eurydice has similar concerns. She is not an artist, but she *is* a woman. She, too, resists fixity, she sees in her artist-husband a man who threatens to cast outline over her—to give her a narrative, which implies a finish, ultimately. Moreover, he threatens to "seal . . . the edges down," by giving her an identity within the continuum of time—"saying I know you from somewhere darling, don't I, / saying You're the kind of woman who etcetera—"

Yes, Graham's poem addresses the crucial act in the myth of Orpheus and Eurydice—his looking back and losing her to hell again—but the poem finally speaks more to an aesthetic that Graham—a poet and a woman, a fusion of Orpheus and Eurydice—evinces throughout her work, namely, an aesthethic that resists closure, and that seeks to calibrate the very nature of art (which is to *represent,* and in so doing, to give it *fixity*) with the human consciousness and fear of mortality, and the consequent urge (both human and artistic) toward its opposite, an immortality in which there is no notion of fixity, because neither time nor space exist as points of reference.

It's not difficult to see that Ashbery's priority in "Syringa" is *not* the myth of Orpheus and Eurydice; the crucial part of the myth is dispensed within the first three lines, in a single understatement: "Then one day, everything changed." Ashbery is more interested here in using the myth as a way of understanding how to approach the making of art—or, perhaps more accurately, how the artist should deal with two anxieties that plague him: the fact that art, being subjective, cannot ever be satisfactorily judged; and the fact that he can never know whether or not the art he makes will outlive him. One tenet is to remember that "it is the nature of things to be seen only once"—to accept the transience, the mortality with which human existence is informed. As Ashbery says, "That's where Orpheus made his mistake." Another tenet: ". . . it isn't enough / To just go on singing . . ." That is, there must be an end to singing, because nothing can be fully judged as to its value until it's complete. That completeness includes the necessary departure of the singer, without his ever knowing whether he will find stellification or not, whether anyone will even bother to ask "But what about / So-and-so?"

When I read the lines about how ". . . an arbitrary chorus / Speaks of a totally different incident with a similar name / In whose tale are hidden syllables / Of what happened so long before that / In some small town, one different summer," I think of myth and fable, of their archetypal nature. What Ashbery suggests is a limit to the number of stories—a notion that brings us back to where we started, with Joseph Campbell's theory, a theory with which Ashbery is here very much in agreement. Another point of agreement: if there is a limit to the number of stories, there is no limit to the number of variations to be made *of* those stories, even as every human life is different. I draw that analogy because I think—with Campbell—that each life is a variation on the finite number of patterns available to a life. Also, because I think that to live *is* to fabulate; we make our story as we go through life—essentially, we *tell* ourselves through. Art is what we make from a life. Remember the title of Ashbery's poem—"Syringa," recalling Syrinx, the nymph who sought escape from the god Pan and was transformed into reeds, across which what else could Pan do? He made a music.

No Rapture:
The Psalms and Restiveness

To be human is to know—within oneself as well as in the relationship of the self to society at large—contradiction, or a conflict of several competing interests. We want what we can't have, or what we shouldn't have, or have been told we should not want to have. In short, we have instinct. But what distinguishes humans from animals is an awareness of that instinct and of its possibilities, if left unchecked. Or perhaps another way to see it is that humans have, among their many instincts, an instinct to reconcile contradiction. Hence, the creation of laws, morality, religion, and other means of giving some generally agreed-upon boundaries to human behavior.

If the artist is human, what makes the artist unique among humans is a seeming unwillingness to reconcile contradiction. I say "seeming," because finally it's less a matter of unwillingness than of inability. Since inability is not correctable (as opposed to unwillingness, which is susceptible to persuasion, whether in the form of punishment or of pleasure), it's not surprising that artists are the first to be held suspect within society—original artists, I mean. For it is the original artist who—again, because of an inability to do any differently—will always challenge rather than reinforce societal convention. His originality means from the start a unique way of seeing the world, and of expressing that vision; and convention is not about uniqueness, but about conformity. The artist is at one moment dangerously intransigent (Emily Dickinson's soul accepting, for example, no society but her own), at the next moment frustratingly flippant (Walt Whitman's "Do I contradict myself? / Very well, then, I contradict myself, / I am large, I contain multitudes"). An inability to speak in harmony with received tradition easily translates into a refusal to do so—a hostility *toward* that tradition.

For the artist, there is less an impulse to reconcile contradiction than to plumb and sound contradiction's depths; and the result (given luck, gift, and vision) can be an art that refreshingly deepens and enlarges the beliefs and sensibilities of the very society it—inevitably, necessarily—also threatens.

—∽—

I have always been powerfully drawn toward the contradictory. It brings with it the unexpected; and the surprise of the unexpected may be pleasing or painful, but it will never be tedious—which is the business of perfection.

To allow for contradiction is, it seems to me, to be more honestly human; or perhaps the most human of contradictions is that between the instinct to reconcile contradiction and the temptation to yield to the contradictory. The reason why the Greek tragedies still resonate with meaning is because of an honesty that has to do not with the absolute and consolidated nobility of the characters but with the unexpected unraveling of that nobility—and it's a ragged nobility that I am after.

The contradictions were what most fascinated when, as an adult and as someone of no particular religious background, I first read the Bible—and it was to the Psalms that I found myself most often returning.

Of course, contradiction abounds throughout the Old Testament, and is most often traceable back to God and the actions by which he manifests himself. The chief contradiction, it turns out, is not within God but between God and man, and the contradiction has entirely to do with what distinguishes one from the other, namely, mortality or the lack of it. To be mortal is to be vulnerable: weakness or flexibility—by whichever name, it is inherent to human nature. Whereas God, though capable of creating weakness and of giving it human shape, is apparently himself incapable of understanding it. If God is all-knowing, then I would refine that a bit and limit the knowing to the intellectual kind. Sensual knowledge is presumably not possible without flesh, which is vulnerable. Nor is it possible to understand—except, again, intellectually—the gestures that spring from such aspects of vulnerability as sorrow, regret, longing, the sorts of things that figure, for example, into the choice of Lot's wife to look back at the home she is leaving, despite the command of God that she not do so. To the inflexibility of perfection, such gestures can only translate into defiance—hence the punishment the wife receives, for no reason that seems *humanly* logical. This is the only limitation I can find to being not only the dispenser of divine law, but the divine law itself. It makes sense that the God of the Old Testament is merciless; from his perspective, what can mercy be?

A fair number of the Psalms are psalms of praise, of thanksgiving to God, for his having spared the speaker—for having been merciful and responsive to the speaker's hopes or prayers. But that seems to me misguided. What seems constant in the Old Testament is the fact of a divine plan or pattern, inscrutable to the limited vision of humans, but in place all the same. And those who do not conform to or assist that plan will not be spared. This is the mercilessness of efficiency, bracing, not random at all, and perfect.

The Psalms are arguably the most human book of the Old Testament because they spring entirely from a human inability to accept the possibility of God as merciless and responsive only to a will or plan of his own. Prayer may be one-directional on the surface—audible prayer does not tend to receive audible answer—but it has been human to want to believe in a response, in some form, to prayer. If George Herbert likens prayer—in his poem *Prayer (I)*—to a "reversèd thunder," he also ends the poem by equating prayer with "something understood,"—understood by another, the listener presumably, whom he would believe God to be. If our belief in response is willed and desperate, it is desperation; if confident, we call it faith. Both occur in the Psalms, and it is an example of the book's necessary contradictions. For every psalm of praise, there seems as well a psalm of railing despair, rising from the human inability to understand God's ways. More bluntly, the psalmist praises God when things go well, and doesn't when they don't. True faith, as I understand it, has little room for this sort of inconsistency, any more than perfection—given its inflexibility—has room for bargaining.

And yet a sense of bargaining or wager is everywhere in the Psalms; and again, I would say this, too, is uniquely human, because to bargain is to assume persuadability or flexibility: human characteristics, not divine ones. Hence, the opening line of Psalm 30:

> I will extol thee, O Lord; *for* thou hast lifted me up, and hast
> not made my foes to rejoice over me.

Or, from 51 (11–14):

> Cast me not away from thy presence; and take not thy holy spirit
> from me.
> Restore unto me the joy of thy salvation; and uphold me with thy
> free spirit.
> *Then* will I teach transgressors thy ways; and sinners shall be converted
> unto thee.
> Deliver me from bloodguiltiness, O God, thou God of my salvation:
> *and* my tongue shall sing aloud of thy righteousness.

And again, from 116 (1–2):

> I love the Lord, *because* he hath heard my voice and my supplications.
> *Because* he hath inclined his ear unto me, *therefore* will I call upon him
> as long as I live.

The words I've italicized above are surely from the syntax of bargain, of consequence, of conditions put forth and variously met, unmet, or in the balance. Perhaps faith can only be conditional among the empirically minded. We require proof, or at the least we have an instinct toward proof. I'm willing to say that bargaining is not the only word for what's at work in the psalms I've cited: Psalm 30 is also an articulation of thanksgiving, an *ex-voto*; 51 is a lovely example of repentance, of a willingness to atone; and perhaps 116 can be seen as an instance of spiritual awakening, of recognition and consequent action in accord with a new appreciation for God's gifts. But these, to my mind, are nevertheless all versions of bargain, testimonials to a call having won or still hoping to win a response.

As the psalms of praise in the face of suffering are written in the immediate wake of having received the requested answer to a cry for help, so are the psalms of bewilderment or despair written in the wake of the *withholding* of deliverance. They carry the sensibility of one who feels his part of the agreement has been upheld, while God has failed on his own side. In Psalm 22, the psalmist falls back on an ancestral history of there having been a fair relationship between God and man, and this is put forward as a way of showing how God has faltered in terms of reliability:

My God, my god, why hast thou forsaken me? why art thou so far
from helping me, and from the words of my roaring?
O my God, I cry in the daytime, but thou hearest not; and in the night
season, and am not silent.
But thou art holy, O thou that inhabitest the praises of Israel.
Our fathers trusted in thee: they trusted, and thou didst deliver them.
They cried unto thee, and were delivered: they trusted in thee, and
were not confounded.

(1–5)

In Psalm 44, the history is not ancestral but more immediately personal.
And the tone is decidedly more accusatory, beginning with a list of sufferings
directly attributed to God, then moving on to a record of how devoted the
sufferers have always been—therefore undeserving of such suffering—and
turning finally from there to questions that, by implication, demand of God
some explanation:

Thou hast given us like sheep appointed for meat; and hast scattered
us among the heathen.
Thou sellest thy people for nought, and dost not increase thy wealth
by their price.
Thou makest us a reproach to our neighbours, a scorn and a derision
to them that are round about us.
Thou makest us a byword among the heathen, a shaking of the head
among the people.
My confusion is continually before me, and the shame of my face
hath covered me,
For the voice of him that reproacheth and blasphemeth; by reason of
the enemy and avenger.
All this is come upon us; yet have we not forgotten thee, neither have
we dealt falsely in thy convenant.
Our heart is not turned back, neither have our steps declined from
thy way;
Though thou hast sore broken us in the place of dragons, and
covered us with the shadow of death.

If we have forgotten the name of our God, or stretched out our hands
    to a strange god;
Shall not God search this out? for he knoweth the secrets of the heart.
Yea, for thy sake are we killed all the day long; we are counted as
    sheep for the slaughter.
Awake, why sleepest thou, O Lord? arise, cast us not off for ever.
Wherefore hidest thou thy face, and forgettest our affliction and our
    oppression?

(11–24)

Is this faith, on the part of man? If so, it's a qualified one, to be sure—not unswerving; conflicted, therefore. But I begin to think that that's one of the (no doubt unintentional) effects of the Psalms when read as a whole: they serve as nothing less than an honest record of human faith, complete with its flaws, its tendency to sway and buckle, to yield as easily to fear and anger as (when things go well) to joy, praise, and appreciation. I call the record honest because it seems to me that this muddled kind of faith is the only kind of which a vulnerable, flawed creature such as man is capable.

And perhaps faith, finally, is in the utterance alone. Whether bargaining with, praising, or railing against, the majority of the psalms are utterances directed *toward*—which is to say that even to utter is to show a belief in a listener or to show a *desire* to believe in such a listener. Many of the psalms speak to or about a God who is said to have hidden himself or have turned away; nowhere does the psalmist doubt that God exists. This is human faith, as I see it, one that argues that a belief in God need not mean an unshakable allegiance to and acceptance of all of the *ways* of God. Humans are distinguishable from other animals by self-consciousness—by ego. And it is ego that makes humans the only creatures capable of articulating a felt worship of God; it is also ego, however, that makes a robotic allegiance to God impossible. Presumably, God knows this, as he knows his presence could not be fully understood without, occasionally, his seeming absence.

An untested faith isn't worth that much, it seems to me. Nor does a natural impulse to test God himself seem a mark of faithlessness. Somewhere in how we release and check that impulse—in the ongoing calibration of release and restraint—there lies devotion.

The trajectory—psychological, emotional—of the Psalms is that of restiveness itself. It is true that the book as a whole ends with an uncharacteristically consistently held note of joyful praise (from Psalm 145 through 150, the last). But crescendo isn't always conclusion; and if we have read the entire book, we cannot help but understand that the only constant here is fluctuation, the ease with which astonishment gives way to joy, joy to fear, fear to despair, and despair again—and temporarily—to joy. This is the restiveness of what it is to be human and perishable. To be flawed. To be alive.

Maybe an absolutely unqualified, unquestioned belief in deity is like those limits in calculus, the point that a line approaches infinitely without intersection, though theoretically intersection must occur eventually. Call belief the point of intersection, call the ever-approaching line the will to believe. Say the point of intersection is shared by God *and* belief—belief in God occurs *at* God, and vice versa. And the ever-approaching line, that we are calling the will to believe? Say another word for that is faith.

⁓ᴧ◡

What the soul apparently wants of the body is the perfection of absolute obedience. But the body comes equipped with instinct; and instinct, more than having a will of its own, *is* that will. Is devotion the same as obedience? Must it mean the giving up utterly of the self to another power? What is the difference between apprenticeship and thralldom, except the degree of submission? How far is folly?

In Virgil's *Aeneid,* Dido—the queen of Carthage—has made a vow of chastity, a devotion to the memory of her dead husband Sychaeus. Soon after the arrival, however, of the hero Aeneas, Dido realizes that she has fallen in love with Aeneas, and she recognizes the conflict between what she has promised the dead and what she feels toward the living. It's a conflict between *types* of devotion. Dido consults with her sister, who encourages Dido to enjoy life—and love—while she can. But the world—or perhaps only Virgil's notions of it?—was more rigid back then: a vow was a vow, and to break it was sacrilege, and it is disappointing but not surprising as we watch Dido descend swiftly the steps of the doom awaiting her, in the form of death by self-immolation on a burning pyre.

But the contemporary world—or perhaps this is only my own notion of it—is one of flexible morality, for better *and* worse. Devotion to the dead, to the living, to a deity, or to a desire to believe that there *is* anything like deity: why do we have to choose? What is so unreasonable about thinking of devotion as many-faceted, multidimensional? That trajectory of restiveness graphed out across the psalms: if the restiveness of being human, why not also the restiveness of devotion? Why not say that there are to devotion, as to being human, many parts, and necessarily they won't be absolutely reconciled in this life?

These weren't questions that occurred to me when I first read of Dido in my senior year of high school. But about twenty-five years later, I did think of such questions while I was visiting Herring Cove Beach in Provincetown, Massachusetts. Typically, for high summer, the beach was packed. I had settled for the day on that part of the beach that, by some unwritten, unspoken law, has always been occupied primarily by gay men. Here and there, I'd see a man lying on a large beach towel, with a small pile or ring of stones beside him—as if the stones were sharing the man's towel. It turned out that these were meant as cairns of a sort, tangible representations of a partner, friend, or lover who had died. In effect, the men were spending the day at the beach—the beach the two of them had often enjoyed together—with the dead, with the (concretized) *memory* of the dead.

What was devotion, if not this?

But the more closely I observed these men, the more I realized that devotion had not meant a diminishment in sexual desire. Each man was keenly aware of the others around him, and the charge in the air was decidedly sexual. If not actually cruising, the men were certainly not indifferent to the *possibility* of sex—there was at the least an openness to it.

And it seemed to me then that sexual attraction to the living need not compromise our devotion to the memory of the dead. Perhaps—even more dangerously—sexual attraction need not compromise our devotion to the living, either. These men did not seem undevoted; rather, they seemed what some might call divided in their loyalties. For me, they were granting devotion—like morality more broadly—a flexibility without which how can we begin to call ourselves human beings, not perfect, only perfectly human?

⁓

In so many books of the Old Testament, we find a prescription for correct human behavior, or narratives behind which such a prescription stands implied. The Psalms provide us with the enactment of all types of human behavior, and there is none of the reconciliation that attends prescription—no easy "if X, then Y" mathematics. That is, the Psalms allow us to believe in *ourselves,* in the many parts of which we are made, including that part that would like to believe there is something more, finally, than just ourselves.

For some of us, one of the larger parts is the one that would like to make art; or more exactly, the part that makes what it would like to believe is art—and perhaps even have others believe, as well. I began this essay by speaking of art and the making of it because I see a parallel between the contradictions that the artist is drawn to, contains, and enacts, and those contradictions that make up the sensibility of the Psalms. The sensibility of the Psalms is, finally, an artistic one—which should not surprise: the psalmist was an artist, after all.

Another way to read the Psalms is as a graphing of that trajectory of restiveness that belongs particularly to the artist. Like God, art is not quantifiable—publications, exhibits, reviews notwithstanding, it is impossible to define precisely what art is; or, if art, whether good or bad art. The ultimate subjectivity of art makes it as distant and abstract as God, and I would equate the urge to make art with spiritual faith: we believe, or want to, that somewhere there is the equivalent of answered prayer, of divine attention; we call it audience—something that, even if we aren't conscious of it during the act of creation, we must somewhere have in mind. When I write a poem, it's because I have something I need to say, and wish to; and it seems only reasonable that to say something is to believe in someone or something to say it to. Utterance, again, as a form of faith.

Among the many things feared by the psalmist, two stand out. One is the fear of becoming "a reproach of men," in particular for having had faith at all:

All they that see me laugh me to scorn: they shoot out the lip,
    they shake the head, saying,
He trusted on the Lord that he would deliver him: let him deliver
    him, seeing he delighted in him.

(22:7–8)

But the fear is broader than that, a fear of reproach of many kinds: sometimes the shame of defeat,

> O my God, I trust in thee: let me not be ashamed, let not mine
> enemies triumph over me.
>
> (25:2)

sometimes mockery,

> But in mine adversity they rejoiced . . . they did tear me, and ceased not:
> With hypocritical mockers in feasts, they gnashed upon me with their
> teeth.
>
> (35:15–16)

> Let them be desolate for a reward of their shame that say unto me,
> Aha, aha.
>
> (40:15)

and sometimes slander,

> For the mouth of the wicked and the mouth of the deceitful are
> opened against me: they have spoken against me with a
> lying tongue.
> They compassed me about also with words of hatred; and fought
> against me without a cause.
>
> (109:2–3)

The other fear often expressed in the Psalms is of abandonment by God:

> But mine eyes are unto thee, O God the Lord: in thee is my
> trust; leave not my soul destitute.
>
> (141:8)

Lord, why castest thou off my soul? why hidest thou thy
face from me?

(88:14)

Why withdrawest thou thy hand, even thy right hand? . . .

(74:11)

O God, thou hast cast us off, thou hast scattered us, thou hast
been displeased; O turn thyself to us again.

(60:1)

What is the artist most bedeviled by? On one hand, the fear that a belief in the art he makes will turn out to have been a misplaced one—the anxiety that surrounds the art, once it's put out into the world: what will the reaction be? Mockery? Hatred?

Another fear: the fear of abandonment, in the form of indifference, not only from the audience but—worse—from no less a force than the Muse herself, analagous to God, when it comes to artists. What if there is nothing else forthcoming? What if she who brought us here should turn her face? One of the shrewder examples of this particular anxiety occurs at the end of "The Wish," a poem from Louise Glück's *Meadowlands.* Estranged husband and wife have each made a separate wish. He imagines that what she wished for was for him to return to her, and for the two of them to be together again. Her response:

I wished for what I always wish for.
I wished for another poem.

(9–10)

Anthem

Trapped bee at the glass.

A window.

Instinct is different from
to understand.

Is not the same.

The window is not the light
it fills with—has
been filling with—

What the bee ascends to.

Is full with.

To ascend.
To have been foiled.
To be consistent.

Instinct making
its own equations.

The window is not, for the bee, a window.

Is a form of resistance

not understood
because not understandable,
not in terms

of reason.
A felt force.

A force entirely:

And I said Yes. That it
had been

like that. Resistance
equaling,
at first, the light—And then resistance

as only one of the light's more difficult

and defining features.

⁓

Resistance is attractive for those with an appetite for challenge—more than attractive, it is necessary: such resistance draws forth and routinely exercises that combination of imagination and stamina that we call the will to believe, whatever the object of that belief may be—deity, words, the flesh. Part of the lesson of the Psalms is that without resistance, surrender would be meaningless. And without surrender—the willing submission to a force more powerful and intractable than our own—no faith, no risk, no poetry. No rapture.

Anomaly, Conundrum, *Thy-Will-Be-Done:*
On the Poetry of George Herbert

But I am lost in flesh, whose sugared lies
    Still mock me, and grow bold:
Sure thou didst put a mind there, if I could
    Find where it lies.

                       ("Dullness," 21–24)

    To have my aim, and yet to be
Further from it than when I bent my bow;

                       ("The Cross," 25–26)

He seemed to me, at first, subversive. I was younger then. Of George Herbert,
what I knew was he'd been a priest. Of devotion, what I imagined was: how
difficult can it be? Only cross belief with enough discipline—
    Also honesty—love—somewhere figuring . . .
    About the flesh, I understood as much as about ambition: truly, nothing at all.

The Temple, comprising essentially all of Herbert's poems, seems increasingly a private record, even as the prose work *The Country Parson* was intended—for himself as much as for others—to be a publicly available instructional work: "a complete pastoral," as Herbert puts it in his note to the reader. In the prose, we are told that the parson "condescends to human frailties both in himself and others" (ch. XXVII); also, that

the parson, having studied and mastered all his lusts and
affections within, and the whole army of temptations without, hath ever so many sermons ready penned, as he hath
victories. And it fares in this as it doth in physic: he that
hath been sick of a consumption, and knows what recovered
him, is a physician so far as he meets with the same disease
and temper; and can much better and particularly do it,
than he that is generally learned, and was never sick.

(ch. xxxiii)

Thus, the more objective stance of the purposefully didactic prose. It is in
the poetry, however, that we see the frailty of the pastor—of, finally, any
individual—laid bare, that we see him engaged in the very wrestling from
which he will emerge experienced (not just "generally learned") and will
consequently give to the poems themselves a degree of earnestness that I
find in the work of no other seventeenth-century poet.

What becomes clear in the prose is that Herbert believes that the pastor
should have suffered bouts of affliction, but that he is not to advertise such
moments; rather, the fact of the parson's private experience, to the extent
that it is evident at all, will be most evident in the quality of the guidance
and wisdom that he is able to extend to his parishioners. That is, there is a
distinction in the prose work between Herbert's era and our own, in which
the exposure of their private flaws would seem to endear us all the more to
our public figures. By the above logic, the poems of *The Temple*—in showing
the would-be devoted sometimes wrestling with, sometimes all but yielding
to, finally admitting to *having* yielded to temptation; and in capturing the
same speaker unrepentantly railing against God or, presumably as blasphemous, inquiring into and challenging the fairness of God's ways—in all of
these respects, the book reads as a private record, one that, in its overall
design suggests less an author who has in mind the best way in which to
please and thereby win a readership, and more the irregular, unpredictable
shifts of heart and mind that are what it is to be human. It is thus that,
as with the best of the lasting writers (just now, Emily Dickinson, Gerard
Manley Hopkins come to mind), what takes its origin in personal experience becomes a touchstone for human experience more generally. And it is
in this regard that I tend to agree with Anthony Hecht and others who have

described Herbert as a confessional poet. He *is*—both in what approximates the liturgical sense of that word (the Reformation having made confession technically unavailable for Protestants), and in the sense that was celebrated as a seemingly new literary movement three centuries later. Herbert's poems seem written *toward* a need to understand, for *himself,* the ways of God and how they figured into his own life; they are an honest and, to a large extent, self-interested inquiry into questions whose answers did not entirely accord with personal experience. In the course, however, of exploring these questions, their answers, and the further questions that the answers raise, Herbert produces poetry that is not only revelatory of individual struggle but remains, as well, powerfully relevant to human experience today.

⟶⟳

Why affliction?—why, inevitably, our suffering? These are questions Herbert asks repeatedly in *The Temple,* even as he—characteristically—knows that the answers are not so far from hand; the problem, rather, is in their being at best fickle comforters. Looking at *The Church,* the central part of *The Temple* [and ignoring the two bookending parts, each a single poem—"The Church-Porch" and "The Church Militant," respectively (which, as Louis Martz has pointed out, "seem rather imposed on either side than organically related to the whole," p. xxv)], it is worth noting that Herbert opens the main portion with "The Altar," then immediately follows it with "The Sacrifice," a poem (not coincidentally, the longest of Herbert's poems, at 252 lines) that details the event that makes the altar so significant to Christian thought, Christ's crucifixion. The next eight poems all meditate on both the crucifixion and what man's response should accordingly be to it:

> Then for thy passion—I will do for that—
>   Alas, my God, I know not what.
>
> > ("The Thanksgiving," 49–50)

>   I have considered it, and find
> There is no dealing with thy mighty passion:
> For though I die for thee, I am behind;
>
> > ("The Reprisal," 1–3)

O my chief good,
How shall I measure out thy blood?
How shall I count what thee befell,
And each grief tell?

("Good Friday," 1–4)

Clearly, Herbert means to suggest that it is imperative to remember the passion of Christ adequately; we are duty-bound to respond, inasmuch as it is by the death of Christ for man that man has access to salvation. But how to respond? One way is by seeing Christ as a model for imitation; this includes approximating, as much as we can, the very affliction that Christ suffered. In so doing, we more worthily enjoy the resurrection that Christ won for us:

With thee
Let me combine
And feel this day thy victory:
For, if I imp my wing on thine,
Affliction shall advance the flight in me.

("Easter-wings," 16–20)

Another justification for affliction is related to why sin is necessary, a fact that emerges when we look at two poems that appear one after the other and, as a pair, present an important aspect of Herbert's thought. First, the poems:

Mattens

I cannot ope mine eyes,
But thou art ready there to catch
My morning-soul and sacrifice:
Then we must needs for that day make a match.

My God, what is a heart?
Silver, or gold, or precious stone,

Or star, or rainbow, or a part
Of all these things, or all of them in one?

    My God, what is a heart,
That thou shouldst it so eye, and woo,
    Pouring upon it all thy art,
As if that thou hadst nothing else to do?

    Indeed man's whole estate
Amounts (and richly) to serve thee:
    He did not heav'n and earth create,
Yet studies them, not him by whom they be.

    Teach me thy love to know;
That this new light, which now I see,
    May both the work and workman show:
Then by a sun-beam I will climb to thee.

Sin (II)

    O that I could a sin once see!
We paint the devil foul, yet he
    Hath some good in him, all agree.
Sin is flat opposite to th' Almighty, seeing
It wants the good of *virtue,* and of *being.*

    But God more care of us hath had:
If apparitions make us sad,
    By sight of sin we should grow mad.
Yet as in sleep we see foul death, and live:
So devils are our sins in perspective.

In "Mattens," Herbert says that despite the many blessings provided by God (as celebrated in stanzas 1–3), man chooses—or has, as an empirical creature, no other choice—to study not the invisible creator, but his more immediately knowable, because visible, creations. Having said that, Herbert goes on to ask that God himself be made as visible as his creation—"May both the work and workman show"—and that the visible be further rendered into something tangible—"Then by a sun-beam I will climb to thee"—an unlikely event, and one which, given the earlier stanzas of the poem, Herbert already knows to be inappropriate to wish for. Where, after all, is faith?

Equally unseeable, says the next poem, is sin, which Herbert would also have be made visible, until reaching the conclusion that "devils are our sins in perspective." Even as devils offer a perspective by which to understand sin, so does the poem on sin offer a perspective on the subject matter of "Mattens," namely, God's blessings. This is why sin is necessary and—to return to the original discussion—it is an explanation for the existence of affliction in our lives: how else, Herbert would ask, better to understand salvation (by which we are to be released from affliction) than by affliction itself, affliction being a modified version of salvation's opposite, damnation? And again, sin provides the perspective by which to know, via our own afflic- tion, the greater affliction of Christ ("like stones [sins] make / His blood's sweet current much more loud to be," Herbert says in "Church-lock and Key," 11–12).

Thus, the rationale. But reasoning notwithstanding, there remain for Herbert two difficulties with affliction. One is that affliction is ultimately inadequate when it comes to knowing Christ's affliction in its entirety. For, not least of the distinctions between Christ and man is that it is via sin that man is subject to affliction (beginning with Original Sin); Christ suffers in a state of sinlessness. As Herbert puts it, "I am behind," by which I take him to mean that man, in his efforts to imitate Christ, is at an insurmountable disadvantage from the start; all of those efforts, therefore, will necessarily fall short.

The second problem with affliction is less sophisticated, but no less true: namely, affliction doesn't feel good.

❧

In "The Windows," Herbert describes man as "a brittle crazy glass" (2)—by "crazy," meaning cracked, flawed. We are also told, however, in "Repentance," that "Fractures well cured make us more strong" (36). In light of what Herbert says about affliction, sin, and their places in our lives, it seems reasonable to understand by this glass metaphor that sins—and the afflictions we suffer as a consequence of sin—can be ultimately good for us. If we are bettered by sin—made "more strong"—can't there be made an argument for indulging in sin, the more thoroughly to know the blessings of God? How can it be that we are made better by the very sins that we are instructed to rail against? Is it true that we are so bettered, or is this the only recourse, when it comes to thinking about the matter—given that, for the Herbertian Christian, sin is as inevitable as our yielding to it, as is our consequent suffering for having yielded? Not the least aspect of Herbert that wins for him my allegiance and trust—and that makes him a distinctly earnest poet among his contemporaries whose work too often can seem mere flourish—is his silence in the wake of these questions.

⌁

Justice (I)

I cannot skill of these thy ways.
Lord, thou didst make me, yet thou woundest me;
Lord, thou dost wound me, yet thou dost relieve me:
Lord, thou relievest, yet I die by thee:
Lord, thou dost kill me, yet thou dost reprieve me.
　　But when I mark my life and praise,
　　Thy justice me most fitly pays:
For, I do praise thee, yet I praise thee not:
My prayers mean thee, yet my prayers stray:
I would do well, yet sin the hand hath got:
My soul doth love thee, yet it loves delay.
　　I cannot skill of these my ways.

How often it is that Herbert's poems will on one level argue—and persuasively—against the very arguments they no less persuasively put forward on a more immediate level. The poem "Justice (I)" can be seen, in terms of its form and rhyme, as a balance or set of scales, in which the weights are God and man. An inability to understand God (1) is by line 12 replaced with the confession (admission?) that man does not understand his *own* ways; the implication is that the correct gesture, on our part, is not to attempt to understand God, not to question his ways, but to consider what—in asking that God justify himself—is being said about our own inadequacies, about our presumption and arrogance. The notion that God is finally superior to—and not answerable to—man is conveyed in the respective rhyme schemes of the two longer-lined "quatrains" that serve as internal frame for the poem. In lines 2–5, which address the responses of God toward man, the rhyme scheme is *a-a-a-a,* the single rhyme suggestive of solidity, that which is unwavering, is fixed—as consolidated in its tonal position as in its strength. Lines 8–11, which examine the responses of man to God, display a *b-c-b-c* rhyme scheme. If the earlier quatrain gains its strength from its sustaining a single note, as it were, then the second quatrain is arguably more suggestive of wavering, straying, of suffering a weakness because of a lack of comparative unity of sound. In short, the poem can be said to argue—on both the level of content and of the rhymes by which that content is conveyed—that man is inferior to God, and is shown to be all the more so by his reluctance to acknowledge his subordinance to God.

However, can't we also say that a rhyme scheme of *a-a-a-a* is finally monotonous, redundant, unimaginative, oppressive in its lack of tonal variation and, accordingly, sophistication? By this logic, isn't a *b-c-b-c* scheme more melodic, more advanced because more varied?

—If the poem is a scale, then: God, or man, who tips it?

～◈

"Justice (I)" is one of many Herbert poems whose ambiguity deepens with each reading. There are, as well, many poems that deliberately do not progress forward—they begin in a moment of despair or of confusion and end in a similar moment. Or perhaps it is more accurate to say that these poems have as their trajectory the trajectory of prayer, which is one-directional, and upward [a "reversèd thunder"—"Prayer (I)," line 6]—any return, in the form of answer (as, again, with prayer) happens in response to, which is to say *outside of* the poem. What is being withheld is the easy resolution that a less reflective or more arrogant poet would be quick to offer. In not resolving the questions that arise, Herbert gains more authority, inasmuch as he seems to say the most honest thing to be said about the conundrum of God and of man—that conundrum is the fact: God punishes and rewards, as man both wins and falls from grace; and the line between reward and punishment, between plummet and ascent, is decidedly blurred. This is everywhere apparent in *The Temple,* whose poems move with relentless accuracy to the irregular strophe of the human spirit, which is to say, to the rhythm of all our human strengths and weaknesses. In *The Country Parson,* Herbert speaks of

> a double state of a Christian even in this life, the one
> military, the other peaceable. The military is, when we are
> assaulted with temptations either within or from without.
> The peaceable is, when the Devil for a time leaves us, as
> he did our Saviour, and the angels minister to us their own
> food, even joy, and peace, and comfort in the Holy Ghost.
>
> (ch. xxxiv)

That is the prose statement of a dilemma, not a resolution to it. *The Temple* is the poetic enactment of that dilemma. To read the poems is often to wade more deeply into dilemma; to meditate, in turn, on those dilemmas is in a sense to experience a kind of affliction in the form of seeing clearly our fallen condition. And yet, haven't we seen in the poems that there is no affliction that does not bring with it instruction? Conversely, no instruction without affliction—

~⁊ఎ

Governing movement of *The Temple:* strophic, decidedly and inevitably, in keeping with the emotional, psychological, and intellectual shifts of an individual trying to bring into equilibrium the unknowable nature of God and the nature of man, which is finally predictable. An impossible task—for if the distinguishing trait of man is his intellectual curiosity, it is also that very trait that must lead him routinely counter to God (see Genesis; and, after that, history itself). It is no coincidence that strophe and antistrophe define the choruses that are standard in Greek tragedy, those plays in which what aspect of human nature isn't in some way thrown into light?

Herbert, of course, no stranger to the classics.

~⁊ఎ

To every great poet, there is a particular arrogance whose nature is twofold: it permits the poet to write with the conviction of one who believes he is in possession of the truth; and it nevertheless does not blind the writer to his own potential failings. It is the latter quality that produces the earnestness that, in turn, distinguishes the merely bombastic from the credibly authoritative.

If questioning the ways of God is one of the items with which Herbert openly wrestles throughout *The Temple,* another as well is writerly ambition. As with the two poets mentioned earlier—Hopkins and Dickinson—Herbert seems (quite reasonably) aware of his gift; the problem is, what to do with it? How to temper it according to how best to serve God and not oneself? How to fashion the perfect offering and then avoid a dangerous pride in one's own achievement? How to be a virtuoso of form and metrics and yet seem less to be flaunting than appropriately harnessing that talent?

The question of the artist's responsibility is raised early in *The Temple,* shortly after it has been established that as human beings we are responsible for following the model of Christ in his suffering—a resolution that was no sooner reached than there rose the question of *how* to approximate such a model, given our human disadvantages. Similarly, in "The Temper (I)," Herbert both announces that the artist (by which he means, of course, his own case, that of the Christian artist) is responsible for praising God, and proceeds to ask how such praise should be put forward—again, given the spiritual instability that attends being human:

> How should I praise thee, Lord! how should my rhymes
> Gladly engrave thy love in steel,
> If what my soul doth feel sometimes,
> My soul might ever feel!
>
> (1–4)

> Yet take thy way; for sure thy way is best:
> Stretch or contract me, thy poor debtor:
> This is but tuning of my breast,
> To make the music better.
>
> (21–24)

The two stanzas argue for, at the very least, a parallel between spiritual and artistic devotion; for Herbert, it seems clear that the two are in fact not parallel but one and the same. The well-tuned breast (that is, the spiritually responsible one) will inevitably produce the music (literal music, but also music as metaphor for a fitting devotion) appropriate to God. But even as the two types of devotion are akin, they inherit the same difficulty, namely, a human instability. Again, the action to take is clearly stated—in "Jordan (I)," in "The Quiddity," but most pleasingly and economically, both, in "Jordan (II)":

> When first my lines of heav'nly joys made mention,
> Such was their lustre, they did so excel,
> That I sought out quaint words, and trim invention;
> My thoughts began to burnish, sprout, and swell,
> Curling with metaphors a plain intention,
> Decking the sense, as if it were to sell.
>
> Thousands of notions in my brain did run,
> Off'ring their service, if I were not sped:
> I often blotted what I had begun;
> This was not quick enough, and that was dead.
> Nothing could seem too rich to clothe the sun,
> Much less those joys which trample on his head.
>
> As flames do work and wind, when they ascend,
> So did I weave myself into the sense.
> But while I bustled, I might hear a friend
> Whisper, *How wide is all this long pretence!*
> *There is in love a sweetness ready penned:*
> *Copy out only that, and save expense.*

(The friend, incidentally, is usually identified as Christ; see Martz, p. 457.) Simplicity, it would seem, is crucial—an honesty of line and of sentiment analagous to an uncomplicated honesty with respect to God: a simplicity of spirit. This last is the point that "Confession" so persuasively makes, arguing against an intricacy of heart, in favor of an openness that will protect us from sins:

> Only an open breast
> Doth shut them out, so that they cannot enter;
>   Or, if they enter, cannot rest,
>   But quickly seek some new adventure.
> Smooth open hearts no fast'ning have; but fiction
> Doth give a hold and handle to affliction.
>
> (19–24)

And yet, as with the inevitably complicated human soul, how is Herbert to adopt a plainness of style when he is so expert at poetic craft? And, in light of the question that he raises in "Providence"—"But who hath praise enough? nay, who hath any?" (141)—mustn't the artist also avoid being accused of stinting on his craft? The line is, again, as blurred as the line between certain vices, the ones "whose natures, at least in the beginning, are dark and obscure: as covetousness and gluttony" (*The Country Parson*, ch. XXVI). Add to all of this that, like human beings, words are themselves at a disadvantage that necessitates their being ever inadequate to the responsibilities demanded of them, inasmuch as words

> Doth vanish like a flaring thing,
> And in the ear, not conscience ring.
>
> ("The Windows," 14–15)

Finally, there is the fact that

> None can express thy works, but he that knows them:
> And none can know thy works, which are so many,
> And so complete, but only he that owes them.
>
> ("Providence," 142–144)

—"owes" meaning "owns" in Herbert's time, with the sole owner being God himself. What is a man of words—and especially of Herbert's facility with them—to do? Just as we have uncovered ways to justify sin, it is possible to argue that a commitment to conveying praise worthy of God justifies an inventiveness of form; the artist is (or should be) engaged in a constant search for the most perfect form in which to cast his offering. My sense is that this was no mere justification for Herbert—he was earnest in his desire to put forward his best, for God. I also find it hard to imagine, though, that Herbert took no pride in such elaborately structured and clever poems as "A Wreath," whose end-words, framing the poem four times over, turn out to form an actual wreath on the page, whose center—formed precisely where the two center lines of the poem make a pivot of enjambment—is the phrase "to thee / To thee," appropriate to a poem that concerns the offering of praise. Here is the poem in its entirety:

> A wreathèd garland of deservèd praise,
> Of praise deservèd, unto thee I give,
> I give to thee, who knowest all my ways,
> My crooked winding ways, wherein I live,
> Wherein I die, not live: for life is straight,
> Straight as a line, and ever tends to thee,
> To thee, who art more far above deceit,
> Than deceit seems above simplicity.
> Give me simplicity, that I may live,
> So live and like, that I may know thy ways,
> Know them and practise them: then shall I give
> For this poor wreath, give thee a crown of praise.

A similar sense of satisfaction must have been part of Herbert's reaction to what he had been able to accomplish with only two rhymes—and only the same four words with which to generate them—throughout his "Clasping of Hands," the first stanza of which is:

> Lord, thou art mine, and I am thine,
> If mine I am: and thine much more,
> Than I or ought, or can be mine.
> Yet to be thine, doth me restore;
> So that again I now am mine,
> And with advantage mine the more,
> Since this being mine, brings with it thine,
> And thou with me dost thee restore.
> > If I without thee would be mine,
> > I neither should be mine nor thine.

And consider the first couple of stanzas of "Paradise," which enacts in endwords the poem's subjects—that man is ever enclosed within Christ, who is in turn contained within God (as the word with which the first line of each tercet ends proves to enclose two other words), and the way in which man's blessing lies in how he is refined gradually, pared away by the knife of God:

> I bless thee, Lord, because I G R O W
> Among thy trees, which in a R O W
> To thee both fruit and order O W.

> What open force, or hidden C H A R M
> Can blast my fruit, or bring me H A R M,
> While the inclosure is thine A R M?

As with many a question in Herbert—in this case, how to temper an ambition to serve God as expertly as possible with an ambition, as an artist, to surpass what one has done before or is capable of doing in the future—to this question, too, Herbert offers a silence that is as humble as it is honest; honest, because Herbert understands that the demands of art and of piety—inasmuch as these are tempered, necessarily, by human nature—will often be in a conflict that, to reconcile, would at best be artistry—but never art. Even as to try to reconcile the ways of God is the stuff of science or of logic, or perhaps philosophy. None of these is faith.

❧

Poems like those just mentioned, in particular like "Paradise" or like Herbert's translation/version "Coloss. 3.3 Our life is hid with Christ in God," whose pleasures lie as much in the play of word as of typography:

> *My* words and thought do both express this notion,
> That *Life* hath with the sun a double motion.
> The first *Is* straight, and our diurnal friend,
> The other *Hid* and doth obliquely bend.
> One life is wrapped *In* flesh, and tends to earth:

The other winds towards *Him,* whose happy birth
Taught me to live here so, *That* still one eye
Should aim and shoot at that which *Is* on high:
Quitting with daily labour all *My* pleasure,
To gain at harvest an eternal *Treasure.*

—these are play and they are also not *mere* play. Part of the message in Herbert's work is the message that is the title of the poem just cited. The human desire may be to have everything be made visible; this is not only evident in "Mattens" and "Sin (II)," but I note, too, how the poems that immediately follow those two poems in *The Temple* are almost all, for several pages, poems whose center is a concrete, tangible aspect of the church: "Church-monuments," "Church-lock and Key," "The Church-floor," "The Windows"—as if in response to an urge for a more concrete understanding of God. But the fact of it, Herbert suggests, is that the ways of God are abstract and ungraspable—this would seem to explain why those very concrete-in-subject poems are immediately followed by the poems "Trinity Sunday," "Content," "Humility," "Frailty," "Constancy," "Affliction (III)"; it also, to return to the poems of wordplay, suggests that much of what Herbert intends in those poems is a reminder about the elusive, the hidden meanings of God—some more attainable than others. In "Coloss. 3.3 Our life is hid with Christ in God," a clear message lies italicized within the plain-face type; the poem itself is thus a concrete means of speaking about the abstract and hidden. (If it does not unveil the ways of God entirely, it gives us a way in which to approximate such a discovery, on the level of words—a pleasure smaller than but analogous to the reward of knowing God more entirely after death.) So, again, there's an ambiguity. A poem for which the poet could be accused of self-indulgence—brandishing with less than appropriate pride his knack for crossing wit and intellect—can also serve as evidence of the poet's commitment to speaking earnestly of his God. This is not unrelated to the earlier discussion of "Justice (I)," whose message continues to show new sides of itself with each re-reading. Is it arrogance or humility at work there, is the message blasphemous or devout?

For me, whether he does it through wordplay, through metrical dexterity, or through a gift for argument that recalls how dangerously close is rhetoric to sophistry—in all of these instances, Herbert suggests that there is nothing merely superficial, nothing absolutely clear when it comes to God, the soul, the body's restiveness, temptation, and how to reconcile them all. There are always other layers—which is why devotion requires vigilance, patience, both—as there is eventually always a point *ne plus ultra*: this is where acceptance is required—faith, presumably, about which Herbert says:

> Faith needs no staff of flesh, but stoutly can
>   To heav'n alone both go, and lead.
>
> ("Divinity," 27–28)

I have said that the constant inventing of new forms and rhyme schemes can be understood as mimetic of the devoted's tireless searching for the vessel most fit to present to God—a God whose desires, like his methods, are unpredictable, ever-elusive. But I also see the poems as physical enactments, on the page, of the body's restlessness, as much in the face of temptation as before the facelessness of God. Without reading the words of the poems, only looking at them in terms of their shifting lines and morphing shapes on the page, they return to me again and again the same questions: what is the body's proper conduct? What of the soul?

⁓

As with poets, so too with poems: some remain more interesting than others. Much has to do with the reader: if I continue to prefer Dante's Hell to his Paradise—what, then? Likewise, with the poems of Herbert. In poems such as "Business," with its patience-straining trochaics and its decidedly pat ending—

> Who in heart not ever kneels,
> Neither sin nor Saviour feels.

—do I resist easy conclusion? What is it about a metrical regularity that (here, anyway) is offputting? I have a similar ambivalence about a poem like "Vanity (I)," whose argument follows a rather conventional tripartite structure, each part presenting an allegory, essentially the same one (man—whether as "fleet

astronomer," "nimble diver," or "subtle chymick"—seeks to know everything), which is then countered by a final stanza whose question—"What
hath not man sought out and found, / But his dear God? . . ."—is predictable enough. "Constancy," "Sunday," "Avarice" . . . I'm not unaware that the
poems that appeal to me less are in general also those that take on as subjects
sins to be on guard against, or holy days, or religious duty. (A notable exception is "Prayer (I)," in part because it includes—surprisingly, at first—sin
as a component of prayer, and in part because it moves associatively from
image to image, each increasingly more vague, the final definition of prayer
being only, and abstractly, "something understood." That is, it pretends to
no simple answer.) What these particular poems lack is an agony that would
mean a speaker who has survived experience, which would in turn produce
the earnestness that characterizes most of Herbert's poems. They also tend
to be delivered in third person—i.e., they lack the "I" whose intimacy will
render a genuine agony even more so.

Another way of looking at the less satisfying poems—recalling what
Herbert says in *The Country Parson* about the two sides to every Christian,
"the one military, the other peaceable"—is that these poems issue from the
peaceable side of Herbert. And peace somehow never seems quite to warrant long attention from us, compared to strife. Or, in saying so, do I speak
more of my own than of the world's tendency?

Or perhaps the poems are meant to seem somewhat predictable, routine—and, in reading them, the effect perhaps not coincidentally suggests
the child or the not especially committed adult who in church can be found
repeating from memory the psalms and hymns whose words he may know,
but whose meaning he has never stopped to consider. Are the poems intended as a kind of example-in-negative of "correct" behavior? And yet,
Herbert remarks with disapproval how "many say the catechism by rote,
as parrots, without ever piercing into the sense of it" (*The Country Parson,*
ch. XXI). Is it again, then, myself? Most often, these poems seem Herbert's
way of reminding us that we cannot yield entirely to affliction, that even
attending to our souls out of duty if not always out of commitment is an
effort in the right direction—in the opposite direction from sin.

Whatever the reasoning, what prevents these poems from seeming, in
the end, aberrations of naïveté is their *placement* within *The Temple*. If we
encounter one of the potentially naïve or sermon-like poems, we are never

very far away from a poem that offers a speaker questioning the very sentiments that have been earlier expressed. As a result, the poems that lack agony read, to me, like a self all but rehearsing, going through the rote motions of what it knows to be "right," even as we can sense the self's lack of conviction; the effect is of a self understanding instinctively that there's a big difference between religious expectation and what is possible, given human limitation. For example, "The Pearl. Matth. 13.45" speaks of a balance that has finally been achieved, a correct acceptance of the relationship between God and man:

> My stuff is flesh, not brass; my senses live,
> And grumble oft, that they have more in me
> Than he that curbs them, being but one to five:
>> Yet I love thee.
>
> (27–30)

But it is immediately followed by "Affliction (IV)," which opens on a note of wrenched outcry:

> Broken in pieces all asunder,
>> Lord, hunt me not,
>> A thing forgot,
> Once a poor creature, now a wonder,
>> A wonder tortured in the space
>> Betwixt this world and that of grace.
>
> (1–6)

The placement of the two poems has its implicit argument: any sense of balance, any temper ("the due or proportionate mixture of elements or qualities," says the *OED*) must needs be temporary. It will always be the case that "I cannot skill of these thy ways" ("Justice [I]"), that our inability will be but one aspect of our affliction, and that all respite from affliction throws affliction into relief only—it does not end it.

Considering how, save for a single line, all thirteen of its stanzas consider the same point in the same way—man is foolish, his hands foul, his eyes blind to God's greatness, therefore entirely unworthy even to serve God, never mind the receiving of blessings—the poem "Misery" should be among the poems that I find less appealing, more dogmatic and too indifferent to a very real, human agony. Why is this not the case?

For a long time, it seemed to have to do with how the third person, in which seventy-seven of the lines are cast, is abandoned for the first person, in the poem's last line:

> But sin hath fooled him. Now he is
> A lump of flesh, without a foot or wing
>   To raise him to a glimpse of bliss:
> A sick tossed vessel, dashing on each thing;
>   Nay, his own shelf:
>   My God, I mean myself.

(73–78)

By means of a simple shift in point of view, Herbert—with an honesty that is the more devastating for seeming to have been accidentally stumbled into—implicates himself in the very behavior that he has spent all this time denouncing.

That is part of it, yes. But also, I think the poem succeeds by what I shall call its mathematics. As a poet, I place great value on a poem's title, and on its last line, and on the relationship between the two. Given how, in the poem, Herbert suggests that the misery of the poem's title refers to the miserable condition of man; and yet, how he also includes himself as an example at the poem's end—I have sometimes seen all of the poem's lines between the title and the last line as an equals sign. One level of the poem's mathematics is: misery = myself.

Punctuation is another of a poem's aspects with which I am always concerned; it creates the silences, in the form of variously timed pauses, in which at least half of a poem's meaning, I am convinced, resides. The last line of "Misery" is: "My God, I mean myself." I read the line two ways: "My God" is meant as apostrophe, i.e., God is the addressee of the remark that follows—"I mean myself;" but also, in the pause that the comma means, a temporal space is opened up—and, inside it, there is time to wonder if Herbert could possibly also have in mind the comma as equals sign. That is, another translation of the line is: by "my God" I mean "myself." In that sense, the line suggests a boldness or arrogance that we have, after all, seen in plenty of Herbert's poems, those in which man cries out in Job-like fashion against the inexplicable ways of God, demanding that those ways be justified.

More math: misery = my God = myself. I mean by this an equivalence in terms of ideas, rather than of "merely" numerical play, though it is worth noting that "misery" and "myself" are each seven letters long—as is the phrase "my God," if we include the space between those two words; and why not, given the weight that seems particularly to attach both to Herbert's punctuation and his use of pause within a given line? In either context, the equation reinforces the theme that we have seen in poems of typographical play, that there is an inextricable relationship between God, man, and suffering—we have only to pare away one to find another enclosed, in an impossibly circular fashion: impossible, because the circle never changes (it being the nature of a circle to remain unbroken), yet its coordinates are in constant shift.

⤙⤚

[Last night]
    Favorite poet?
        George Herbert.
    Favorite poem by?
        "Artillery."
    Best line in?
        "Then we are shooters both . . ."
    Favorite line:
        "Shun not my arrows, and behold my breast."

⤙⤚

Of "Artillery," this mostly: that it is one of many Herbert poems that present human life as an ongoing process of bargaining (even when, as here, the speaker knows that there is no real bargaining—"no articling with thee"—to more than speak of) between God and man. Most often, the bargain is one-directional—that is, Herbert puts his terms forward in a poem, and the poem ends; in these instances, the poem resembles—no, it *is* prayer, when it isn't psalm, which is praise sent in one direction. Both figure, here:

Artillery

As I one ev'ning sat before my cell,
Me thoughts a star did shoot into my lap.
I rose, and shook my clothes, as knowing well,
That from small fires comes oft no small mishap.
    When suddenly I heard one say,
    Do as thou usest, disobey,
    Expel good motions from thy breast,
Which have the face of fire, but end in rest.

I, who had heard of music in the spheres,
But not of speech in stars, began to muse:
But turning to my God, whose ministers
The stars and all things are; If I refuse,
    Dread Lord, said I, so oft my good;
    Then I refuse not ev'n with blood
    To wash away my stubborn thought:
For I will do or suffer what I ought.

But I have also stars and shooters too,
Born where thy servants both artilleries use.
My tears and prayers night and day do woo,
And work up to thee; yet thou dost refuse.
    Not but I am (I must say still)
    Much more obliged to do thy will,
    Than thou to grant mine: but because
Thy promise now hath ev'n set thee thy laws.

Then we are shooters both, and thou dost deign
To enter combat with us, and contest
With thine own clay. But I would parley fain:

Shun not my arrows, and behold my breast.
    Yet if thou shunnest, I am thine:
    I must be so, if I am mine.
    There is no articling with thee:
I am but finite, yet thine infinitely.

Just as bargaining involves two, so does prayer—even in those cases like "Artillery," in which (unlike, say, "The Collar," "Jordan (II)," "Dialogue," among others) God himself does not respond with counterterms. In fact, it seems that God is most present for Herbert in those poems (the majority) in which God is not actually a "character" or speaker. If anything, there is a heightened intimacy—the intimacy of two in one corner of the same very large room: one is speaking, one listening . . .

And in the poems in which God does in word or as *dramatis persona* or via messenger (again, "Artillery") appear, it is never in the word, the representation, or the messenger that I detect the truer presence of divinity. It's elsewhere, in that part of the poem that Stanley Kunitz calls a poem's "wilderness"—he means, I think, the necessary part of a poem that eludes analysis because it has to, and that makes its presence known to our sometimes-too-rational selves only by its very resistance to those selves. That resistance is of course not visible, but it is palpable; to feel it, though, the flesh alone is for once as helpless as—

as I think Herbert would say it always will be—

—◦—

"But I have also stars and shooters too,"

And yet—what can it mean, but folly, to place confidence in the weapons available to us, if we know the weapons themselves to be inferior—if they have intentionally been made so—if the maker is also our opponent—

"Then we are shooters both—"

Yes, except one of the two parties—and that party not our own—holds finally all power; what point, then, in shooting at all—to pass the time that will pass anyway—any event—without us?

"Thy promise now hath ev'n set thee thy laws"

By promise, default, oversight, pity—how is it victory, if secured thus? Conversely, what is victory to the one who can only find defeat, each time, a stranger?

"I am but finite, yet thine infinitely"

All victory, then, as meaningless—and ours finally—and not our own. As for defeat: that it is ultimately not possible—just immediately so.

—◁▷—

Anomaly, conundrum, *thy-will-be-done:* all three, says Herbert, whom I find not so often embracing as standing braced, human, frightened, cocksure, and full of questions before—what, exactly? That which he cannot understand?

If Herbert would know the mystery that is God, he is also just as baffled by and at the same time in awe of the mystery of himself—sometimes more so. After all, the invisible and unsubstantial must by definition elude us, at least in terms of the eyes, of the hand. But how much more frustrating, not to be able to understand what—being flesh—requires relatively little to know?

There are mirrors; or you could touch me.

Here, where you see I touch my very self.

—◁▷—

The Pulley

When God at first made man,
Having a glass of blessings standing by;
Let us (said he) pour on him all we can:
Let the world's riches, which dispersèd lie,
　　　　Contract into a span.

So strength first made a way;
Then beauty flowed, then wisdom, honour, pleasure:
When almost all was out, God made a stay,

Perceiving that alone of all his treasure
  Rest in the bottom lay.

  For if I should (said he)
Bestow this jewel also on my creature,
He would adore my gifts instead of me,
And rest in Nature, not the God of Nature:
  So both should losers be.

  Yet let him keep the rest,
But keep them with repining restlessness:
Let him be rich and weary, that at least,
If goodness lead him not, yet weariness
  May toss him to my breast.

The particular beauty of "The Pulley" has to do with the impurity of the comfort it offers. It is difficult to know how to feel about the news that our restlessness is essentially God-given. On one hand, there's a comfort in knowing that the restlessness that makes us stray sometimes from God is of his own making—we are refreshingly blameless. But there's a perverseness, isn't there, to such a God? How else to understand a deliberate withholding of blessings? What does it mean about God and about man, if any bond between the two can only be achieved through stratagem?

  Yet, perverse or not, the God of "The Collar" endures thirty-two lines of man's restlessness, lines of outcry against God, which God then counters with a single word, *"Child!"* In which word I hear admonishment, welcome, fear, intimacy, the tone of what forgives as much from pity as from respect . . .

  I have said how Herbert withholds easy solution. The way, in the poems, God does? Or perhaps Herbert searches earnestly enough, but does not find, in the end, easy solution—in which way, he recalls our best selves . . .

⤙⤚

I once described my own poems as "advance bulletins from the interior," by which I meant that over time they delivered to me a meaning other than—more troublingly personal than—the meaning I had more consciously intended or at least thought I'd intended. To the extent that the poems have some relevance to their readers, I am grateful. That they also deliver their own confessions—for they do not seem my own entirely—makes me aware of the ways in which poetry can correctly be called dangerous. This is why to write requires great care, on so many levels. It also requires, incongruously, a certain appetite for risk. One proceeds with honesty. At risk, always, is the truth itself.

I mention this, because how I view my own poetry, how I approach the reading and writing of it, cannot help having something to do with how I respond to and come away from Herbert's work. Don't we, necessarily, see the world and everything in it (literature included, of course) through the lens of ourselves, each self responsively shaped according to the world's actions upon it? As far as I know, we step free of the world no more easily than we relinquish the lens through which we see it—by death alone. Necessarily, in this life, I *am* that self.

⤙

For what I would, that do I not; but what I hate, that do I.

(Romans, 8:15)

Herbert persuades by the very thing with which his poems so frequently are ill at ease: his flawed self. It is not so much that he admits to flaw (as much is said in the prose), but that he brings flaw into view as instructive example (one definition, incidentally, for confession)—an instruction intended, I believe, primarily for himself. He persuades by openness, even in those poems in which high artifice figures—if anything, the elaborateness of form often throwing the directness of personal cry into greater relief.

If there is an overall message by the end of *The Temple,* it seems one that emerges not from intellectual or literary engagement, but from a life that has with no little difficulty come through to the farther end of hardship of body and soul—much to its own surprise:

> O my only light,
> It cannot be
> That I am he
> On whom thy tempests fell all night.

("The Flower," 39–42)

Lines like

> The fineness which a hymn or psalm affords,
> Is, when the soul unto the lines accords.

("A True Hymn," 9–10)

speak in part toward the need for something as seemingly obvious as committed feeling—in poetry, it's otherwise all form and function. And in part, the lines address the hymn—in the form of correct behavior—that we are told we should strive to make by calibrating our souls to the lines drawn out for them by God.

What is not said is that any of this is without its difficulty. It is mostly strife, which in "The Banquet" we are instructed to love, though how to do so is never stated in practical terms. My sense by the end is that we essentially learn to live with what will, anyway, be there—be it God, strife, our human frailties.

In the final poem of *The Temple* (again, I omit "The Church Militant"), the soul is "guilty of dust and sin," but is nevertheless encouraged by Love (God, I have always assumed) to "sit down . . . and taste my meat":

Love (III)

> Love bade me welcome: yet my soul drew back,
>   Guilty of dust and sin.
> But quick-eyed Love, observing me grow slack
>   From my first entrance in,
> Drew nearer to me, sweetly questioning,
>   If I lacked anything.
>
> A guest, I answered, worthy to be here:
>   Love said, You shall be he.
> I the unkind, ungrateful? Ah my dear,
>   I cannot look on thee.
> Love took my hand, and smiling did reply,
>   Who made the eyes but I?

Truth Lord, but I have marred them: let my shame
        Go where it doth deserve.
And know you not, says Love, who bore the blame?
        My dear, then I will serve.
You must sit down, says Love, and taste my meat.
        So I did sit and eat.

Absolution?

Salvation?

Or, having admitted to his share of the blame, God's peace offering?

Or consolation, but too late?

As in so many places in Herbert—and what brings me again and again back to the poems—a silence, one that I don't want so much anymore to penetrate or (related, I begin to suspect) I don't need to, no. Increasingly, may it be enough to hear it.

Poetry, Consciousness, Gift:
The Model of T. S. Eliot

⟿

That nothing of art be accidental
That nothing of God be random
That no step—back, nor fore—be minor

⟿

Nothing of T. S. Eliot's sequence, "Landscapes," seems random, accidental—
or indeed minor, despite Eliot's choice to group these under the heading
of "Minor Poems" in his *Collected Poems*. Like "The Waste Land," like the
individual quartets of *Four Quartets,* this sequence is in five sections—
reminiscent of the number of acts required by Aristotle (and adhered to
by Shakespeare) for drama—for tragic drama in particular. And certainly
a drama is afoot here, one whose trajectory proves a useful one for understanding Eliot as a poet, as part of a larger tradition of poetry, and as a
model for those poets writing today who hope to contribute meaningfully
to and to further that tradition.

The first landscape, "New Hampshire," opens with the image of "Children's voices in the orchard"—at once presenting us with one of the central
themes of Eliot's work: human beings and their relationship to the natural
world. There are many difficulties to that relationship, but Eliot usually
has two in mind. One has to do with our supposed superiority to the
natural world. Unlike animals, who perforce live according to what nature
provides, humans are able to shape and condition those provisions—an
orchard, for example, is not a natural phenomenon, but a systematization
of natural occurrences. What allows for all of this is the human characteristic of being rational—self-conscious—not purely instinctive, which is

to say, animal. But while an orchard may be a harmless-enough product of human reasoning, there are more distressing outcomes, such as the scene presented in the fourth landscape, "Rannoch, by Glencoe," where "the crow starves, . . . the patient stag / Breeds for the rifle," a landscape whose psychological topography includes the "Listlessness of ancient war / Languor of broken steel, / Clamour of confused wrong. . . ." It is as if the trajectory of this drama were from the recognition of a harnessing of gift, to the perversion of gift—that is the implication, when sections I and IV are examined beside one another—a choice I don't make arbitrarily. It seems not at all coincidental that these two sections are the only ones twelve lines in length—and that they are the only ones in which humans have any actual presence—even as sections II and V, each being thirteen-line sections, seem meant to be considered together, for reasons I'll come to shortly. But first, I did mention two difficulties of the relationship between humans and the natural world. The first—our seeming superiority to the natural world and the detrimental effects, ultimately, which the natural world suffers at the hands of that superiority. The second is how in the course of a life, it becomes apparent that nature—that the animal world—is not so inferior as we had thought; gifted with reason, with self-consciousness, we are also burdened by it, by its translation also as consciousness of time and therefore of the end of a life, as an ability to know and therefore anticipate loss, and suffer in that anticipation. The children who open the first landscape are as close to animal as we can hope to get—like the orchard, they, too, are "Between the blossom- and the fruit-time"—they have not reached the point of adulthood, a consciousness of time, of present vs. future, they are not yet conscious in the way that our speaker is, who says: "Twenty years and the spring is over; / To-day grieves, to-morrow grieves, . . ." The children are far still, as well, from the landscape they are destined for, that of section IV, scape of memory only, and a snapped pride.

Part of the drama of this sequence concerns the progress from the recognition of nature's superiority to a decision to approximate nature—and a gradual acceptance that such a decision is a doomed because impossible one, and that the history of being human is one of longing. All of this becomes clearer when we examine sections II and V in tandem. Not only equal, as mentioned earlier, in line length, they are the two sections that most concern themselves with the natural world, the landscape in its unpeopled state. Or, more accurately, people do figure in these sections, but as departing figures: in "Virginia," the speaker appears toward the end, but as an example of what must pass into and become subsumed by the river that ultimately contains everything (is superior to it), even as it frames the section itself:

> Ever moving
> Iron thoughts came with me
> And go with me:
> Red river, river, river.

> (10–13)

Similarly, in "Cape Ann," the human being present by implication—the addressee of all those imperatives—is instructed to "resign this land at the end, resign it / To its true owner"—nature, manifest as "the tough one, the sea-gull."

A third factor—in addition to content and line length—suggests we are right to pair sections II and V, namely, their strategy is most overtly one of repetition, significantly more than section I, which does have some repetition, and than II and IV (no repetition, and three instances, respectively). To what effect? Here is the section in its entirety:

> Red river, red river,
> Slow flow heat is silence
> No will is still as a river
> Still. Will heat move
> Only through the mocking-bird
> Heard once? Still hills
> Wait. Gates wait. Purple trees,
> White trees, wait, wait,
> Delay, decay. Living, living,
> Never moving. Ever moving
> Iron thoughts came with me
> And go with me:
> Red river, river, river.

There is a calmness to the repetition here—a prayer-like peacefulness to it that has to do with how the repetitions are distributed; how words like "still" and "will" and "wait" are repeated, but scatteredly, throughout the poem; also, how the repetition is not just at the level of words, but of vocalic sound—the short "i" occurs nineteen times; also, how the lines limit themselves to either three or four stresses (the penultimate line, of two stresses, is the only exception—and I would argue that this is deliberate, as if the white space after that line's colon were meant both to be the understood missing stress and to represent absence itself, for the content's effect)—this is the stress pattern of the hymn, is it not? As for the source of this hymn-like peace, it seems to lie in the fact of the natural world's elements being themselves only, as opposed to being aware of themselves. The heat, the mocking-bird, the waiting hills and trees that no more *know* they wait than they can know what they are waiting for, namely, "decay," and passage back into a river that seems so much to equal something like time, time's continuum; but note how insistent Eliot is in that last line "Red river, river, river," a line that reminds me of Stein's rose—in both cases, the thing is the thing itself. All the resonances and connotations of it are imposed on it, by human consciousness.

That this difference between the natural and the human states has been understood is clear when we consider the different effect of repetition in "Cape Ann." Here, the repetitions—all occurring in significantly longer lines—occur closely together, more anaphorically, at the level of words:

> O quick quick quick, quick hear the song-sparrow,
> Swamp-sparrow, fox-sparrow, vesper-sparrow
>
> (1–2)

Instead of assonance, there's an emphasis on alliteration, which oddly gives not so much an insistent effect (as in the last line of "Virginia"), but the effect of frenzy—also, the effect of stutter, of stall—at least when this is combined with actual word repetition. I think that has to do with the speaker's having understood clearly his inferiority to nature—or the futility of his attempts to master it. In the line "Red river, river, river," the emphasis was on how the river is river, plain and simple and somehow ineffable. In a line like "hear the song-sparrow, / Swamp-sparrow, fox-sparrow, vesper-sparrow," note how a tension occurs between the constant of "sparrow" and the ever-shifting prefix word by which the sparrow is rendered more specific. I see here, on the level of the words themselves, an argument being made that goes something like this: we, as humans, may attach any number of names to it, but the sparrow is finally sparrow—we are the ones who seek to possess by naming, but in the end, being mortal, we possess nothing. Granted, the sparrow dies, too, but it does not *know* this. In this sense, the sparrow "wins." The final section of the poem, with all its imperatives—yet another level of repetition, of course—is urgent enough, as if we had very little time, indeed, to approximate nature (so as to leave our inferior selves behind), to follow (i.e., imitate) the goldfinch's dance, imitate the whistles of quail and bob-white, or make ours the itineraries of the walking water-thrush, the flying purple martin; but in the end, this is seen as useless anyway, no choice but to quit the attempts, all of which have been reduced to palaver, and even that now finished—confined to a mortality we cannot stop ourselves from being aware of, hence the poem's frequent references, as well, to time—not just "vesper," "dawn," "dusk," "noon," but the anaphora of "quick quick quick, quick" and at line 11 the prepositional phrase "at the end."

Speaking of the imperative—it's worth noting that of all the grammatical moods, it is the most frustrated or static. On one hand, it has a force to it that is forward-looking—there's a momentum: do X implies that X may be done. But if it does get done, the evidence of that lies outside, unseeably, the command itself, at least when written. This is true of the interrogative, but questions are from the start less forceful than commands, so the momentum is less. Also, less tension exists between question and answer, because both are verbal, whereas the "answer" to an imperative is usually a physical, visible response of some sort: a relationship is being conducted on two separate planes, as opposed to a single one. Even the subjunctive is more stable because it always makes clear what could/would/might happen or what could have/would have/might have happened—a response is understood. Eliot's heavy use of the imperative in "Cape Ann" serves him well in conveying the thwartedness of human effort, how at the end of any urge toward action, the result is stasis, the stasis of consciousness, the consciousness of the ultimate stasis, that of death itself. It would seem that the sequence's final line—"The palaver is finished"—refers to all that the final section has suggested in terms of remedy; the palaver might, as well, be the list of instructions that have preceded—palaver, because futile. In which case, this is a decidedly unhopeful poem.

But an alternative translation for the palaver becomes apparent if we bear in mind the section we have yet to discuss. Section III, "Usk," is the central section, the sequence's pivot, in terms of actual position. Unlike the other sections, it has no match in terms of line length; at eleven lines, it is distinct both structurally and positionally. To these facts, add what we considered earlier about the assignment of five acts to a Greek tragedy, and we have every reason to believe that something climactic should occur at this position— though, given all that was said about the imperative, which also governs this section—any climax or turn will at best be subtle.

What "Usk" instructs against is any false notion of escape, rescue, fantasy—the poetic, on some level, or the poetic versions of rescue, images such as that of "The white hart behind the white well," the Arthurian lance. All of these Eliot reduces to the single phrase "Old enchantments," and I would suggest that these are also what Eliot means by the "palaver" of "Cape Ann." There is, though, in addition to that which we're instructed against, another element we are directed *toward,* and that is the spiritual—not, however, in its conventionally concretized forms, "the hermit's chapel, the pilgrim's prayer," but in something neither human nor animal, not of that natural world which finally decays, as we have been told in "Virginia," but locatable only within the timeless and double continuum of light and the space it finds, that place "where the grey light meets the green air." We aren't told what this spiritual thing will be—not the Grail, presumably another of the Old enchantments. But I find an element of hope, albeit undefined, in this section. For one, this section's imperatives aren't negated in a final imperative such as "resign this land," as in "Cape Ann." Nothing in "Usk" suggests that a responsive action to the imperatives is not possible. Unlike section V, where the imperatives (in concert with that section's use of anaphora, alliteration, and references to time) generate the effect of stalled momentum, here the effect is closer to that of prayer, one-directional, yes, but propelled by hope, which in turn implies belief.

~⁊~

Is "Landscapes" a pastoral sequence? Yes, in a couple of senses of that tradition. One is the Herbertian, if we recall how Herbert, in the preface to his prose work *The Country Parson* referred to that work as "a complete pastoral," a treatise on the pastor's duties. And I believe the duties to which we are instructed by Eliot are reducible to a few lines from "Usk," the three lines whose brevity, relative to the lengths of all the other lines, causes them to stand out as is nowhere else apparent in the entire sequence. Those three lines, also the only three in dimeter, are 2, 7, and 9, and put together they read thus:

Hope to find
· · · · · · · · · ·
Lift your eyes
· · · · · · · · · ·
Seek only there

A very pastoral message, indeed—and no surprising one, given the shift toward spiritual solution that is apparent in the great poems "The Waste Land" and "Four Quartets," poems to which this smaller sequence seems respectively an echo and a preparatory study.

"Landscapes" is also pastoral, of course, in the Virgilian sense, if we recall how the natural landscape in Virgil's *Eclogues* becomes the backdrop against which to understand the horrors and aftermath of civil war, part of whose effect is not only the carving up of the land (and the consequent dispossession of its rightful owners) but a stripping away of the idyllic—perhaps idealized—psychology with which the life inside that landscape once was charged. Eliot's pastoral, too, suggests a lost ideal, one of near pre-consciousness, of children's innocence ("New Hampshire"), against which is held up a landscape of war and broken steel—a shift from the golden age to that of iron. Interestingly, Virgil's sequence also locates at its center, or near-center, a space for hope in the form of the spiritual—I refer to the fourth eclogue, which speaks of a messianic rescuing figure, whom many scholars have tried, at least, to identify as Christ.

⟞∿

What would it be like to live by instinct entirely, to have none of the human powers of reason, the self-consciousness, intellectual and bodily, that separates human from animal? Keats is hardly the first to have asked the question, but perhaps most famously did so in his "Ode to a Nightingale," a poem that surely hovers behind "Cape Ann," the final section of Eliot's "Landscapes." As both Keats and Eliot soon learn, to ask the question is to understand the futility of having asked; the problem is that in losing our self-consciousness, we would not become animal, i.e.,

> quite forget
> What thou [the bird] among the leaves hast never known,
> The weariness, the fever, and the fret
> Here, where men sit and hear each other groan;
>
> (21–24)

the solution isn't that easy. Rather, to lose the human element is to suffer death as a human—to die, essentially if not actually, which is presumably why when Keats casts about for something analogous to the nightingale's state, in human terms, what come most immediately to mind are hemlock, the "easeful Death" to which it can lead, and the river Lethe for the forgetting *after* death. Even at poem's end, when Keats seems to have sung himself into that desired state of unconsciousness, he asks "Do I wake or sleep?" and in doing so he shows that he has in no way succeeded at approximating the animal. The nightingale would never ask that question.

⟜

It isn't, however, as if humans have no animal qualities, or the ability to manifest them—in *Prufrock* and in the 1920 collection simply entitled *Poems*, Eliot frequently discusses humanity in terms of animals—but the humans acquire no peace as a result of being akin to animals. Rather, the manifestation of the animal in the human becomes the evidence by which to understand the effect of social erosion *upon* the human individual. In these earlier poems, Eliot's speakers do not *seek* to become animal. Prufrock, for example, may say "I should have been a pair of ragged claws / Scuttling across the floors of silent seas", but that is less a statement of longing than one made after the fact of recognition that such longing would be ineffectual. Rather, while Keats seeks to attain nightingale-hood, but is prevented by human self-consciousness, Eliot's Prufrock seeks himself, but is prevented by societal consciousness, as it were—society's notions of what a self should be, namely, not individual. This seems to be the meaning of the line with which that poem concludes—"Till human voices wake us, and we drown"—the more intimate, more personal "we" drowning as a *result* of the more communal "human voices." More often, what happens instead of drowning is that, for Eliot, the human gets rendered partly animal, the part of being animal that Keats does not mention, the part which is indifferent, necessarily, to suffering—including its own—in any rational way.

We find many examples, throughout the earlier poems, of humans being aligned with animals: Mr. Apollinax likened to a centaur (itself a creature half-human, half-animal); the uncorseted and lusty Grishkin is likened to "the sleek Brazilian jaguar" whose "feline smell" is apparently not "so rank" as Grishkin's own (in "Whispers of Immortality"); there is, of course, Sweeney, sometimes "orang-outang" in his gestures, sometimes "apeneck," "The zebra stripes along his jaw / Swelling to maculate giraffe." But one of the most disturbing instances, and one which particularly highlights what I have said about the animal as that to which the human gets *eroded* by the ills of society, occurs in these lines from "Rhapsody on a Windy Night":

> "Remark the cat which flattens itself in the gutter,
> Slips out its tongue
> And devours a morsel of rancid butter."
> So the hand of the child, automatic,
> Slipped out and pocketed a toy that was running along the quay.
> I could see nothing behind that child's eye.
> I have seen eyes in the street
> Trying to peer through lighted shutters,
> And a crab one afternoon in a pool,
> An old crab with barnacles on his back,
> Gripped the end of a stick which I held him.

> (35–45)

As with the singing of the nightingale, the crab here grips the stick out of instinct, because of its own inherent nature, which is in turn to seize what could be food; likewise, the cat devouring the rancid butter. But the child who pockets the toy with the same eagerness as the cat would seize the butter (or the crab the stick) is a child who has been forced by deprivation to act animalistically—to perform what he would recognize as theft if he were thinking humanly, but he is lost to the human, for which reason we are told there is nothing, now, behind the child's eye.

Any agony of an existential sort is not suffered by human-animal hybrids— that is one blessing, anyway, their being unable to fully understand what they have been reduced to. No, the ones who suffer in these poems are the speakers, the observers of those individuals who unfortunately have *not* been so eroded as to be blind to suffering. When Eliot speaks in "Preludes" of "The notion of some infinitely gentle / Infinitely suffering thing" (50–51), he means presumably that human being whose consciousness has not been blunted, who *knows* suffering, and whose powers of reason enable him to know the impossibility of escaping consciousness without becoming un-human, a form of death-in-life. The poet, too, is something between human and animal, differently though from the less-than-human figures we've seen earlier. Unlike those figures (who are human in body only), the animal component, for the poet, has eroded everything *but* consciousness of reason; the result is a capacity for tragic illumination, a clear window onto the reality of which, as Eliot tells us, "human kind / Cannot bear very much" ("Burnt Norton").

The single instance I find of such a creature in Eliot's poetry (besides the speakers of the poems) is the figure of Philomela who appears in "The Waste Land," the woman metamorphosed to nightingale, but decidedly different from Keats's bird. Philomela is bird in form, but human in her ability to be aware of her own suffering—having been raped by her brother-in-law and had her tongue cut out; and, like the poet, is doomed—or fated?—to bear endless witness to and sing her suffering (at least as portrayed in sections II and III of "The Waste Land") without being able to change that suffering. Interestingly, when she was human she had the speechlessness of animal-bird—because of the lack of a tongue; once she becomes bird, Philomela *can* speak, but the irony is a bitter one indeed:

Twit twit twit
Jug jug jug jug jug jug
So rudely forc'd.
Tereu

  (203–6)

she sings, carrying always in her mouth the name of her rapist and would-be murderer. It is by becoming the nightingale that Philomela escapes that murder, but she leaves behind none of the consciousness of which Keats's nightingale can have no idea.

❧

Would it be better to be a hollow man? I used to think the speakers of "The Hollow Men" were a sort of chorus made up of those psychologically alienated people from Eliot's earlier poems. Now, the hollow men seem—well, not *unhappy*, nor blind either, to the reality that is theirs. They are higher, so to speak, than the other figures, because less animal—their reason has not been blunted, they do not act by instinct alone—but they are clearly less than human, if only bodily, being both things: hollow, but also stuffed, but the stuffing itself straw only, nothing human *or* animal. They also seem better off than the poet-figure as we've suggested it, and better off than poor Philomela.

The hollow men live in some in-between, limbo-like state, or perhaps closer would be whatever we might call a purgatory *preceding* death—since these men have not died yet. I say purgatory because, unlike hell, purgatory offers the hope of eventual paradise and ultimate salvation. And I see something approaching this kind of hope in the hollow men's description of their environment, a shadowland

Between the idea
And the reality

  (72–73)

· · · · · · · · · · · ·

Between the emotion
And the response

(80–81)

. . . .

Between the desire
And the spasm

(84–85)

This may not seem fraught with hope to many, but I find here a trajectory of possibility akin to the one we assigned to prayer. Idea, for example, implies reality, if only potentially. So long as reality has not yet been arrived at, it has the possibility to exist. Desire, prior to spasm, may be unfulfilled, but it remains possible for the spasm to occur and to be as good or better than we had expected. As Eliot will later point out in "Ash-Wednesday," the torment greater than "love unsatisfied" is the "torment / Of love satisfied." Existentially, the trajectory of the hollow men is forward, upward—from the first step toward fulfillment to the second step by which the success or failure of the first will be known for certain. And in the not-knowing lies the possibility, which is hope—a lack, as yet, of despair.

The hollow men seem smarter, incidentally, than does Keats in his longing to be the nightingale. They recognize that such a transformation would be death itself, and that the trick is to skirt death, not step into it; hence, their wish to come no closer to death (as I translate the phrase "death's dream kingdom") than becoming merely what is acted upon, and escaping not consciousness but bodily responsibility—hence their desire to be not only like scarecrows (after all, they're already stuffed with straw) but disguised as them:

Let me also wear
Such deliberate disguises
Rat's coat, crowskin, crossed staves
In a field
Behaving as the wind behaves
No nearer—

(31–36)

Such an existence amounts to a succumbing to, a giving over of selfdom to another power; this can sometimes seem lack of responsibility, or indifference, or self-imposed slavery—or, in the wake of the recognition of another power's inevitablity, variously surrender or trust. I think it may be a bit of all of these in *this* poem, but the leaning, as I read it, seems toward a surrendering of self *trustingly* up to the authority of God, given the refrains of "For Thine is the Kingdom," and in particular what is identified in Part IV as the only hope available to empty men, "the perpetual star / Multifoliate rose" attached to visionary experience, especially Christian visionary experience. Concerning submission, I consider the following lines:

> Yet take thy way; for sure thy way is best:
> 　Stretch or contract me, thy poor debtor:
> 　This is but tuning of my breast,
> 　　To make the music better.

The lines are Herbert's, of course, from "The Temper (I)" (21–24). But how different is their sentiment from that which is voiced by the hollow men? Not just at the scarecrow lines, but even in the poem's concluding lines that seem less an acknowledgment of defeat than of a fact arrived at and accepted, rationally bowed down before.

⁓

To be a nightingale is to live instinctively and bodied, without the consciousness of it. To be a hollow man is to live consciously but bodiless—or at least freed of the body properly understood. To be human and hope for either of these states is finally folly, part of what Eliot seems to refer to at the conclusion of "Ash-Wednesday" when he prays "Suffer us not to mock ourselves with falsehood." "Ash-Wednesday" is the poem where Eliot most overtly makes the turn toward a third gate, as it were, namely that of religion. The turn is, in and of itself, predictable enough as a response to moral crisis on a societal level: the spiritual, in all its forms, credible and the "usual/Pastimes and drugs"—as Eliot will later say in :s"—that "always will be, some of them especially / When nations and perplexity / Whether on the shores of Asia, or oad[.]" I think of the rise of mystery cults during the shift

from republic to empire in ancient Rome; or of the turn away from matters imperial to the private interior of Stoic meditation on the part of Marcus Aurelius; or indeed of the alarming increase of focus on the censorial role of religion, in response to a perceived laxity of morals in contemporary society. But Eliot's turn is not toward a religion that equals escapism—from the ills of self *or* of society. The prayer early in "Ash-Wednesday" may be to escape self-consciousness:

And I pray that I may forget
These matters that with myself I too much discuss
Too much explain

(27–29)

But by the end of the poem, this is yet another falsehood—and is understood as such. We return to lines with which the poem's first section ended— "Teach us to care and not to care / Teach us to sit still"—but at poem's end those lines equal not a prayer for indifference or for consciouslessness, but rather for the ability to find "Our peace in His [God's] will." Eliot's peace is not oblivion; it's something more like an ability to temper an inevitable awareness of self and of desire and of will with a consignment of the will to an authority whose existence depends entirely on faith; which is to say, it depends entirely on our corralling the part of our identity that is empirical-minded. The good poet stops there, and in his silence is the implication that solution has been found. The great poet—of which, of course, Eliot is one—understands that to recognize solution is not the same as having it. Herbert and Dickinson distinguish themselves as poets because they acknowledge the metaphysical wrestling as an ongoing event, whose end won't be understood in this life, the life itself a form of apprenticeship to what is not humanly attainable; yet, in the striving is a form of victory, a refusal of the pat and complacent. There is also—back to "The Hollow Men"—the pleasure derived from not completing the trajectory, that deferral of arrival that keeps hope possible.

By hope, I mean nothing of the naïve variety, however, the kind of hope that Eliot describes as being as deceitful as is despair in Part III of "Ash-Wednesday," a section that is especially relevant here. The entire section can be read as a map of the unfinished trajectory under discussion. In this case,

we are at a very small and middle portion of an ascending trajectory, the
space climbed from the second to the third stair, and the implied—but not
realized within the poem itself—fourth stair. (Or we are in the shadowland,
again, between idea and reality—also, that "dreamcrossed twilight between
birth and dying," as Eliot will call it in Part VI of this poem.) The deferral
of arrival at anything certain is what leaves the trajectory open and fraught
with potential. Yes, Eliot toward the end of the section announces twice
"Lord, I am not worthy," but he concludes with "but speak the word only,"
and in so doing he both concedes inadequacy and an impetus to act *beyond*
the acknowledgment of that inadequacy, by speech, even if speech itself is
inadequate, is mere approximation, hence that word "only" tagged on at the
end. The speaking is a version of prayer, or will be equivalent to that by the
end of the poem proper, when "but speak the word only" seems to find its
translation in the concluding line "And let my cry come unto Thee." Again,
the cry goes out, but is not answered, not on the page at least—Eliot does
not provide answer, but allows for its possibility, which is different from
complacency or naïve hope. Eliot also dismisses despair here as deceitful,
by which I think he means that it, too, can be naïve, or another version of
escapism—just as, by the way, Eliot dismisses pastoral of a certain kind here
as well, recognizing it as a faded ideal (as did Virgil):

> And beyond the hawthorn blossom and a pasture scene
> The broadbacked figure drest in blue and green
> Enchanted the maytime with an antique flute.
> Blown hair is sweet, brown hair over the mouth blown,
> Lilac and brown hair;
> Distraction, music of the flute, stops and steps of the mind over the
> > third stair,
> Fading, fading; . . .
>
> (109–115)

What is the pastoral, finally, but "Distraction," so Eliot says, from the task
at hand, namely to take on the responsibility that both hope and despair
refuse to—the responsibility to look honestly, with relatively little or no
flinching at all, at the very reality that humans ordinarily find unbearable?
To do so is not necessarily to court disaster, nor to claim with certainty its

opposite. As Djuna Barnes says in her novel *Nightwood,* "The unendurable is the *beginning* of the curve of joy" (italics mine).

—⊸

Many contemporary poets—younger ones, especially—seem to hold Eliot in suspicion, somehow. Much of this has to do with his turn toward religion, and with the prevalence of thinking of religion only in its more opiate and/or ecstatic manifestations. And yet it seems to me that the spiritual life, of any faith or denomination, finally concerns itself most with methods of discipline by which to lead what instinctively and intellectually waivers through the steps of pilgrimage—if not literal, then existential—toward what exists only insofar as we believe it does. Hardly a drug, religion can make the world all the more visible for its being thrown into the light of what may or may not exist beyond it. "Garlic and sapphires in the mud."("Burnt Norton").

Also problematic for many: the association of religion with intellectual naïveté. But, far from a gesture of naïve, ecstatic throwing of self up to another, Eliot's notions are more along the lines of patient—and wide-eyed—waiting to see. As he says in "East Coker,"

> I said to my soul, be still, and wait without hope
> For hope would be hope for the wrong thing; wait without love
> For love would be love of the wrong thing; there is yet faith
> But the faith and the love and the hope are all in the waiting.

> (124–127)

There is a general suspicion of the authoritative—of which religion is but a single version—in contemporary poetry. Statements of any conviction are considered arrogant, emptily hieratic, often overbearing *because* intellectual and reasoned. And yet, if anything, poetry should have authority—why speak, if we hardly believe in what it is we're saying? The key, I think, in bringing authority to a poem is in remembering that authority is not divorced from vulnerability—any more than the intellectual precludes the sensual (or vice versa). In fact, the wisdom of intellect that is evinced *convincingly* in a poem will always turn out to have come from the consequences *of* vulnerability. In Eliot's early work, I find an unattractive cyni-

cism that smacks mostly of the swagger of eager youth. By early, I mean
prior to "The Waste Land." The exception of course is "The Love Song of
J. Alfred Prufrock" (and possibly "Gerontion"), where we are not for a moment allowed to forget that the speaker is mired in self-doubt, not until
the final few lines, whose authority—precisely *because* of the honesty of the
authority with which the speaker maligns himself—goes unquestioned. I
am willing to trust, about religious experience, the poet who opens a poem
(in this case, "The Dry Salvages") with reasonable doubt:

> I do not know much about gods; but I think that the river
> Is a strong brown god— . . .
>
> (1–2)

These lines move seamlessly from *not knowing* to *thinking* to near-actual-
ization of a statement that would be "The river *is* a strong brown god."
Or consider the wavering of self that shifts toward authority but whose
authority is borrowed, finally, in Part III of the same poem:

> I sometimes wonder if that is what Krishna meant—
> Among other things—or one way of putting the same thing:
> That the future is a faded song . . .
>
> (124–126)

The speaker does not think or believe, but wonders—and then only sometimes—*if* that is what Krishna meant. What is being considered is then
deferred by two moments of qualification ("Among other things—or one
way of putting the same thing"). The lines themselves become exemplary
of a hesitant but persistent, sometimes wrenched-with-doubt, but forward
movement toward an authority to be eventually stepped into as the speaker's
own. They are a graph by which the mind is tracked in the act of processing
psychological, intellectual, and experiential evidence and shaping all of it into
eventual idea. There are several available phrases to describe this particular
activity: to reason, to quest intellectually, to be rational. To be conscious of
our mortal condition, and to instinctively want not to *be* conscious of it. To
be human.

All of Eliot's work serves finally as a model for how the poet has a responsibility (and perhaps an innate tendency?) to be something *more* than human—namely, to move *past* a longing to turn away from an unbearable reality, and learn not so much to solve as to bear it.

Why bear it? Why not yield to whatever might most readily blind or blunt us to what is difficult? Why, as poets, strip and thereby make visible difficulty instead of satisfying the majority of people by veiling it? Because poetry is not only what reminds us that we *are* human, but helps ensure that we don't forget what it *means* to be so. In an ever more technology-minded (how human is that?) society—and the latest millennium has only just gotten started—poetry is one of the means left by which the genuinely human is spared extinction. Granted: in the being spared lies, incongruously, the peculiar torment that is what it is to live consciously. "Who then devised the torment? Love."—says Eliot toward the end of "Little Gidding." He recalls Herbert yet again, in whose poem "Love (III)" Love, symbolic of God, confesses that he was himself the cause behind the weary supplicant's travails: "And know you not, says Love, who bore the blame?" (15). For both poets, the spiritual—of a very particular kind—is turned to, but not so much as the solution as a *direction-toward-which,* a context for quest whose end is ever elusive. Is it fair to say that all great poetry—the writing of it and the reading of it—is spiritual, inasmuch as it is finally a quest (for truth, clarity of vision) for which vigilance—attention—devotion are required? I think so. And how else is devotion to be tested unless by hardship?

To this question, let Eliot's words from "The Dry Salvages" (168–169) serve, fittingly, not as answer—no, but as clear-eyed, unconsoling, hortatory chorus:

> Not fare well,
> But fare forward, voyagers.

Association in Poetry

All poetry is at some level associative. What seems to lie behind the impulse to write poetry is that we feel/see/hear/touch/taste, in some way perceive something, and our desire to articulate that perception is not satisfied with the immediately available language; to say "I feel bad," as a means of expressing that I feel bad, is not likely to satisfy a poet. In the course of trying to be more specific, we tend toward an image, some parallel situation, that our bad feeling approximates, and that's where we associate. "Feeling bad reminds me of the time I was forced to eat liver while running in place," the poet might say—or some version of "X is like Y"—and by assembling the things that are similar to it, we give our particular bad feeling a context, and context always helps bring an object into greater clarity.

This assembling of a group of images that are related is key to the lyric method, is what makes lyric resemble an extended simile or set of them suspended in time, so that the lyric poem implies a larger narrative, of which the poem is intended as a fragment—representative, and not entirely so, of the larger narrative. The gathering together of images can be likened to a musical chord—several notes held simultaneously to produce a meaning that in music is called harmony; in lyric poetry, we call it resonance, which is more than just meaning—it's more like meaning with a lingering haunt to it, or (back to music), meaning with a vibrato.

By associative poetry, I mean poetry that works almost entirely by means of association—no connecting narrative pieces, often no syntactical connection, poetry that is characterized by leaps not just from stanza to stanza, but from one image to the next in ways that do not immediately make sense because their relatedness to one another is not clear. The reason for this lack of clarity is that the associative poem (to quote Barbara Herrnstein

Smith from her book *Poetic Closure*), often seems "to represent not overt speech but transcription, as it were, of an interior monologue," a map of the life of the mind. But—to return to Herrnstein Smith—"the life of the mind is not always so orderly; we are not always thinking about something specific, and our thoughts may develop from each other through casual associations and lead nowhere in particular" (pp. 139–140). There would seem to be greater freedom, then, to the associative poem—if the monologue is interior, then we are freed of the need to explicate points that are only privately referential, since *we* know what *we* mean. It's a dangerous freedom because it's the freedom to be arbitrary. And yet, if we are writing poems, we hope to communicate something to others than ourselves. The task for the writer of the associative poem is to give the impression that something has been written in total freedom when in fact that freedom has been necessarily compromised by the need to bear in mind the degree to which what we are writing is intelligible to an audience we are pretending does not exist.

❧

Say that we put next to one another a barking dog, a boom box on which is being played a recording of a toilet being flushed, and an idling lawn mower. Is this a chord of music? Less so, at first, than the several notes held together earlier; since the sounds don't seem to go together except by coincidence, and since none of the sounds is locatable in our received idea of music, the sounds do not initially generate the musical equivalent of meaning—namely, harmony. And yet, the sounds are not unrelated to one another: each, for example, is the sound of something connected with human civilization—the domestication of animals; the domestication of such natural acts as defecation, as a means of making such acts socially more acceptable; the manufacture of machines like lawn mowers, which are also tools of domestication. Slowly, several possibilities for meaning become possible. A statement is perhaps being made about human culture; the absence of any humans here may argue for how the products of human culture have crowded the human out. And so on.

Part of the point in the associative poem is that the reader *should* be unsettled, should not know at first what to make of what has been read. As poets, when we liken X to Y—unless we are resorting to cliché—we are presumably the first to have made such a connection. Which means it may not be immediately intelligible to the reader—but it should be eventually accessible. Otherwise, we are guilty of a self-indulgence that, increasingly, it seems to me, mars much contemporary American poetry, producing work that calls itself oblique or mysterious or vatic, when in fact it is merely obfuscated, not very well thought-out, is suspicious of meaning, and privileges the arty over art itself. However, when applied successfully, the associative method makes for a poetry that demands—both of poet and reader—that the mind be athletic, not just able to negotiate the leaps, but able to find in such leaps a restorative vigor that is among the pleasures of reading great poetry.

～

It's no accident that the same generation that gave us Imagism—those poems that focus exclusively on a cluster of images and put all the burden of expression on the images themselves—is the same group that introduced into English and American poetry the Japanese haiku and tanka, along with the Chinese poets Li Po, Tu Fu, and others. What they all have in common is a stripped-down quality that employs association rather than overt narration; their meaning depends wholly on the degree to which the assembled images continue to resonate past the poem's apparent ending. Linda Gregg acknowledges the influence of the Chinese masters in her poem "Growing Up," then goes on to employ their method:

> I am reading Li Po. The TV is on
> with the sound off.
> I've seen this movie before.
> I turn on the sound just for a moment
> when the man says, "I love you."
> Then turn it off and go on reading.

Skillfully crossing the associative method with the method of reportage, the poem makes its first leap in the first line, as the great poetry of the eighth-century T'ang Dynasty is juxtaposed with the comparatively banal, technological world of TV. The relationship between them is not apparent—makes no immediate sense—and therefore the mention of TV seems random, at first, as does the mention of there being no volume; for that matter, we might ask what meaning or relevance is to be gleaned from knowing that a television is on and someone is reading a book at the same time. But Gregg has chosen to give us in reverse the information that makes the mention of no volume clear: she's seen the movie before, there's no need to hear it, the dialogue's memorized—so much so, that she knows exactly when "I love you" will be said. That this is the only line she listens to suggests that she has winnowed out what isn't necessary (to her) in the movie, down to this single phrase. She is free then to return to her reading. Working associatively, Gregg moves quickly from Li Po to TV; taking advantage of the flexibility of association, she offers information in another order than the one we'd expect in straightforward reporting or narrative. She then offers information that seems only of personal relevance: she favors a particular line in the movie, we are not told why, then all returns to where it began. But Gregg's poem is, in fact, very structured, and this is what prevents the poem from being mere self-indulgent anecdote. The poem is framed, at beginning and end, by the act of reading Li Po. Within the frame of reading, Gregg seems to say, TV is contained—TV may inevitably exist, but it will have its place, which is to be contained by literary endeavor, not to overwhelm it. The reading is a box that contains the TV; the TV contains the movie; the movie contains many lines, but again Gregg has determined which line will be permitted to exist as a *heard* one—it happens to be one of the oldest lines in any language, and could be in *any* movie at all; as with the Li Po poems, the line exists *outside* of television, has had a life independent of and prior to technology. Going from large box to smaller, to smaller still, we reach the heart—the line "I love you"—which not incidentally is related, by timelessness, to the Li Po poetry. To reinforce that relationship, Gregg then ends with an immediate leap back to the act of reading.

As with Li Po's work, Gregg's poems are physically small and can initially seem like random anecdote. But they are always more than this, precisely because nothing is random about them. They exemplify one of the truths about associative poetry: the associative poem, if successful, will always show evidence of a governing order or pattern behind it. It is in this ordering/patterning process that both art and vision figure.

I have been thinking of the famous line from Wordsworth's preface to *Lyrical Ballads:* "poetry is the spontaneous overflow of powerful feelings; it takes its origin from emotion recollected in tranquillity." Too many poets have forgotten that last bit, about recollection in tranquillity.

⁓

Another method often used in associative poetry is that of improvisation, by which term we can see that the associative poem can be related to a critical technique of jazz, whereby the musician riffs off of the previously played few bars of music, in a sense letting the music take him or her where it wants to. Bear in mind, though: in music, improvisation that goes nowhere has other names—variously, practice, tuning one's instrument, noodling . . .

Associative writing is often discussed in the same breath as stream-of-consciousness writing, which we are told is meant to be reflective of the mind caught in the act of thinking. But the truth is that successful stream-of-consciousness writing cannot be an exact transcript of the brain—it would be so random that it would make no sense at all to the reader. When William Faulkner, in his novel *The Sound and the Fury,* not only employs stream of consciousness but for a considerable portion of the book gives us the consciousness of a retarded boy, he succeeds because he is selective in which thoughts to include so that a communicable pattern emerges, which translates into meaning for the reader. We are in the mind of a retarded boy *via* the controlling lens of the author—that's the art part. It is not true to fact, because art is never fact entirely. It's a manipulation of fact.

In the context of improvisation and stream of consciousness, here is Yusef Komunyakaa's "Back Then," from his 1984 collection *Copacetic:*

I've eaten handfuls of fire
back to the bright sea
of my first breath
riding the hipbone of memory
& saw a wheel of birds
a bridge into the morning
but that was when gold
didn't burn out a man's eyes

before auction blocks
groaned in courtyards
& nearly got the best of me
that was when the spine
of every ebony tree wasn't
a pale woman's easy chair
black earth-mother of us all
crack in the bones & sombre
eyes embedded like beetles
in stoic heartwood
seldom have I needed
to shake a hornet's nest
from the breastplate
fire over the ground
pain tears me to pieces
at the pottery wheel
of each dawn
an antelope leaps
in the heartbeat
of the talking drum

Most immediately noteworthy is the absence of punctuation; in effect, the poem is an extended run-on sentence and, as we look at the content, we find that the imagery is likewise run-on—perhaps it's more true to say that the imagery is delivered in a cascade which, because of the lack of punctuation, forces us (especially if we are *hearing* it, and not reading it) to experience in a wash, as it were, a group of images, rather than having the opportunity to examine each individually; the poem doesn't allow for that stopping time. Therefore, before we can entirely "take in" the notion of fire as edible, we are expected to consider breath as a bright sea, and immediately let go of that image for the equally challenging one of memory as a hipbone.

Time, as well, is blurred. We have the initial "I've eaten," which suggests a *habitual* activity in the past, then (line 5) "& saw a wheel of birds," suggesting a *particular* event in a past that was prior to the one of the poem's present place in time—which is somewhere after the era of slavery, but prior to the present of the poem, in which "pain tears [the speaker] to pieces," and each dawn (a way of implying the future) contains elements (the antelope, the talking drum) that belong to a more atavistic past that seems not to have yet encountered the development of civilization to the point of considering human slavery a commercial enterprise.

And yet, the poem begins and ends in the natural world—as remembered, in the poem's first six lines; and as dreamed of / imagined, in the last six lines of the poem. They form a frame that contains the history that, more complicated, is allotted more lines—sixteen, to be exact. Is it an accident that the central lines of this section, the two lines that form the poem's hinge, are precisely the ones that juxtapose a symbol of commerce with the natural world whose stripping is the price exacted by that commerce: "a pale woman's easy chair / black earth-mother of us all"? In a sense, those two lines represent the argument of the poem overall: nature vs. civilization, and the inability of the two to coexist without some eventual suffering on the part of both, a sort of mutually erosive symbiotic relationship. Komunyakaa's poem, if improvisatory, if like a stream of consciousness, is also at each point deliberate, controlled—an example of the associative poem at its best.

⸜⸝

In George Herbert's entirely associative (and entirely fragmented) "Prayer (I)," it is the method of association itself that provides the poem with its argument:

Prayer, the Church's banquet, angels' age,
    God's breath in man returning to his birth,
    The soul in paraphrase, heart in pilgrimage,
The Christian plummet sounding heav'n and earth;
Engine against th'Almighty, sinners' tower,
    Reversèd thunder, Christ-side-piercing spear,
    The six-days' world transposing in an hour,
A kind of tune, which all things hear and fear;
Softness, and peace, and joy, and love, and bliss,
    Exalted manna, gladness of the best,
    Heaven in ordinary, man well dressed,
The Milky Way, the bird of Paradise,
    Church-bells beyond the stars heard, the soul's blood,
    The land of spices; something understood.

If the poem is a list of definitions, it is more accurately a list at war with itself. On one hand, we have a list that works inclusively—that is, the gesture is one of defining prayer and constantly elaborating on that definition, finding it necessary to keep expanding it, as if the more one understood about prayer, the more one had come to realize the impossibility of including everything that prayer apparently includes. And on the other hand, we have a list whose gesture is one of constantly rejecting, in search of exactness of definition: prayer is X; no, prayer is Y; no, keep trying. And in that final definition, "something understood," the poem seems to argue that the human impulse to define (in a sense, to impose pattern, which is what the sonnet form seeks to do here with the information that keeps threatening to overwhelm it) is itself the problem, and that prayer is finally that which is understood as itself utterly. Inclusive of everything, and like nothing that it contains.

To give a list is one thing, to report is another. Some poems proceed in a purely reporting fashion—delivering bits of information from line to line, the bits themselves easily connected, clearly related to one another—only to make a wildly associative leap at the end, the leap all the more bracing to us as readers because we have been so conditioned to the reporting method that has governed the poem. One of the more remarkable examples in English is James Wright's "Lying in a Hammock at William Duffy's Farm in Pine Island, Minnesota":

> Over my head, I see the bronze butterfly,
> Asleep on the black trunk,
> Blowing like a leaf in green shadow.
> Down the ravine behind the empty house,
> The cowbells follow one another
> Into the distances of the afternoon.
> To my right,
> In a field of sunlight between two pines,
> The droppings of last year's horses
> Blaze up into golden stones.
> I lean back, as the evening darkens and comes on.
> A chicken hawk floats over, looking for home.
> I have wasted my life.

Essentially, the poem is a list of what the poet sees around him. When he suddenly tells us "I have wasted my life," it is shocking, there's no reason to have expected a shift at all, let alone such a bald statement of failure—nor is it immediately clear how or why the scene that the poet envisions must lead inevitably to the realization of that last sentence. No small part of the force of the last sentence—of the leap—is that Wright isn't leaping from image to image in that final leap; rather, the leap is from the world of imagery itself, which has been the space inhabited by the bulk of the poem, to the world of mental or emotional climate—or of psychology. We are forced to try to reconcile the poem's final statement with all that has preceded it—which can be done, ultimately, and in a variety of ways. This reconciling is what one does in the wake of epiphany. The poem itself is an instance of another axiom about association: a small admixture of associative method to what has been entirely narrative or report-like in method will yield epiphany, if it is also the case that a line can be feasibly traced back from the moment of epiphany to the material that has preceded it. Note the difference if we substitute, for Wright's last line, "I am ready for dinner," which becomes another announcement in present time and does not resonate with any meaning beyond the actual information that it contains. Or we might end with "Last night, the neighbors' barn burned down"—but again, though we have shifted in time, the information itself doesn't resonate; thus, it continues the list, and the poem remains static. We might even substitute the last line of the poem that lies behind Wright's poem (and whose strategy informs it), Rilke's "Archaic Torso of Apollo," whose famous last line is "you must change your life." This might work, if it were understood as being addressed to the speaker—by God? by the chicken hawk? by the speaker addressing himself?—but a big part of the poem's success has to do with the movement from the exterior, what surrounds the self, to that most private part of the self in which personal failure is bracingly admitted to; a second voice, even of another part of the self, implies dialogue and, accordingly, less of the intimacy that is finally the particular intimacy of existential aloneness in a world whose indifference to us is palpable, even as it is strangely lovely to look at.

Another example of this method is Frank O'Hara's "The Day Lady Died":

It is 12:20 in New York a Friday
three days after Bastille day, yes
it is 1959 and I go get a shoeshine
because I will get off the 4:19 in Easthampton
at 7:15 and then go straight to dinner
and I don't know the people who will feed me

I walk up the muggy street beginning to sun
and have a hamburger and a malted and buy
an ugly NEW WORLD WRITING to see what the poets
in Ghana are doing these days
                                        I go on to the bank
and Miss Stillwagon (first name Linda I once heard)
doesn't even look up my balance for once in her life
and in the GOLDEN GRIFFIN I get a little Verlaine
for Patsy with drawings by Bonnard although I do
think of Hesiod, trans. Richmond Lattimore or
Brendan Behan's new play or *Le Balcon* or *Les Nègres*
of Genet, but I don't, I stick with Verlaine
after practically going to sleep with quandariness

and for Mike I just stroll into the PARK LANE
Liquor Store and ask for a bottle of Strega and
then I go back where I came from to 6th Avenue
and the tobacconist in the Ziegfield Theatre and
casually ask for a carton of Gauloises and a carton
of Picayunes, and a NEW YORK POST with her face on it

and I am sweating a lot by now and thinking of
leaning on the john door in the 5 SPOT
while she whispered a song along the keyboard
to Mal Waldron and everyone and I stopped breathing

Here, the leap is from the ordinary, banal daily activities to the more shocking—because not expected—news of the death of Billie Holiday. Again,
the method that governs the poem is a combined form of reporting and

associating: we are given a report of each stage of the action, and each stage is governed entirely by the speaker's whim—until the news of the death, which is *outside* the speaker's ability to decide or reject. And within that leap from controllable activity to the uncontrollability of death itself is the leap (signaled at the level of tense-shift) from conscious engagement with the present to the world of memory, which both allows us to possess something of the past and at the same time is a reminder that what is remembered is available *only* to memory. And the death of the remembered singer means that there will be no more moments of experience out of which to take away parts of that experience in the form of memory.

This method—of combining associative method with report—I distinguish from narrative because narrative traditionally has its beginning, middle, and end. The method in O'Hara's poem—and in Linda Gregg's earlier—I trace back to Whitman, and I would call it *cumulative:* the poem ends up being a list of actions, sequential but finally only a fragment of narrative. The danger, however, is that in the course of saying "I'm doing A, now B, now Q, and I'm considering Z"—in the course of this, we risk writing what amounts to personal anecdote, to which the reader might well ask: "Who cares?" But isn't a pleasure of writing precisely in the taking of risks, pushing at them, and managing to survive them? And the successful poem makes the reader care about it, even before the reader has quite understood why he or she *does* care.

⟶⟳

A particularly pleasing type of associative poem is the one that is governed by wordplay. But wordplay being a potentially self-absorbing and therefore self-indulgent activity, there's always a risk here of generating nonsense in the name of play or experiment (this is why there is good Gertrude Stein, and there is bad). Here's a successful example by Pamela Alexander, from her collection *Navigable Waterways*. The poem is called "Vines":

A.
Acacia. flowering and an archway.
A round ambush = an abyssinian cat.
Consider lines as small events:
a curled cat uncurling.

Consider events as places to live, and
        paragraphing
                as paper sculpture.

A polygon has many angels.
How many cousins to the ounce?
How many weasels to the once?
Consider the shapes breath makes: words   clouds
coins in the blood
florins.

A flourish.

II.
Two parts. Often it does.
mountain and river.
First loss lasts
and fills itself
with glosses.

B. the glass blower.
His breath closes open air, makes
shapes into shapes.
Bottles   clear or amber
a green glass
a blue dress:
he says can I look at them all
all at once.

      Eyes
small rooms to hold worlds   cities, woods
and the wide shadows of words travelling toward the sun.
She says may I look at you.

IV.
Ivy that is.

Had you forgotten.
X.

Winter a white angle.
A gable.
Gabriel at the table, upon it
is oil.   precious.   pressure.
In a brown bottle a crush of prehistoric fern.

V.
The leaves he showed her became the first she'd seen.
She is a shape in space containing many things;
where his eyes burned her there is
room for tigers
       the Tigris

      irises
      one ibis

      two.

The poem is held together, barely. The poet here lets herself be carried away entirely by how each line can somehow be made a variation of (or pun on) the line before. Perhaps, then, it's more an exercise. But there *is* a kind of pattern—beyond that of consistency of method. The poem's structure resembles that of an outline: A, then II, then B, then IV, then V. A play, according to Aristotle, should have five acts; meanwhile, it is common enough for an act of a Shakespearean play to close with the stage direction "a flourish," which is the close of part I (or A) of Alexander's poem. For dramatic characters, there's B. the glassblower, and there's a woman un-named, probably introduced at the line "a blue dress" (part B), but clearly so at "She says may I look at you," the line with which that section ends. The bringing of the two together is the action of the drama, which would seem to conclude with the two of them continuing as two-in-one—"one ibis // two" or, bearing in mind that "bis" is the Latin for twice," we might say: one [but] I (one) twice = two. The play is a romance. It is also a poem whose ostensible subject, Alexander reminds us in section IV, is ivy, which winds and twists about arbitrarily—as the poem has, or has not? How did we get here?

~

Associative poetry is more difficult to read than more straightforwardly narrative work, for the same reasons that metaphor is more demanding than simile—the link has been removed, the sense of sequence; a greater leap is being made, which parallels the psychological gap between "he is like a cantaloupe" and "he is a cantaloupe," the latter forcing us to consider it literally at first.

~

One strategy used by many writers in the associative mode is to assign the poem a title and/or thematic scaffolding that will, if not explain the actual meanings of each leap in the poem, at least give the reader some sense of why such leaps are to be expected. At its worst, this can serve as a cover for what would otherwise be deemed a sprawling mess, in the guise of a poem intended as a mirror of the poet's inner turmoil or of the chaotic careering of civilization itself. But at its best, this use of title or theme can serve as an ordering device for the poem by providing each of its elements a shared context. To some extent, this is how the title "Vines" works for the Alexander poem. Differently, here is "Spring Drawing 2," from Robert Hass's *Human Wishes*:

> A man says *lilacs against white houses, two sparrows, one streaked, in a thinning birch,* and can't find his way to a sentence.
>
> In order to be respectable, Thorstein Veblen said, desperate in Palo Alto, a thing must be wasteful, i.e., "a selective adaptation of forms to the end of conspicuous waste."
>
> So we try to throw nothing away, as Keith, making dinner for us as his grandmother had done in Jamaica, left nothing;

the kitchen was as clean at the end as when he started; even
the shrimp shells and carrot fronds were part of the process,

and he said, when we tried to admire him, "Listen, I should
send you into the chickenyard to look for a rusty nail to add
to the soup for iron."

The first temptation of Sakyamuni was desire, but he saw that
it led to fulfillment and then to desire, so that one was easy.

Because I have pruned it badly in successive years, the
climbing rose has sent out, among the pale pink floribunda,
a few wild white roses from the rootstalk.

Suppose, before they said *silver* or *moonlight* or *wet grass,*
each poet had to agree to be responsible for the innocence
of all the suffering on earth,

because they learned in arithmetic, during the long school
days, that if there was anything left over,

you had to carry it. The wild rose looks weightless, the floribunda are heavy with the richness and sadness of Europe

as they imitate the dying, petal by petal, of the people who
bred them.

You hear pain singing in the nerves of things; it is not a song.

The gazelle's head turned; three jackals are eating his entrails
and he is watching.

The title suggests the poem will be a verbal attempt to equal a pictorial representation of a particular season, spring. To the extent that whatever Hass
does here will be verbal, and not pictorial, the task is an impossible one. And

it's the impossibility of it that prepares me for—explains—what seem at first to be not entirely related (or not immediately so) prose stanzas; I read the white space as the place where the poet acknowledges the unsuccess of the last stanza (rather like the list that keeps rejecting each definition of prayer in the Herbert poem earlier), and is gathering strength for the next stab at it, which will occur in the form of the next stanza. In the course of these attempts, though, a theme emerges: that of waste, glanced at in stanzas 2–4, then (as if without intention) drifted back to around stanzas 7–8, where the earlier, personal instinct of the poet to *avoid* waste (stanzas 3–4) is slowly transformed into something like a good purpose for *any* poet, not to waste anything—the innocence of the suffering or, as the poem proceeds, the act of suffering itself which, according to Hass, is not gratuitous, like song, but inevitable, like pain. That final image is finally not so startling: if the poet is to waste nothing, he must include his own suffering, and be able to look at it as squarely as the gazelle can watch its own destroyers.

Is this a drawing of spring? It's at least a meditation on an aspect of spring, that of growth, a natural instinct *not* to waste, vs. the human, societal notion of the ability to be wasteful as a mark of social position. It's also a lesson *from* spring—for the poet not to be wasteful, to be as resourceful as nature itself, which includes holding onto verbal fragments like those in the first stanza, even if they never find their way into a sentence.

It is not the title that helps us with L. S. Asekoff's poem, "Delta," which appears in his collection *Dreams of a Work:*

Take off these jewels
The moon weighs too heavily on my breast
What is our blood but a skein of deceit & desire

He came to me saying
I proposed to one married the other
I'm your son but I could have been your father
Life I said is filled with pointless coincidence
The deeper we dig the more dirt gathers

Still where there's smoke

The last I saw of him
Was a shadow waving from the metal detector
Gold flight bag under his arm

Here the weather lyric electric
A lighthouse wandering among rocks
Pale horses of the sea dash against breakers
& each morning arrives like the miner's gray mule

They called it feeding the beast
Inside the machine I could almost sense a flicker of feeling

Whose curse is this

Look she says
I am the left-handed sister
A cougar crouches beside a pool of yellow flowers

Sister I say Mother
This is the darkest delta
I am riding on the back of a white ox
The sun floats like a nun in a coffin
A black sail drapes the forsaken daughter

As we read through it, it is hard to know who is speaking, why she is speaking; however, there are enough clues to give a sense of a narrative: someone spoke to the speaker, then he left (flight bag under his arm), now she's somewhere that includes electric weather, a lighthouse (but a wandering one, suggesting unreliability to those things that provide both orientation and warning against danger), some marine environment that is no refuge from the curse whose source the speaker questions. By the end, someone is dead, or perhaps only the speaker is, and perhaps only figuratively. Despite this retrievable narrative, though, the poem is highly associative; incidents, bits of dialogue, sudden expostulations, geography are all presented with seeming randomness—in effect, we have a collage of abandonment and of the suffering that comes in its wake. This is enough to appreciate the poem's beauty, I find. But look what happens when we are given some context via the note that Asekoff includes on this poem at the end of the book: "Delta," he says, "is best understood as a fevered dream of Phaedra," the woman who, in Greek mythology, was driven by a curse of the gods to feel sexual attraction to her stepson, and hung herself in frustration and grief, but not before leaving behind a note for her husband suggesting—though falsely—that the son had attempted to rape her. The poem is an example of how a certain context can, again, validate what might seem like erratic association. It is also a way to impose order on the poem. Asekoff's skill is apparent when we consider the lengths to which he *could* have gone, in the name of fevered dreaming. I think he is correct in withholding the specific context from the reader. It allows the poem to resonate beyond the particulars of one story—*and* to address that story. As well, the story has served as a means of establishing parameters for the poet in the writing of the poem.

John Ashbery's "Meditations of a Parrot" does not offer a context where there are clear parameters, and as a result the poem veers dangerously close to straining belief on the reader's part:

Oh the rocks and the thimble
The oasis and the bed
Oh the jacket and the roses.

All sweetly stood up the sea to me
Like blue cornflakes in a white bowl.
The girl said, "Watch this."

I come from Spain, I said.
I was purchased at a fair.
She said, "None of us know."

"There was a house once
Of dazzling canopies
And halls like a keyboard.

"These the waves tore in pieces."
(His old wound—
And all day: Robin Hood! Robin Hood!)

Parrots, of course, cannot meditate. To suggest that they can is to enter the world of fantasy. It also makes the poem unassailable. If we question whether or not a parrot would think of the sea as "blue cornflakes in a white bowl," for example, the poet can remind us that parrots can't meditate; if we have made it to the second stanza, we've given some credence to the title, and having agreed that a parrot can meditate—in a poem, at least—he can also think figuratively. The bit of remembered dialogue between the parrot and the girl has something of loss to it; there was a beauty that the waves later tore in pieces—we are not told the context for that: is it the wound referred to in the final stanza? The only answer we get is "Robin Hood! Robin Hood!"—which makes no sense. But the poet might reasonably ask what sense have we expected from the meditations of a parrot?

We are in the neighborhood of surrealism, here, which is often confused with the associative poem. Surrealism removes all contradiction from the world—exists beyond the real world, by definition—there is either nothing that does not mean, or, more disturbingly, there is nothing that means. Ultimately, the associative poem will yield meaning.

⟜⟝

In the case of Ashbery's poem—like many of the poems in the book in which this appears, *Some Trees*—I think part of the point is to question such literary conventions as the meditation, as well as to question epistemology and inquiry. But it is easy to see how Ashbery's well-thought-out project might be misunderstood, and viewed as an excuse for other poets to write anything at all in the name of elevated spoof or wry commentary. This is the ever-present danger of the associative method, and can only be avoided via a certain amount of control, which is the artist's vision, a kind of tightening of focus. As Brenda Hillman says, in lines from two poems in *Loose Sugar* ("Remembering Form" and "Two Brothers," respectively), "Early life was a looseness; // even if your preferred mode is fragment, you need syntax to love", and "'To think' means: the looseness is taken away." In the successful associative poem, a line can usually be drawn (distinct from a line of narrative) by which we get from beginning to end—the element of sequence as a planned thing (if only subconsciously) is hard to avoid. And in fact, when we avoid it entirely we end up with a sprawl of language that may be realistic in terms of stream of consciousness, but isn't art, which never becomes nonsensical.

Another way to say this is that if we can agree that poetry is less a mirror of the culture it springs from, than a group of voices which, in coming from a culture, to that extent speak for it, represent it, then we must agree that the ultimate goal should be meaning. And perhaps the meaning may turn out to be meaninglessness itself—babble. Babel was also, you'll remember, the name of a city that—like art that finally isn't art at all—did not last.

A Brief Stop on the
Trail of the Prose Poem

The *Annals* of Tacitus, the first-century AD Roman historian whose writings are much of the source for what we know of Rome's early imperial period, is a prose work—a history. The one exception is its first line, which looks initially like any other line of prose. But if we scan—metrically parse—the first line, it turns out to be a line of pure dactylic hexameter: the meter then used for epic verse. In using a meter of poetry as part of a prose work, Tacitus is able to say, without saying, that this work that we are about to read will be more than a history of the early Roman empire—it is to be an epic, in the manner of the *Iliad* or *Aeneid;* which is to say, if we agree that, among other things, epic is a touchstone for a particular culture, this history—which turns out to be a wry and bitter look at the criminality of all the principals of Rome's ascent into empire—is a reflection of the society from which Tacitus is writing. As well, this is the meter of didactic, instructional verse—and certainly Tacitus means for his outlining of imperial flaws (and human flaws, more generally) to serve as instruction for how, if not to avoid those flaws, then to be able to recognize them in the future.

The *Annals* is hardly a prose poem. But it is an early example of how the tools of poetry can be incorporated into prose to various effects, of which—left to itself—the prose might not be as capable. It seems to me that any good piece of literature finds—or we find for it—the form that will allow it to be most effective in conveying its information. That is, we should cast a poem into rhyming quatrains not because it might be fun, but because that is the only form that we deem appropriate for what the poem wants to mean and to say. Another way to put it is that the form of a poem should finally be inevitable. If a writer has chosen to write a prose poem, then, there are presumably unique properties to that form, without which any hoped-for meaning will be less fully attained.

Increasingly, though, I encounter prose poems whose form seems less inevitable, and more a choice made out of laziness and/or confusion: "I didn't know quite *what* to do with the words as lines, so I thought I'd put them into prose" is a comment I've often heard from students, as if the prose poem weren't itself a form to be turned to not for random but for particular reasons (just as free verse, if done well, will everywhere display a sense of control and a sense of deliberateness, however intuitive the form may initially appear). Another reason given for choosing to write a prose poem is vaguely political: there is a notion that to write a poem in prose somehow takes a stand against the "Old Guard," as represented not only by traditional form but by those who choose to write in actual lines; my sense is that this line of thinking is connected to the unfashionableness (and fear) of exercising authority among many younger poets. To make a line, especially in free verse, is to make a choice for which one is willing to be held accountable, or should be. Isn't it easier, always, to turn away?

~✵~

In her debut volume, *Infanta,* Erin Belieu offers the rare opportunity to consider the ways in which poetry and prose differ in their strategies, by presenting us with two pieces that address the same material, but one in prose, the other in poetry. Here are the two pieces:

Part of the Effect of the Public Scene Is to Importune the Passing Viewer

FOR EXAMPLE:

walking past the Ritz a girl may be sitting on the last
step crying as if alone and you notice, even in this
cocktail-hour light, the little rips and shreds of her
chapped lips and that she has no Kleenex and no one

stops to offer one and you feel damned if you do or don't, not wanting to intrude, as a man is standing maybe only three feet away, his profile approximating a little shame, some discomfort, but mostly a sphinx-like composure, or boredom, perhaps, indicating they *are* together, together in that way you're not completely sure you'll ever want to know about again and you're ashamed, too, with nothing to offer but to gaze intently at the fascinating streetlamp as you walk by.

PROBABLY YOU'VE CAUSED A SCENE YOURSELF:

public or private, at a bar or in a strange apartment, when suddenly you became conscious of the drama, of the real pleasure in your tears, the catharsis of the wail and rage, the screams, the "trashing of the joint," because that's what's next, snipping up his Liberty of London ties, ripping off her nightgown, pushing her out naked on the patio for the neighbors' judgment who are there, to be sure, either by accident or rubbernecked design, keeping score or scared for their own property. Or instead you've been the impetus, unfaithful, deceitful, maybe only the hapless object of some other person's desire thinking that, for all their protestations of love, you might as well be a bathroom fixture or book-end. In either case,

IT'S HARD TO MAKE A GRACEFUL EXIT:

as all scenes peter out in awkward ways. Someone's left thinking of the perfect remark, a remark that'll sink like an ax blade, the kind that are never on hand when needed, so that you end up shouting, spluttering *Oh yeah?! Oh yeah?! Oh Yeah?!* like a moron, like a damn fool, crying on the last step, in front of strangers, without a Kleenex.

Outside the Hotel Ritz

The ripped girl gathers herself,
draws into the recess of a downtown
highrise, then cries as if alone into
the body of an indifferent building.

The black feathers of her party dress
forsake her, dead flutter falling round
her arms. Having flown through many autumns,
in other clear, martini dusks, their circles

kept growing smaller till they settled
at nothing, save decoration. Now currents
are senseless and wind, still sweeping warm
across the public ponds, just wind.

Around the corner a man in a tuxedo looks
bored, always waiting. She's borrowed
his handkerchief. Profile of the Napoleonic
sphinx, yes. Yet something struggles

beneath the dial of his face. He craves
the crowd, its wandering breach and flow,
hears a genuine laugh bob up and wants
to follow it home, all the way through

the city, to any lit place beyond him. Night
is pending. Its tributaries flow, spilling
fast onto the sidewalk; something wet and plumed
to catch him. Like feathers raining. Like wings.

The basic material: a woman is crying in public; the man who probably
made her cry is standing embarrassed and fairly useless, apart. That's it. But
consider the differences in treatment, how "the little rips and shreds of her
chapped lips" (a literal image) in the prose version become in the poetry

version the figurative phrase "the ripped girl." Or how the Kleenex of the prose becomes the handkerchief of the poetry version. The casual inclusion of "but mostly a sphinx-like composure, or boredom, perhaps" (as if an aside) in the prose is less lofty than the fragment we encounter in the poetry: "Profile of the Napoleonic/sphinx, yes." I don't mean to suggest that poetry is necessarily an elevated, loftier form of prose, but that would seem to be part of the thinking for this particular poet in the context of these two examples. The two pieces have different intentions, as well, and this has everything to do with the different treatments of the material. Characteristic of the lyric mode, "Outside the Hotel Ritz" resists closure, instead presents us with partially sketched portraits of two figures who are and are not connected to each other; and it is largely in that undefined space between them that the tension—the narrative—of the poem gets deployed: a narrative that stops just short of resolution. "Part of the Effect of the Public Scene," in contrast, begins with the man and woman as a couple, but then uses that as a stepping-off point to present—about couples—an argument with which the "you" (the reader?) is assumed to be familiar. The prose piece is working not lyrically, but didactically, via express example. It even sets itself up as a kind of proof in three blocks of prose, each heralded by a generic introductory heading. The scheme, structurally: here's the public example; here's the contrast to and comparison with private experience; here's the moral, as it were, which results from the synthesis of the two earlier discussions, a lesson that is intended to transcend such divisions of experience into public and private. It is a rhetorical structuring, not surprisingly. Although there is much rhetoric to be found in poetry, rhetoric has its origins in prose speech—specifically, in oratory; rhetoric functions to organize and modulate one's material in order to more effectively persuade one's audience. Rhetoric is the prose equivalent of poetry's line break and stanza break, in that they are all structuring devices.

We are conditioned to expect certain things from prose—it will be narrative or it will be annunciatory of information deemed significant: legal documents, histories, religious tracts, newspapers. The lyric is likely to infer information by having the bulk of the information delivered via resonance from a small number of images, and by the arrangement of those images. We won't as often encounter statements like "it's hard to make a graceful exit," "you become conscious of the drama," and "that's what's next, snipping up his Liberty of London ties," for example. Rather, we are left to understand that by "ripped" the author means the girl is a broken, torn figure, stripped of something like pride, dignity, rescue. We are not told that the man and woman are together as a couple in the poem—but we know it, or suspect it. By comparing the night, at poem's end, to feathers, then to wings—and we have been told that the woman's dress includes feathers—we have to wonder to what extent the feathers that, we are told, have forsaken the woman will be sufficient safety net for the man, should he require (and again, we suspect he will) such a net. The result is that the poem—more indirectly, figuratively, subtly—allows the material to suggest loss, a state of rescuelessness, that neither man nor woman can escape; and we can wonder, as readers, if we can reasonably hope to be excluded from a similar fate. The prose version also has a conclusion that it reaches, but it is difficult to say that this one comes to us by inference and by surprise. The piece has been laid out in so outwardly programmatic a fashion, and delivered via prose that is so bare of imagery and other figurative devices, that the writing can't help but be more direct: figurative devices are a way of amplifying a statement, offering an additional filter through which to receive and understand a piece of information. Removal of that filter makes for, if not always greater clarity, at least an increase of directness. "Part of the Effect of the Public Scene" offers a variety of awkward scenes. Its conclusion is that there are many awkward scenes, whose endings are equally awkward, and that if there's a purpose to these scenes at all, it is that they may garner the participants some attention to—though no rescue from—the scene in which they are embroiled. Perhaps this is a reason not to consider Belieu's prose piece a prose poem. It participates too entirely in the devices of prose, does not employ figurative language—there are similes, but none that resonate or amplify much. It is prose, highly rhetorical in its structure, very straightforward in the delivery of its information and of how we should think of that information.

So the prose poem must employ the strategies of poetry to some (perhaps undefinable) extent. The only clearly forbidden strategy is that of deliberate line break. But—as a start to fleshing out a definition for the prose poem, insofar as that is possible—the prose poem will likely include figurative language (figurative language is not *exclusive* to the realm of poetry, but it isn't *required* for prose). A second characteristic of prose poetry will be a general avoidance of completed narrative, which is absent from purely lyric poetry and which is specific to prose. As Ross Feld has said in "Timing and Spacing the As If: Poetic Prose and Prosaic Poetry," "poems are entitled to picture themselves as pure Middles"—or, as I like to think of it, the lyric poem is a torso. Without the extremities of arms, legs, head, the torso has to serve as representative of all that's missing, has to resonate in the manner of Rilke's archaic torso of Apollo. Similarly, the lyric poem will tend not to have a marked beginning and ending—when it succeeds, we as readers are not frustrated by the lack of these two things. This torso or middleness quality is almost always key to the prose poem. And, conditioned as we are to expect narrative when we see prose, the tension generated between the expectation of narrative (because of a prose poem's visible shape, its exterior) and the decided avoidance of narrative *within* the prose poem can lend to the prose poem the sense of epiphany, resonance, and subtlety that we more commonly encounter in lyric poetry.

⊶∿

Part of Eve's Discussion

It was like the moment when a bird decides not to eat from your hand, and flies, just before it flies, the moment the rivers seem to still and stop because a storm is coming, but there is no storm, as when a hundred starlings lift and bank together before they wheel and drop, very much like the moment, driving on bad ice, when it occurs to you your car could spin, just before it slowly begins to spin, like the moment just before you forgot what it was you were about to say, it was like that, and after that, it was still like that, only all the time.

In her piece above, Marie Howe manages to have both narrative and middleness. Eve is telling a narrative, certainly. But it is the middle of a much larger narrative that we are expected to know, namely, that of Genesis in the Old Testament. This prose poem doesn't require beginning or end, because it relies on its ability to resonate against and within a larger tradition. All the writer gives us, here, with which to identify the piece's subject is the first word: "It," the ultimate understatement for the Fall and the expulsion from Eden. But "It," as it turns out, is enough—so much so that Howe can make use of anachronism (the spinning car) and trust that she won't throw her reader off. "Part of Eve's Discussion" is a prose poem because it partakes in the middleness of lyric poetry, but remains prose in its visible shape. It eschews narrative. It engages, instead, in the associative leaping that lyric can sustain, and that narrative—if the writer really hopes to be understood—cannot, at least not for very long. Much of that associative leaping is done via the rhetorical (prose) device of anaphora—the modulating repetition of a particular word or phrase; therefore, we find "like the moment" and "just before" repeated throughout, each repetition marking a renewed attempt to recover precisely the irrecoverable moment, to possess that moment by naming it exactly, which proves impossible. This combination of poetic device (associative leaping) and rhetorical device (anaphora) is part of what makes this piece both prose and poetry—a prose poem.

Amy Gerstler's "Saints" is an example of a prose poem that leaves narrative entirely behind, to become a kind of meditation on or obsessing about a single topic:

> Miracle mongers. Bedwetters. Hair-shirted wonder workers.
> Shirkers of the soggy soggy earth. A bit touched, or wholly
> untouched living among us? They shrug their bodies off and
> waft with clouds of celestial perfume. No smooching for
> this crew, except for hems, and pictures of their mothers . . .
> their lips trespass only the very edges of succor. Swarms of
> pious bees precede her. One young girl wakes up with a ring
> on her finger and a hole in her throat. Another bled milk
> when her white thigh was punctured. All over the world,
> a few humans are born each decade with a great talent for
> suffering. They have gifts that enable them to sleep through
> their mistreatment: the sleep of the uncomplaining just,
> the sleep of the incomplete. Our relationship to them is

the same as our relationship to trees: what they exhale, we breathe.

For the most part, this is mere listing—a device more of prose than of poetry—and a listing, mostly, of fragments at that. There are a couple of fragments of potential narrative: "One young girl wakes up with a ring on her finger and a hole in her throat," and "Another bled milk when her white thigh was punctured." Each of those sounds like the beginning of a story, but the story itself is withheld from us. Instead, we move into the mode not of narrative but of authoritative statement, or lesson, about the nature of saints. The ending has the ring of summation, but it isn't the summation of the events of any narrative, which would make this that other prose form, the fable. Instead, we have a summation of a type of person—a saint—beside which, just as the piece is ending, Gerstler places us, and leaves us, so that we have no choice but to ponder alone, beyond what happens on the page, our own character in relationship to that of a saint, the particular symbiotic relationship with which the piece ends. It is this pushing of the reader past where the words stop that gives to the prose of "Saints" the resonance of lyric. This resonance, along with the associative thinking in the piece and the heavy use of assonance and alliteration to create a music in the language—all of these give the prose its poetic quality, and help situate the piece in the realm of the prose poem.

❧

Suddenly

it's night and Tom
comes in and says,
"It's pouring buckets
out," his blond hair
diamond-dusted with
raindrop fragments.

Technically, we can't say that James Schuyler's "Suddenly" is a prose poem. After all, there are line breaks. But the line breaks seem fairly random—the lines range between four and five syllables, but randomly. There are no particular brilliances that flash from a line break the way they can when line break is done skillfully. If we write out the ostensible poem, we see it for the banal sentence it is:

> Suddenly it's night and Tom comes in and says, "It's pouring buckets out," his blond hair diamond-dusted with raindrop fragments.

A flat sentence, with perhaps some elevation at "diamond-dusted," and with the description of raindrops not as drops but as fragments—so, briefly, we break out of the language of conversational prose into something more figurative. What happens when the sentence is lineated as a poem is that the line breaks operate as a pacing device; they create a fairly regular series of hesitations, and force us to let the sentence's individual elements accumulate, creating the effect of crescendo, so that when we get to the two more lyric moments—the last two lines—we have worked toward them in a modulated fashion, something that the sentence, when written out as prose, would not have allowed for without an artificial use of commas. Here, timing becomes everything. The result: a prose sentence in poetry lines—but not prose poetry, if only because of the lineation. And yet the piece's sensibility is not unrelated to that of the prose poem.

⤳

Yet another anomaly. Here is Amy Hempel's story "The Lady Will Have the Slug Louie," from her collection *At the Gates of the Animal Kingdom:*

> My dog—I found him on the dining room table, stepping around the bowl of fruit, licking the beeswax candles.
>
> My cat is another one—eats anything but food. I watch her select a tulip in a vase. When her teeth pierce the petal, I startle her away with sharply clapped hands.
>
> A moment later, and again the cat stalks. She crouches in front of the next flower over, tasting the four-inch petal of a parrot tulip as if she is thinking, *That* one is the one I am not supposed to eat.
>
> My brother keeps a boa constrictor for a pet. The prey-

ing snake suffers from a vitamin deficiency, so my brother buys a large jar of powdered high-potency supplement. Before each meal, he dips live mice in water, then drops them in the jar. He shakes the covered jar until each mouse wears a healthy coat of vitamins A through E. Then he feeds the coated mice to the snake.

When my brother and I were young, I mixed dirt with his scrambled eggs. My mother let me feed him in his high-chair on the porch. I would leave my brother alone and go off into the garden. I'd return with a handful of soil from under the pansies; with the dirt and whatever things lived in the dirt, I laced his eggs.

For years, in seafood places, my brother ordered for me. "The lady will have the Slug Louie," he told the waiter. "And please, if it's no trouble, she would like her roll 'au beurre.'"

All my life I have been afraid of milk. I thought that if you drank too much, your bones would outgrow your skin, your teeth overrun your lips.

There is a story that mothers read to their children wherein the little girl speaks and the mother answers back:

—Mother, what do witches eat?

—Milk and potatoes and *you*, my sweet.

I call this a story, because the author so identifies it on the cover of her book. But how far is it from being a prose poem? The strategy throughout the story is purely associative. We expect we'll get narrative at every turn, only to have those expectations not be met. Instead, the majority of the paragraphs introduce an anecdote that seems initially to have no context—as if this were merely a listing of present and past actions: "My brother keeps a boa constrictor for a pet," "When my brother and I were young, I mixed dirt with his scrambled eggs," "For years, in seafood places, my brother ordered for me," etc. Each paragraph begins to take us somewhere, narratively, but the next paragraph is never apparently that somewhere. Eventually though, it becomes clear that each paragraph shares the subject of eating, on one level or another. This places it in the meditation/obsession category of prose poetry, of which Gerstler's "Saints" was an earlier example—except without the use of poetic devices or language, no metaphor or simile, elements that did indeed figure into the Gerstler piece.

But those last two lines of the story: does Hempel realize that each is in tetrameter—the first in trochees, the second, for the most part, dactylic? And, as a rhyming couplet, the last two lines suggest closure, in the way that a Shakespearean sonnet often does in its final couplet. And yet there is no closure, here, in terms of narrative. As with all the other tales within this short story, there is only calling—the responses are left out, which does create a resonance, in that the reader is tempted to think beyond each of these broken narratives in search of an ending. I think the magic of Hempel's ending is that the couplet's sound causes us to pause briefly in satisfaction, as if everything had been neatly tied up. Then comes the realization that nothing has been tied up at all, and it is in that disturbing ripple of recognition that the reader is unseated from complacency and the story begins its life beyond the page. Again, this is the result of using the strategies and language of prose—setting up narrative expectations and not meeting those expectations—and certain strategies less associated with narrative prose than with associative poetry; and finally, there's a bit of rhyme and meter thrown in as contrast to the prose that for the most part, here, gives little attention to rhythm, let alone rhyme and meter. Something in me resists calling this a prose poem, though, despite the loose bits of definition that we've arrived at and to which this piece conforms.

Whatever lies behind that resistance, paragraphing is not a part of that. Although prose poems more often than not appear in a solid, unparagraphed block, the paragraph does appear in prose poems, as early as Baudelaire's in many ways genre-shaping *Petites poèmes en prose*. And the paragraph is everywhere used by Russell Edson, a writer who has written exclusively in the prose-poem genre his entire career, and who is often pointed to as one of the few masters of the prose poem. It is Edson's paragraphs that set the reader up immediately to expect narrative. But the pieces eschew narrative entirely, meanwhile employing a slippery symbolism and often-surreal imagery as a means of widening even further the possibilities for interpretation, making it nearly impossible to settle on any one interpretation for very long. That is, they avoid closure, as we have come to expect with the prose poem. Here are a couple:

Clouds

A husband and wife climbed to the roof of their house,
and each at the extremes of the ridge stood facing the other
the while that the clouds took to form and reform.

The husband said, shall we do backward dives, and into
windows floating come kissing in a central room?

I am standing on the bottom of an overturned boat, said
the wife.

The husband said, shall I somersault along the ridge of
the roof and up your legs and through your dress out of the
neck of your dress to kiss you?

I am a roof statue on a temple in an archaeologist's
dream, said the wife.

The husband said, let us go down now and do what it is
to make another come into the world.

Look, said the wife, the eternal clouds.

The Fall

There was a man who found two leaves and came in-
doors holding them out saying to his parents that he was a
tree.

To which they said then go into the yard and do not
grow in the living-room as your roots may ruin the carpet.

He said I was fooling I am not a tree and he dropped his
leaves.

But his parents said look it is fall.

And yet, if these are prose poems, and if the prose poem should somewhere
also employ some of the strategies of poetry, where are those strategies in the
two pieces above? The imagery, where it occurs, is not more characteristic

of poetry than of prose. And the language is straightforward—perhaps more highly pitched, more rhythmically modulated, but certainly nothing like the rhyming couplet effect in the Hempel story. "The Fall" employs what might or might not be stanza breaks—they seem arbitrary, though; I have no difficulty imagining the piece without those breaks, which is to say nothing different happens as a result of the breaks that doesn't happen in "Clouds," where those breaks don't occur. The sensibility of Edson's pieces is closer to that of fable or parable, but without the closure of moral summation—a sort of surreal variation on the sayings of the Desert Fathers or on Zen koans. The lack of closure is certainly part of what we have come to expect in a prose poem. Interestingly, Edson seems in his later work to want to intensify that lack of closure: he has all but abandoned the period at the end, punctuating the end of almost every piece in his most recent book, *The Tormented Mirror,* with ellipses instead (and where this doesn't happen, his choice is usually the question mark, allowing the piece to end on an interrogative note forever unanswered). So, if more prose than poetry in their strategies, are these prose poems? The author himself refers to these pieces as prose poems—so aren't they?

⌐ん

"I have called the prose poem a medium because it is not a form," says Michael Hamburger in his translation of Baudelaire's prose poems, and he points out that the prose poem was instead, for the French poets of the nineteenth century, the only medium prior to the "arrival" of *vers libre* that allowed for the freedom of expression the genre would later provide. But the prose poem has surely become a form since then, perhaps not as fixed a form as a sonnet, but perhaps one of the closest forms to free verse, whose forms are countless. To my mind, that makes the prose poem one of our most organic, challenging, and potentially frustrating forms today. Frustrating, if we insist on codifying it, at least on the level of craft. There is a psychology of the prose poem, it seems to me—even as a villanelle brings with it a psychology unique to the villanelle. All forms bring with them a particular psychology, or way of articulating psychology—it is why more than rhyme scheme distinguishes the Italian from the English sonnet, and why certain themes more easily inhabit the sestina than do others. What makes the prose poem different from any of our more established, traditional forms is that it resists, again, definition at the level of craft—it may or may not be in paragraphs, there may or may not be complete sentences, it may work associatively, and may not. It does seem to insist on avoiding closure—but so do the majority of free-verse poems being written today. Here is what Edson has to say in his prose poem "On the Writing of a Prose Poem":

> When thinking of writing a prose poem it seems more
> than natural to think of suicide; to think of someone at
> last exposed to the God of things who might thunder, as I
> imagine it, from the sky, you have ruined my thing, now I
> shall ruin your thing.

Edson and/or the speakers in his prose poems are, at best, slippery characters, and not always to be trusted. But here Edson, in suggesting (as I interpret it) that the prose poem is the result of pitching ruin against ruin, offers a direction of thinking about the prose poem that might be the most reasonable one available. If we can think of mortality as an ongoing form of erosion—and I do—and of erosion as a form of ruin (not without its possibilities for beauty along the way), then perhaps the prose poem is simply another proof of what art does best and, for me, was meant to do: in the making of poetry, we have captured one thing and, in so doing, we have briefly, mercifully, staved off another.

II

Interview
(Conducted by Nick Flynn)

Carl Phillips is the author of five books of poetry, including, most recently, The Tether, *a movement of work as a whole as deep into the unknown and perhaps ultimately unchartable realms of desire, of wanting, of mortality, as any we are likely to encounter. In following, or being led by, his precise and sinuous lines, one is always aware of and often surprised by the dangers encountered, the illusions, the false steps inherent in such a journey. Meditative on the most essential, most elemental aspects of existence, both high and low, earthy and graceful, we are led to the edge of the unknown and then challenged as to why we followed. What was it we hoped to find? There are answers here but none of them are what was expected at the outset.*

Ten years ago Carl and I were in the same workshop together, led by the poet Alan Dugan, in Truro, Massachusetts. Ongoing, for years it seemed, Dugan's workshop was near legend, somewhat unstructured, with students appearing and disappearing over the course of each summer. Carl appeared one day, seeming at once both calm and restive, restrained and passionate, and read his poem as if it wasn't part of him, with his head to one side, as if surprised by what it contained. It left the rest of us awed, open-mouthed.

I have followed his work closely since, and with nothing less than that initial awe. His poems enact the edict that it is in the saying, as opposed to what is said, by which the poet will lead us further into the unknown. By following the language down, or up, by tracing the erotics of syntax, we witness again the interaction of consciousness and flesh, a deep yet tangible mystery we too often sleepwalk through. His work instructs us in ways that are hard to name, like desire can instruct, or joy, a fleeting knowledge that, once attained, proves difficult to hold onto, or even to return to, but has left us, thrillingly, changed.

I have thought, since, of
your body—as I first came
to know it, how it still

can be, with mine,
sometimes.

(from "Parable," in Pastoral)

This epistolary interview was conducted by e-mail and old-fashioned fax, between Saint Louis and Provincetown, from January to February of 2001.

Nick Flynn: When you spoke last year at the Bread Loaf Writers' Conference on the seventeenth-century poet George Herbert, you said, "how we read a poem is a form of confession." Was your reading of the subtext in Herbert's poem "Sin,"—"if sin makes us better, isn't it possible we should indulge in sin . . ."—a confession?

Carl Phillips: It's more a speculation—but the fact that I make that speculation must say something about (betray) my own thinking, at which point it becomes a confession of sorts, right? That's what I was thinking about when discussing my reading of Herbert, the ways in which we can only see anything through the layers of the various selves we are. . . . As for sin and things sinful—whatever those may be—it was in Milton's "Comus" that I first encountered the idea that good can never be known until evil is also known, by which logic the person who wants to be sensually and intellectually whole will want to have had experience with evil. That works fine, maybe, for the age of Milton, but it becomes dicier—in equal parts more thrilling and more perilous—to bring that way of thinking into the current age, one of moral flexibility.
    Confessed?

NF: Not yet. First, is this a morally flexible age? I know we're all living on *Temptation Island,* and the language of good and evil has more gray tones, but it seems, if we are talking of sex, that the risks are at least as great now as they ever have been, no? I only bring this up because so much of your work involves desire and the body, which somehow leads my puritan/porn-addled brain into realms of, if not "sin," then whatever we have substituted for sin.

CP: Perhaps I'm overstating my position. I guess what I mean is that morality seems more flexible than we are often willing to suggest—or there's a human instinct toward believing in the possibility of such flexibility, which is as old as (to go back to the first question) Herbert, and then some. Somehow it seems appropriate here to refer to some lines from "Caravan," a poem that appears in *The Tether*, because I think I state my view most cleanly there: "language should be—and / is—flexible, / it recalls, in // this way, morality, / how there's nothing, it / seems, not to be given // in to. . ."

NF: You connect language with morality in this poem that is in part a call to move beyond the given, the clichéd. Yet the way is anything but clear. What is the relationship between what is known to what is unknowable?

CP: It's the same as that between what's easy and what's difficult. It isn't that I court difficulty—in a life, any more than in a poem—but I can't understand complacency, how anyone cannot be restive and still think of himself or herself as living a life of inquiry, which is to say, as living a life at all. You're right: the way is anything but clear, nor is the danger nor are the surprises. But for me, there's an urge to push at ideas with which I've become comfortable, and to keep testing what others might prefer to leave alone. How else do we grow, as writers and as people?

NF: That surprise is one of the reasons I return to your work. Yet it seems more and more your poems are following a syntax beyond even surprise, into the unknowable, to a precipice of sorts. Which is where surprise turns dangerous, perhaps. In the poem, "The Pinnacle," you question a given description of ferns—"you // called a sea"—"but wasn't it also some over- // whelming green argument / whose point was that / not everything requires // light?" How does syntax lead us into this landscape?

CP: First, by our crediting syntax with having some degree of an organic life of its own; and second, by our willingness to take the risks that I think language sometimes wants to take. I'll admit, though, that I remain in some doubt as to whether I'm imposing upon language the urge to push that I mentioned earlier, or whether language's own instincts eventually become my own.

NF: By pushing the language, are you talking about the attempt to create a new syntax, to move the language forward?

CP: First, if there's any new syntax being created in the poems, it's certainly not conscious on my part. The syntax in my poems is simply reflective of how my mind works, at least in that space where a poem gets made. As to what you ask about my pushing language, it's the language itself that does the pushing. It's like dogsledding, the language being the dogs who aren't so much driven as they are given the direction; the force is entirely their own, though. The poet, of course, being the sled-driver.

NF: Your last book, *Pastoral,* has a recurring image of a stag, referenced in the poem "Words of Love" in *The Tether*: "*There was, one time, a stag . . . /* And now there isn't, // is there? / And no, he won't come, /ever, back . . .*" An elegy, of sorts, yet it works on an allegorical level. What do you think about being referred to as an allegorical poet?

CP: I don't mind it, if the same term can be applied to, say, Dickinson or Plath. As I understand it, by allegorical it's meant that the poem's elements (including whatever narrative there may be) are symbolic or more than just what they seem, yes? But wouldn't that then describe any poem that has resonance to it? What makes me uncomfortable with that term is that it seems to imply a single alternative that's merely literal. My poems aren't simply a diary of "what happened," but I also don't want something like a stag to be reduced to a cardboard figure, marked "symbol," marching across the page. It's more accurate to say that I am interested in how much of the world is symbolic *incidentally.*

NF: Well, it adds another tension to the work, which pulls between the actual and the symbolic.

CP: Yes, that's in fact what the larger "point" seemed to be in *Pastoral,* once I'd arranged the poems and looked at them all together—how much is real, and how much is as we imagine it to be because we want it to be real or because something in our brains—as a kind of safety mechanism—refuses to bear reality and transfigures it, as a result. That's what I had in mind in "Autumn. A

Late Music" (from *Pastoral*), where the speaker is slowly coming to understand that all the pastoral symbols, everything that's been translated into mythology—all of that amounts to a grimmer reality in which the body stands naked, transparent, craven. Everything else has just been a means of justifying outrage. Sometimes poetry itself—the making of it—seems to me like an elaborate subterfuge that the brain provides as a way of giving brief containment to the more difficult parts that keep threatening to overwhelm. . . .

NF: From the image of the stag in *Pastoral, The Tether* seems shot through with images of light in all its forms—shadow, brightness, dimming. Could you say something of your process here, of when or if these recurring motifs become something that holds the work together into a book?

CP: This too is probably more incidental than not. Or has to do with something rather ordinary—namely, that I spend a lot of time tracking the light in its different manifestations and degrees. I know this is something that increased once I moved out to the Midwest, where I was struck by the different light one sees out here, as opposed to the light on the East Coast, which is still home for me. I also spend a lot of time outside, in the actual landscape, thanks in part to my partner being a landscape photographer—much of what I write starts in that context, of the landscape and the light's relationship to it.

NF: Has that always been true, the poems starting in landscape and light?

CP: Yes—now that I think of it, that would explain why I almost always write in the morning, and always in a room that has an east-facing window. The view isn't exactly landscape, in Saint Louis, where I look out onto an alley and the back of a row of houses—but there's a lot of sky, and our equivalent of Central Park lies just past the houses. But in the summers, back East, there's nothing but conservation land out back—plenty of woods, deer, the occasional fox, a tribe of coyotes.

NF: If the geography of *Pastoral* could be called "the meadow," then this new work could be "the yard" or "the trail." What is the role of place, of geography, how important is it to be "placed?"

CP: The role of place is crucial to the psychology, at least, behind the poems. I lived in a different place every year for the first ten or so years of my life—my father was in the air force, so our family didn't really settle until I was in high school. I'm convinced that this has made a difference for me: there's an urge to settle, to come to rest; and no sooner is that rest arrived at than it gets replaced by a restiveness, a curiosity about the next space—geographically, intellectually.

NF: I know you split your time between Saint Louis and Cape Cod. I've also read that you're from a biracial family. One a choice, the other a birthright. Do these facts add to the restiveness?

CP: I think the divided-living situation might reflect that restiveness—I feel very grounded in each place, and I find I can't decide which I prefer; each provides something very necessary for me, and for the writing. I have this longing to live in one place and call it home forever, but some part of me seems to *require* longing, rather than the satisfaction of that longing. Decidedly masochistic. . . . As for the effects of birthrights, yes: while my being the product of two racial identities should mean that I am both those identities, I have always found it to mean that I don't get to quite claim either identity but, instead, I live somewhere in between. Not by choice—it has to do with the countless, various, and conflicting conventions about race, what it is to be black, what it is to be white; though I'm at ease with myself when it comes to race, I sense a lot of unease—among blacks and whites—when it comes to how they might go about including an anomaly like me. And somewhere in that between that I mentioned earlier, there's a lot of restiveness, quite reasonably.

NF: Understandably. Brenda Hillman has said that "punctuation marks beg for the sanity of not going forward, of resting. . . ." Could you say something on this? I ask to get to the means you employ to embody this restiveness.

CP: I'd say that punctuation marks are indicative, in equal parts, of the urge to go forward and the urge to turn back and the urge toward stasis—the conflict among the three, when meaningful, can be exhilarating.

NF: I've also heard you describe your relationship with syntax as "erotic"— say more.

CP: For me, syntax has great possibilities for the erotic—there's so much stall-and-deliver, release-and-restraint, or at least that's the kind of syntax to which I've always been drawn, in the Latin of Tacitus, in the English of James. And I don't mean just the wildly sinuous sentence, its conclusion held back frustratingly, teasingly, by subordinate clauses, self-correction, parenthetical addenda, etc., but also the relationship of those particular sentences to the fragment, or to a simple and terse statement, the sudden clarity of a sentence like "Reader, I married him." So much of what resonates with meaning has to do less with the actual content of a sentence than with the relationship of how that content is deployed to how the content has been deployed earlier and will be deployed later. Can't the same be said about sex? To care about syntax—to believe in its infinite possibilities, rather than just accepting the few to which everyone easily agrees—is akin to distinguishing between sex and good sex. Surely that's a distinction worth making.

NF: Well, it certainly layers the experience of approaching a poem one is interested in. You use the word "ambition" at least twice by my count in *The Tether:* in "Regalia Figure" ("And yet, / to let go of it, ambition, / seems as impossible, as / impossible—") and in "Lustrum" ("Anything / left, anymore, private? *Ambition, / like they said: little torch*"). *The Tether* is your fifth book, the second in as many years. What is your relationship with ambition?

CP: The ambition I had in mind in *The Tether* was one of the body, whose ambition I think of as getting expressed in terms of desire. Desire is ambition—both can be thought of as those curves in calculus that move forever toward a point they can never reach, since the reaching itself has no limit. By the end of *The Tether,* I hope what comes across is an understanding of the body's desires, both as folly and as sacred, and as necessary. Stasis, in the world as I've imagined it anyway, is more than a kind of death—it equals death.

But the way you put your question suggests that you're speaking here of literary ambition. In that regard, I can only say that I have great ambition for the poems—that is, that they come as close as they possibly can to achieving what I want for them as poems. That's artistic ambition, maybe. That's what I want, and can control. How the poems fare outside my own space of making them is, as you know, very random and often has to do with many factors beyond the poems themselves. As for two books in as many years, well, I feel fortunate in being able—at least right now—to write in ways that are satisfying to me. I've never planned a book—never had a notion as to what a book would be about, or how long it should be. There just comes a point at which a project announces itself as having been a project all along, and as being finished. That sort of thing has its own time or schedule, I find. I can understand just as easily there being ten years—or more—between one book and the next, according to how it has to happen, not for the poet so much as for the poems.

NF: In describing what you hope the impact of your work will be (in an interview in *Callaloo,* 1998), you state, "What I hope is learned is that we all have the same hungers, fears, needs, etc., and that sexuality and race are just as much the point as they are not." That seems essential to placing your work in a larger context, and the turn at the end makes it an essentially "Carl Phillips" statement. Would you like to add to this?

CP: Just that it's possible for one thing to be both crucial and incidental, when it comes to identity—that's what I was getting at when I made that statement. Necessarily, I see the world from within the context of being biracial, gay, male; but those are only three identity markers, no more crucial—and no less—than where I grew up, or whom I live with, or whether or not I can swim. And when I'm writing a poem, I am as conscious of being gay as of my being a so-so swimmer—that is, not conscious of it at all, though I have no doubt that both facts are somewhere in my brain. They can define identity, but are they defining it at that moment? If yes, then each to a constantly shifting degree—all identity, not just sexual identity, being fluid. But people have a tendency to discriminate among all these markers of identity, to give more valence to some things than to others, to think of these valences as fixed, and to equate valence with value. I'm hardly going to resolve that one.

NF: Although simply by refusing to be anything but fluid within the context of identity, a stand is taken, which perhaps contributes to the dismantling.

CP: I guess I don't think it's possible to take a stand on identity, only on the politics of identity. To be gay (as with being black, for example) is a various and multidimensional fact of identity, not a stand on it. Even how those facts of identity get articulated isn't entirely a thing we can choose; but where choice is possible is where a stand might reasonably be taken.

NF: As with past work, many of the poems in *The Tether* deal with connecting with the lover/beloved. Yet several of the new poems are also about turning away: "I was there—yes—but / I myself touched no one." Has the syntax of connection led us into a more difficult, complex realm?

CP: I think so. I think the difficulty and complexity of connection are challenging, sure, but they can also lead to the instinct to turn away. I spoke earlier of pushing forward, but that gesture isn't exactly a merry romp. It's taken me awhile, too, to understand how little touch has to do with connection, at least sometimes. I guess by nature we're empirical creatures—that doesn't help very much when it comes to negotiating those spaces that resist our usual ways of knowing, i.e., by touch and other senses—trust, leaps of faith. Those are harder tools to manage, but sometimes the only ones available, or so it seems.

NF: Again, we come up against the unknowable. . . .

Your earlier books have a tension, it seems, on one level, between elegance and, well, earthiness. I sense a different tension at work in *The Tether*: "Less and less // am I one of those who believes / *To know a thing, / first you touch it*". The elegance is still present, yet it seems to be pushing against something else.

CP: There's nothing to get the hands dirty with, nothing to muck about in, when it comes to those spaces I've mentioned: what's the connection? What is divinity? What is trust or belief? The earlier work (though I think this changes with *From the Devotions*) concerned itself more with the body, the actual physicality of it. There's a lot to get dirty on, in that arena. Earthiness? Some, of course, say the first body was made from earth. . . .

NF: Though I sense even more psychic dirt, somehow, in coming face-to-face with the limits of touch.

CP: Yes, but psychic dirt is itself a chimera, at least as a term, isn't it? It's just a way of trying to grapple with the abstract by rendering it concrete—but the psyche isn't concrete, and dirt, in that phrasing, is only a metaphor. The hands, to all appearances, rise clean. But we sense that they aren't in fact clean—and nobody senses this but ourselves. That's what's terrifying.

NF: When the actual and the symbolic blur.

Your poems have a lot of weight, yet the syntax—fluid, inverted—often suggests a turning from that authority: "not // only do I respect, I / require mystery." Could you talk about the balance between authority and what might be named "reticence"?

CP: For me, the truth—as one has come to understand it after careful wrangling and consideration—is one of the best authorities. And the truth doesn't have to announce itself with a lot of fanfare and trappings; on the contrary, I tend to give more credence to what simply announces itself and trust that whatever authority it has will be in itself, not in its context. As for what you say about the syntax, I think that my syntax is probably indicative of how carefully, how respectfully one has to approach authority. Mystery, by the way, is also a truth for me—I grant it a lot of authority.

NF: That's another aspect of your work that feeds me, the willingness to linger in mystery. I'm interested in where you come from, whatever you take that to mean.

CP: The poems come out of my need to understand what I can't seem to bring to a point of understanding that stays fixed. Devotion. Desire. The sexual and the spiritual. Hunger. Morality. Mortality—what's past it.

NF: One could argue that these larger concerns have remained consistent threads throughout your five books. How have they changed?

CP: Like everything else in life, they've changed according to those experiences by which we come to understand anew what we thought we understood entirely already. *In the Blood* was written before I'd come out as a gay man (I always say—and believe—that the book outed me), the poems in *Cortège* were written in the immediate wake of falling in love and of my conviction that love had some meaningful governance over the body's resistance. With each book, I've had to start all over in terms of reckoning with those issues that you refer to as consistent threads. What's consistent is their inscrutability, and I approach them with weapons that change each time, though each bears the same engraving: experience. For me, the hardest lessons have been those out of which *The Tether* was written. There's a sustaining arrogance (or confidence, or complacency) about the body in *Pastoral*, as well as about the realization of ambition, the bodily sort that I mentioned—an assumption that the distance between "to want" and "to have" is a small and easily negotiated one. The poems in *The Tether* are the humbly offered evidence of mistakes both recognized and not entirely regretted, even as to see disaster squarely is not necessarily to wish any of it undone, or so it seems tonight.

NF: I'm thinking of the lines from your poem "Little Dance Outside the Ruins of Unreason:" "and the difficult-to- / admit-to disappointment / at the loss of them, carnage's / bright details". And from "The Pinnacle": "I am remembering // the obvious—trees / mostly, and a hardness of breath . . ." Your use of "the image" often feels like a landscape glanced from a moving train, always in service to the thought. What is your relationship to the image?

CP: Well, maybe it has to do with what I said about being empirical. The image seems the most available way to understand circumstance, and from which to begin to understand the ramifications of circumstance—or predicament—beyond the easily available details (trees, carnage, breath). But I also think of the image as that against which it becomes possible to begin to understand how much is not available to us, is not knowable. I also think there's an impulse to generate an image for the unknowable to inhabit—we feel better that way. Thunder-gods to explain thunder, for example. And of course there's the image generated as a substitute for what we begin to sense we can never have.

NF: That sense of what we can never have is one of the ways, it seems to me, that your work has been tempered.

CP: Merely living—just being flesh and blood—is to be a fact of loss, an instance of it in progress; which means there's only so much we can possess, and what we do possess is ours only temporarily. That can be very freeing when it comes to concrete things like a scratch on a new table, a broken cup—even if the possession is temporary, we can go to the store and replace them with an equally temporary something. But what is joy, for example, and how can we know we have it if we don't know what it is except abstractly? And when is the body not hungry for more, and the mind content to stop its always questioning, except when living itself has ended? I don't find it possible to be alive and not to be aware of all that we can never have—I'm aware that this is not the case for many other people, the majority, it sometimes seems. And that in saying what I've said, I've made yet another confession.

NF: Confessed.

Often I read issues of power and control into your work—of who has authority, of who leads. Can you say something about this? Is this my own confession?

CP: It may well be! But you're also on target about power and control in the poems. I'm interested in those issues on two levels. One is the level of relationships between two people—between lovers. For me, control and the lack of it are constantly the case, if not the point; power is fluid, I believe, shifting variously between two people in the course of trying to make a life together, which is what makes the effort to do so challenging—especially, or so I find, when the two lovers are both men. I tell my students that a large part of the "meaning" in a poem can be found in the relationship between restraint and release—that's true, as well, for lovers. It's very erotic and murky and fraught with the possibility for violence (which in another context might differently be called persuasion). It's also true for the other level with which I'm concerned, the power "dynamic" between human beings and whatever deity (deities) might be said to exist—that, for me, is what Herbert's poems are largely about.

NF: All roads lead to Herbert. In your talk on Herbert, you called him a "confessional poet," in a liturgical sense, in that his confessions were less spoken than enacted. You went on to say that to share our problems is less difficult than to embody them, but that most "confessional" poetry today is more about "sharing." Is the turn away from "the image" into the act of sentence-making an attempt to enact?

CP: Hmm. Well, I'd say that sentence-making is the attempt to give the images an order that makes sense enough for us to use them as a departure point for the kind of thinking that leaves the literal (and the figurative) behind. Maybe sentence-making is, increasingly, consciousness caught in the act of completing the trajectory that can only lead to the dissolution of consciousness itself—past which, well, we'll see if we get there.

Sea Level

Provincetown, November 1995

Where most open, where seawall and brush of any to-be-reckoned-with size give out, they have lined the shore with what must be, given bits of tinsel still stranded among, flashing among the now-brown needles, so many discarded Christmas trees—heaped, then by wire bound down. Almost a year old, and yet the scent is still with them, strong enough to hold its own with the air's salt. I like the notion that what is dead, only a memory for most of the people already caught up in trying to catch up with the fast-approaching holiday season, can find a use in the life beyond it, a space in the world that says, *Yes, I will hold you.*

I have always loved a summer town in the winter, in what they call here the "off" season, or the dead one. I lived for many years in such a town and remember looking forward most to being able to see *things* again. It's why I've come here so late in November, strange month that finds its start with the dead, its end in the giving of all thanks.

Here are this afternoon's things. The water boatless, or only two-boated. The usual many of souls assuming, stepping out of, resuming the shells a life gives: glint of light or drown of it; seaweed in broken bits like distraction, barely seeable fish, a single skate whose moving remembers a scarf dropped and falling through air; birds, various but annunciatory all, of . . .

Of the general hunger too many know . . .

Of what thing *I* would know?

Prior to anything like what is called "coming out" as a gay man, there was sex with other men. Naturally. As if knowing already the difficulties—the baggage—that come with sexuality, morality, consciousness of and the reconciling of the two, the body tends to limit itself to the simpler instinct. And I think hunger—for food as for the flesh—and the correspondent satisfaction that is the result of feeding that hunger—these are, of all our instincts, the simplest. Close behind: fear, in the sudden thicket of danger (close behind because hunger, pitched high enough, will inevitably override fear).

So. Sex.

I suppose everything is finally instructive, and that every lover is a kind of teacher, but it seems especially significant that in each of my rather few forays into the world of homosexual sex, I found myself—in bed, in a truck, on the fallen steps of property entirely abandoned except by the weather and the yard's unchecked strangle—with a professional teacher of one sort or another. A medical school professor (I myself a mere college undergraduate at the time) whom I would later cast, less than subtly, in a poem as Chiron, the mythological instructor to the hero Achilles in the art of becoming a man. Nearly ten years later (and more than half of that into a marriage), a psychotherapist whom I'd hoped could show me how to school my body away from what, as it turned out, we both wanted. A conservationist, the first encounter with whom began as a nature walk through the salt marshes where he instructed school groups (and others, obviously) in the earth's fragility, in the need to always take care. Granted, sex was the point in each of these meetings; the role of teacher was, in each instance, immediately or almost immediately thrown out the proverbial window. I learned, but in the way that any eager-enough, self-motivated student will learn, despite a year in a classroom with a teacher who either never could teach or, after years of steady burnout, has perhaps not lost the gift but forgotten there once was one.

My wife of (eventually) ten years was not a teacher in the way these men were, but I can see that relationship, too, as an example of student-seeks-teacher. We were students together (and, ultimately, each the other's best friend) at Harvard, having met there as freshmen in 1977, a time when I had begun (but only barely) to question . . . not my sexuality but my hungers, which I suppose I then wanted less to satisfy than to permanently undo. This is not to say that when, at twenty-four, I married—never having lived alone and, thanks to a graduate program after Harvard, never having lived in what is called the "real" world, that world outside the academy—I married as a means of erasing homosexual desire. Nor do I mean there was no love. There was love. But I am reminded of the way in which a student with any genuine zeal for learning (and a concomitant frustration with ignorance and/or the unresolvable) loves a teacher—anticipatorially, I want to say. Already grateful for the ease we have known clarity to bring. Already thankful for that clarity that will come, surely, can't we already taste it, and isn't it sweet, for isn't that what we were promised?

It's hard to imagine back, at this hour in high tide, to how bleak it was earlier this morning, when the tide finding its lowest ebb meant also the complete exposure of a usually forgettable (because unseen) world at the sea's floor. Tide flats, I think they're called, the generally exposed areas across which lie strewn the suddenly vulnerable lives of, oh, snails, worms that aren't earthworms (I suppose they are sea worms), tiny crabs, and things that seemed related to them—everything left helpless before the sun's indifference and the collective hunger of scavenger gulls whose hour this particularly is. Here and there a few fortunate creatures have found small pools of water between rises in the seafloor's surface. Brief seas, miniature havens, the pools say everything about how closely circumscribed hope or survival can be.

It's hard to imagine back, except on remembering one beaten and barely red anymore truck in the midst of where, normally, were feet and feet of water. Not only curiosity but human need brought me to walk across the tide flats to the truck. Isn't it human when anything—a lover's heart, a wound, a different world—has been exposed, to want to step inside of it, to know it, before we pass on to whatever's next (and usually predictable)?

He was kind enough, considering: one stranger to another.

As it turns out, he farms quahogs ("Oysters I try each year—more luck with quahogs.") He led me to the netted-down beds he had seeded last year and rummaging the wet sand, he drew several of the quahogs out—each a different size, each variously ready, or not quite, for market.

One was dead. The farmer pointed out a small hole toward where the shell's two halves came to a hinge. Apparently, there's a snail that drills through the shell, draws the meat out, and eats it, leaving the shell empty, the almost indiscernible hole the only sign that there has been . . . violation.

That was hours ago, now.

In the realm of knowledge, the general (instinctive, I want to say) drift is toward the empirical. More precisely: touch is always preferable to hearsay, no matter how often the latter may call itself Wisdom Gathered from Long Experience. (What does it feel like, that gathering, and how will we know unless we become the gatherers ourselves?)

Before I had touched a man sexually, I knew inside of me an attraction to other men. After I had touched a man sexually, I knew it not just inside but entirely. This, for some, is what will amount to a coming-out story.

But a stripping away of doubt as to one's physical attraction toward men is not, in and of itself, what I have found it to mean to be a homosexual man. On the contrary, the results of those physical attractions, the sexual encounters—predominantly (inevitably?) anonymous—with men before and, yes, during the last years of a marriage, had convinced me, not of my homosexuality so much as of my perversion, my abnormality—and of my revulsion from homosexuality *as I understood it.* But how else to understand it, in the absence of a societal openness that might have helped me overcome the fear of investigating the few books that did exist on the subject, or the fear of (what should have been easier) speaking up. In high school, college—sometime, anyway, before the pulling of at least one life, my former wife's, toward a disappointment none of which she deserved, all of which I might have prevented.

When I consider that I was born in 1959—am, in essence, a "child of the sixties"—I'm all the more surprised at my sense of society as closed to sexual openness. Certainly, if I recall correctly, the sixties were at least partly *about* openness, if not—in the face of a turbulence that seemed increasingly insurmountable—about a downright abandon that seems understandable (as I have always understood the ease with which the beleaguered crew of Ulysses at last yielded to the Lotus-Eaters). And if I was a child of the sixties, I was becoming socially and politically aware in the seventies, an era that, for all the bad press it sometimes receives, does seem to have brought women's rights and (to a lesser degree) gay rights more forcibly into the public view.

But the crucial difference, for me, was in being part of a military family. My father was a career air-force man and, until I began high school in 1973, when he retired and we settled in Falmouth, Massachusetts, we moved annually from military base to military base, stopping to rest only in Germany, where we lived for four years—again, on a military base, which could have been anywhere. Germany was there, but how often did everyday life spill into it, given the nature of military bases? Worlds unto themselves, with housing, theaters, mall equivalents, restaurants, schools. One need never leave base borders—which is also to say one need never move outside the realm of military thinking. There was even a separate newspaper, the *Stars and Stripes,* in addition to the daily that each base generated.

Need I say, given the current hysteria surrounding the notion of gays in the military, that there was at no time any discussion of homosexuality in school? To be fair, there was little discussion of sexuality at all, and what little there was made it clear that heterosexuality was not just the norm but the only possibility. What did that make me, waking some mornings from disturbing dreams of lying naked and not fondling so much as fumbling with the guy who later in the day would again be Mr. Richie the algebra teacher?

Just to have heard—and been able to believe—somebody saying, *Yes, what you want, who you are—they're okay . . .*

Instead—no—*therefore* (years later, of course): the windowless bars; downright frightening theaters for the showing of pornographic movies; other places where, if one was curious enough (or perhaps only that human), one could "stumble upon" live pornography on a stage, in a back room. At which point, haven't we come back to the empirical? Men as a matter of how many hands, this tattooed back, that cock, which ass, this one, whose lovely enough brow until dawn or the lamp's light am I forgetting?

This afternoon, walking across town to the old dairy bar/seafood restaurant, I remembered a dream—or whatever to call what lies stationed between dream and nightmare—that I used to have often. Not of a house with windows, but of the windows themselves, alone, freestanding, no house unless air. There are two windows, one shutterless, the other with one shutter the blue that, could I have it, I think I could rest, I could want nothing. From the shutter a fish hangs, as it has done for days. I know this. I know its blue and green iridescence means finally rot and hunger, flies for scales. The fish hangs, its mouth gaping, as if wanting to say . . . who knows what? The dream ends.

It has long since ended.

The restaurant is one of those 1950s types, the pale green so many of the cars seem to have been, back then. Arrestingly bright plastic booths, paper plates only, and, for ambience, the usual nautica: fishing nets, wooden floats, buoys, a whale's forever-agape jaw one passes through to get to the counter and place an order. But the unique thing here, and perhaps my main reason for revisiting the restaurant, is the collection of deformed lobster claws. All is exactly as I remember: the back room as before, the same glass case inside it and, inside that, the lobster claws, each mounted on its little cork stand, each variously misshapen, or lacking or hard-blessed with something extra, useless, half hindering (but only half), the size of each claw attesting to a life that, despite the body, for the usual number of years lasted.

I wept at little, when I saw them, I can't say why.

I wasn't sad.

When I say that being raised in a military family on military bases was crucial to my sense of identity, I should add what was equally crucial: I am the child of a biracial marriage. My father is black, from Tuscaloosa, Alabama; my mother, white, was born and grew up just outside London, England, not far from the military base where my father, a young recruit in the 1950s, would eventually be stationed.

It's an interesting mix. I don't mean the black and the white of it. I mean that my parents, who, in getting married at all in so racially strained a time, could be credited with a certain rebellious, pioneering spirit, should at the same time have fashioned their lives within an institution not particularly known for the acceptance of nonconformity of any kind, least of all in the area of race. And my parents were clearly aware of the racism, no less common in the military than in the world at large. For this reason, my two sisters and I grew up in a very sheltered space, whose borders ended with immediate family. Few, if any friends—of my parents, of us kids—entered the house. Evenings and weekends were spent among ourselves.

One way to look at this is with admiration for my parents' efforts to provide a sense of unity, of our family as a trustworthy refuge from a world that could not be relied on to give us the same shake, fair or otherwise, as the next—i.e., all-white—family.

The other view: essentially, we lived in a tightly circumscribed circle called Family, that circle itself circumscribed by the circle called the Air-Force Base, encircled in turn by that larger ring, the Military. Beyond that—as in the days when the world was presumed flat—who knew? Except a veritable sea of things nameless and better left unnamed.

"Coming Out." "Come out of the closet." I think of a closet as storage space for what is so little used that it has been forgotten (an unfashionable tie, an old Hoover kept as backup should the new and improved model fail) or a place for what is very much and routinely useful (a broom, a favorite coat, the umbrella that still works), but not all-the-time enough to warrant regular display. I think sexuality—we are talking about identity at its basic level; before *Whose am I?* must come *Who and what am I?*—I think sexuality is neither of these things.

"To come out of one's shell" seems closer to, if not quite to be, the point. One's identity is a sort of shell, even as we can understand various aspects of identity to be so many shells we regularly step into, step out of. Now father. Now son. Now teacher. Now lover. Now beloved. Bottom. Top. Every role, as every body, entails an inhabiting of space. The shell image will serve.

Persona means "mask" in Latin. Mask: half a shell.

The shell image will serve, because it must. It had to. How else to explain, for example, that role of husband that I couldn't entirely call mine, or how to explain away the more lurid lives that, I maintain, it was only partly myself living?

What is commonly called "coming out" I prefer to call a stepping into. We step into a shell that is finally and undeniably our own—that we entirely inhabit. This is not to say it isn't fragile, ultimately corruptible, necessarily impermanent. We are human; we do die, after all. But the right shell, stepped inside of, will at least be invulnerable to guilt about one's sexuality. Call that first moment of in-stepping, if you wish, a coming out.

From where I am staying in this small harbor town at the tip of a peninsula, as we shift, all of us, routinely, toward dark, I can watch the lights as they raggedly come—not *on*, it seems, but *to*. The green light marks the stone jetty's single finger extended. There is a house. There . . . is another house. And of course the lighthouse two towns beyond these, but visible tonight.

"Lighthouse, tower of bright, distant witness" I once wrote in a poem from an earlier summer. But the lighthouse is witness to nothing, really, is only a tower proffering flat, unvaried warning, its lamp panning, like long habit, the now everywhere black, as for some somewhere findable gold.

I won't sully it. I won't. That's the way I used to think about my marriage. It's the way I meant to think about my body and then, always, forgot—until after, when it seemed that nothing could wash me clean enough. In this regard, to quote the poem from which the lighthouse description comes seems useful.

The Gods

It is not that they don't exist but that they are
everywhere disguised, that no one space than another

is less fit or more likely:
the lighthouse, tower of bright, distant witness;

the same dull bird as before, still extendedly calling
where has every wing flown

—the sand, the salt grass.
Think of any of those times that they are said

to have assumed the slowing burden of flesh
and done damage; recall Christ, then (all over)

the boy you found lying restive
(among the sand, the salt grass),

naked—save for the words "breakfast included"
lipsticked onto his chest in thick, plum letters;

and that particular beauty that disarms first,
then attracts

(in which way he most resembled any bad road
collision from which the bodies have not yet been

freed, he resembled the bodies).
They are to any of our hungers as, once, the water was

to that Portuguese man-of-war that you can see
is collapsed now, stranded, useless to itself

against any mouth toward it and open.
They were equally to do with your saying *no*

and your saying *no* not because of not wanting but
Because, you thought, *what else can it be, so much*

wanting, except wrong? Their forgiveness
has never been to be sought: it will, or will not

befall us—you are not stupid, you know this.
As you have known, always, their favor: that it is

specific and can be difficult to see, it is that thin
and that clean. Easily it breaks, and it breaks clean.

I continue to be amazed at how densely packed with guilt and paranoia
it all is: the equating of burden with flesh; the idea that the gods (read: judgment) are so ubiquitous that their gaze is inescapable—at all moments, the
subject is observed. Even the sudden object of desire, a young man whose
"included" breakfast promises to include his own ravishing self—even he
is likely to be a god or the decoy of one. We can't know. In such a world,
to arrive at the ability to say no to random sexual temptation is less a
matter of moral uprightness or self-discipline than of plain fear of . . . of
retribution—something in which we all seem to have been conditioned
to believe, in one form or another (even if that retribution is the nothing
that is all the atheist is expecting). For the space of the poem, fear wins out
over hunger, but this moment of conquest can only be temporary. Hence
the other thing with which the flesh is here equated: a damage that, given
historical precedent, is to be expected. There is a poem, in other words,

which we understand to follow and provide the closure to this one. But its predictability has bored us already. Why write it?

Sudden fireworks, a treat I hadn't expected—though it *is* the day after Thanksgiving, official start, I suppose, of one holiday season.

They shoot the fireworks over the water of this same harbor every July, but that's in the midst of a tourist season that brings the town's population to nearly ten times its "normal," off-season one, the streets so crowded, the harbor that night so aglut with spectators that I've never bothered to join them in the drunken fight for any view.

But *this* . . .

Alone in this house on the harbor, in a town that seems comparatively deserted now, the watching of fireworks becomes an entirely different event, almost as if I've never seen them before.

Something I haven't noticed before is the smoke left just behind the actual bursting of the fireworks. I imagine that the cold has something to do with it, the heat of the explosion lingering more visibly on the air's lowered temperature—that old phenomenon that, as children, we called *Look, I can see my breath.*

The other thing accounting for the visibility of the smoke is the moon, of course. Not full; almost nothing, in fact. A shaving of light whose relative lack of brightness, compared to the firecrackers' brilliance, somehow comes out the winner nevertheless (confirming my long-held suspicion that what normally seems only modest—even humble—if consistent can, when juxtaposed with an excess of dazzle, find itself passing for that more elegant kinsman of the humble, subtlety).

Tonight, anyway, the smoke of the fireworks is increasingly a more considerable thing to watch than the fireworks themselves. For whole minutes, the after-smoke hangs in the air as if uncertain about the wisdom of rising. Then it rises imposingly—into the air, across the water—and with what seems (for mere smoke and no fire, anymore, behind it) an odd strength. The right wind bears it away.

To come out, for me, ended up meaning to fall in love with another man. To have sex with a man, as I have said, was to have the initial pleasure, sure, of orgasm. Then, almost simultaneously—seconds after, at most—to find oneself deluged in the usual trinity of waves: guilt, fear, revulsion. The notion that the body doing this cannot possibly be mine, or is mine for now only. When, when can I leave it?

It was unexpected. A cruise on the street four years ago, the sort of thing I had begun to fear could only become increasingly the norm for me. The cruise wasn't unexpected. (Why else was I standing outside a gay bookstore in Boston, all of me frozen except for the eyes that sought for questioning those of each customer coming, going?) Nor was the sex unexpected—that was presumably the point in repairing, immediately after having one's gaze at last met, to the men's room of the nearest hotel with the newfound stranger. But the sense (mutual, I'd later learn) of guilt surrounding the sex was different. This time, guilt stemmed not from a belief that the sex was morally wrong by society's standards but that it was for once not *entirely* the point. Something in this meeting made sex not irrelevant but *less* relevant, transcended the purely physical.

That is why, after the standard exchange of phone numbers, after my standard ride home on the subway that may as well have been powered by my sense of self-loathing *(a married man, a married man)*, I did two things that were not standard—had never, in fact, happened before. I called the number I'd been given and I confessed to having deliberately given a wrong number, lest he should call and my wife answer. Now I gave my right number. I *wanted* to see him again, not for sex necessarily, but for what he'd (genuinely) asked for in giving me his number: the chance to meet for coffee and to talk. What other man had ever asked me for that?

At that moment I understood another definition for homosexuality, one that included—there seems no unsentimental way to put it—love.

The idea that love and homosexual sex could come together had certainly occurred to me, but on the level of fantasy. I'd neither read of nor seen any examples to prove the idea was anything more than an unrealizable ideal. I could say that I found at that moment of falling in love with another man the shell—the life, really; the identity—that was mine, not in parts this time, but completely.

The man with whom I fell in love is the man I still happen to happily be with; but I do not mean to suggest that coming out must mean finding the so-called love of one's life. Doug was—to look at the situation in a manner less romantic—what might result were one to cross, say, a catalyst with a key or a map's legend. (Isn't this, now that I think of it, another definition for *teacher?*) This is why I can honestly say that I did not leave my marriage *for* Doug. When, two weeks after having met Doug, I told my wife that I was gay, it was because I had become able to do more than merely accept or understand (which had probably partially happened already) my homosexuality. I had come to know it as a core part of myself, about which there could be no choosing. This is also why, were Doug and I no longer together, I would not (contrary to what my wife long believed—how much out of love, how much out of bitterness and an understandable fear of being alone?) return to the marriage. A realization of one's sexual identity is something quite different from an affair engaged in out of curiosity, boredom, spit—whatever the reasons commonly thrown up. Doug happened to remain in the picture, as they say, because that moment of my full knowledge of myself as a gay man happened to coincide with our falling in love. "Fate, fate, like a flag, like a novel" is how I have put it in a poem.

Most days, I simply smile and say *gravy.*

"The so-called love of one's life." Is that what I meant by "gold" when I wrote of a lighthouse's lamp as "panning the now everywhere black, as for some somewhere findable gold?" "Panning" as in scanning, the lighthouse as a gay man scanning the bar's darkness for the right body? As any genuine heart seeking its mate, who must be *out there* where we are not?

Yes.

No.

Just as: yes, I did, and I didn't mean anything like being swept off of one's feet, as they say, in that bit about the smoke clouds suddenly carried off by wind. I didn't mean to equate wind with disease or violence and the clouds with the unsuspecting, unprotected, vulnerable flesh. And, yes, I did. It is the logic I mean in a statement such as "to come out is to finally step into, inside."

The travel writer Jan Morris, to a book describing her early awareness that she was a woman born inside a man's body (which is not, of course, the case with homosexuality, but is not unrelated to the homosexual who feels born inescapably inside a heterosexual model) and her gradual setting out on a journey whose merciful ending would be an understanding of transsexuality and a successful sex-change operation—to this book, Morris gives the title *Conundrum.* Nowhere else have I seen the word more beautifully applied, or more exactly.

The waves are stronger on this morning of slow, reluctant leave-taking back to the city. The beach over and into which this small house stands is gone now, covered by the water that—if I didn't prefer the room's heat to the near-zero that would come with opening any door or window—I would hear more loudly meeting, beating up against, half burnishing, half stroking toward rot, the house's supporting posts that, for now at least, last.

From doors looking onto a deck and out to sea, the effect is of the house having finally separated from whatever held it to land and become a boat, moving steadily forward, not so much into and against an adverse current as aslant to one whose only pattern is indifference. Not fair and not brute, either.

Logic says that, if all of it holds long enough constant—current, wind, our little boat of a house and its not so little, almost willful drifting—we will eventually come out of this harbor that all our lives we have been told not to leave: this, the one safe place. And after that—as broad and as precarious, perhaps, to lean on as rumor—the sea. No oars, no handed-down-to-us wings, but—irrevocable, perilous, fraught, too, with joy—a life at last claimed: our own, for to steer with.

III

Boon and Burden: Identity in Contemporary American Poetry

Wave of sorrow,
Do not drown me now:

I see the island
Still ahead somehow.

I see the island
And its sands are fair:

Wave of sorrow,
Take me there.

["Island" (I)]

Not long ago, I began a session of a course on American poetry by reciting this poem, then inviting the students to discuss it. A certain amount of talk ensued about structure—the missing stress of the fourth stanza, for example, serving to reinforce metrically the aborted hopes of the speaker—then about content: a poem that captures the existential crisis of us all, since humans are as mortals doomed to strive past a mortality that can't be got past; a poem about the sorrow of the human condition, the wave as sorrow; sorrow as, variously, what can overwhelm us, can provide us fleetingly with a vision of safe haven, may even be the means by which we reach that haven. Reasonable approaches, all of them. When I then added that Langston Hughes was the author of the poem, however, all of that interpretation was abandoned— the class was certain that Hughes must mean to address slavery and how it figures into the African American psyche, and that this poem must at some level be remembering the Middle Passage, that sea route by which the slave trade was conducted between Africa and North America. Others determined that Hughes was making for himself a place in the Negro spiritual tradition, and making a place for that tradition in American poetry, by referring obliquely to the River Jordan, via which the speaker might eventually reach some better, promised land and lay aside the burdens of having lived in this more troubled one. Finally, I threw into the discussion the likely homosexuality of the poet. Suddenly, Hughes's poem was a veiled expression of a man alienated from the joys available to those belonging to a predetermined norm. Unable to speak honestly, Hughes had been forced to mask frustrations of sexuality in more traditional—acceptable—marine imagery.

Once the particulars of the poet's identity were known to them, the students clung to those interpretations that relied entirely on those particulars, and the possibility that Hughes's poem might be one in a broad tradition of poems in English addressing the human condition was abandoned for the certainty that the poem spoke primarily for two facets of that many-faceted tradition: gays, and African Americans. Rather than enriching the possibilities for meaning, these aspects of identity had prompted readers to impose on Hughes's poem what it might be radical to suggest is segregation—however inadvertent—but I'll suggest it.

It's what Countee Cullen, a Harlem Renaissance contemporary of Hughes, is getting at, I believe, in his "Yet Do I Marvel":

I doubt not God is good, well-meaning, kind,
And did He stoop to quibble could tell why
The little buried mole continues blind,
Why flesh that mirrors Him must some day die,
Make plain the reason tortured Tantalus
Is baited by the fickle fruit, declare
If merely brute caprice dooms Sisyphus
To struggle up a never-ending stair.
Inscrutable His ways are, and immune
To catechism by a mind too strewn
With petty cares to slightly understand

What awful brain compels His awful hand.
Yet do I marvel at this curious thing:
To make a poet black, and bid him sing!

Up until that last line, it wouldn't be unreasonable to think of this sonnet as—if not written by Keats or Shelley, those two pivotal models for Cullen—then clearly influenced by those poets. At the very least, Cullen is suggesting in that last line that the issue of race—of being a minority—complicates one's participation in the tradition of poetry, when the tradition under discussion is unaccustomed to—and/or resistant to—inclusion of said minority. By withholding the information about race until the last line, Cullen gives the reader ample time—and thirteen lines of example—in which to appreciate how formally accomplished the writer is, and how worthy he is to contribute his thoughts to the ever-continuing dialogue concerning divinity and our relationship to it; all those qualifications notwithstanding, however, the final line makes clear that race somehow outweighs them.

When is participation viewed as trespass? When does it become betrayal? Cullen was often enough accused by other black writers, Hughes among them, of working too hard to become, as it were, the other—writing in the language not of daily life in Harlem, but of the white, English, and very much dead Romantics. And trespass or betrayal, by whom is it so viewed? And to what extent can or should the poet finally be concerned with any of this?

In an age in which author photographs—and the author's private life—get as much play as the author's writing, it becomes increasingly more difficult to come upon a poem without bringing to our assessment of it what we know of the author's identity. But ultimately, it should be the identity of the poem, not the poet, that matters; the poem's identity, its virtues or lack of them, must be the focus of our critical scrutiny. When this isn't the case, then the issue of identity only complicates and muddies clear—and fair—judgment on the part of the reader. Often too, the *poet's* judgment becomes muddied. This is why it is difficult to defend as good poetry the bulk of the poems produced by the Black Arts Movement of the 1960s and '70s; it rarely transcends its time in history, or the individuality of the poet, and I am suggesting that good poetry must do at least these two things. The truest poetry speaks to us not as documentation—which is part of the business of prose—but as confirmation—echo—of something essential to being human, flawed, mortal. This is why, when Sappho speaks of being alone with nothing but moonlight and her desire for an absent lover, it is irrelevant that she was a woman, may or may not have been a lesbian, lived about twenty-six centuries ago, spoke Greek, and a dialect form of it at that. For me, the best poems don't so much give us place as remind us that there *is* a place that we don't inhabit alone—the weather of that place is, variously, joy, despair, terror, innocence, trust, mistake . . .

Part of the burden of identity—particularly the specific identity-markers of race, sexuality, and gender—is that once it becomes *either* the focus of the poem's content *and/or* the primary lens through which the poet both sees and deploys the poem's content, the poem becomes charged with the possibility for conspiracy and exclusion, and this accordingly charges and challenges the relationship between poet and audience. A sense of them vs. us governs the poem—which is very different from a poem that considers conflict between two parties in a way that allows both for a meditation on that particular conflict and for one on conflict itself; this latter kind of poem has the additional advantage of making it possible for members of both parties to end conflict through mutual understanding, rather than becoming even more galvanized in their opposition to each other.

This isn't to say that there aren't reasons to limit audience. We may wish to unite a particular group of people, to create a shared consciousness among them, the better to begin showing the size and force of our resistance to particular restraints and prejudices. This was a very large part of the philosophy behind the Black Arts Movement's aesthetic: the poems are to be not only accessible, but directed in particular to a black audience. What I'm arguing is that this aesthetic is finally a limiting one in terms of the making of lasting poetry; it displaces discipline—of music and of argument—without which there can be no clarity of vision, which is the same as no vision, which is the same as no resonance. One of the more bracing examples can be found in Amiri Baraka's "Black Art."

> Poems are bullshit unless they are
> teeth or trees or lemons piled
> on a step. Or black ladies dying
> of men leaving nickel hearts

beating them down. Fuck poems
and they are useful, wd they shoot
come at you, love what you are,
breathe like wrestlers, or shudder
strangely after pissing. We want live
words of the hip world live flesh &
coursing blood. Hearts Brains
Souls splintering fire. We want poems
like fists beating niggers out of Jocks
or dagger poems in the slimy bellies
of the owner-jews. Black poems to
smear on girdlemamma mulatto bitches
whose brains are red jelly stuck
between 'lizabeth taylor's toes. Stinking
Whores! We want "poems that kill."
Assassin poems, Poems that shoot
guns. Poems that wrestle cops into alleys
and take their weapons leaving them dead
with tongues pulled out and sent to Ireland. Knockoff
poems for dope selling wops or slick halfwhite
politicians Airplane poems, rrrrrrrrrrrrrrrrrr
rrrrrrrrrr . . . tuhtuhtuhtuhtuhtuhtuhtuhtuh
. . . rrrrrrrrrrrrrrr . . . Setting fire and death to
whities ass. Look at the Liberal
Spokesman for the jews clutch his throat
& puke himself into eternity . . . rrrrrrrrrr
There's a negroleader pinned to
a bar stool in Sardi's eyeballs melting
in hot flame Another negroleader
on the steps of the white house one
kneeling between the sheriff's thighs
negotiating coolly for his people.
Agggh . . . stumbles across the room . . .
Put it on him, poem. Strip him naked
to the world! Another bad poem cracking
steel knuckles in a jewlady's mouth

Poem scream poison gas on beasts in green berets
Clean out the world for virtue and love,
Let there be no love poems written
until love can exist freely and
cleanly. Let Black People understand
that they are the lovers and the sons
of lovers and warriors and sons
of warriors Are poems & poets &
all the loveliness here in the world

We want a black poem. And a
Black World.
Let the world be a Black Poem
And Let All Black People Speak This Poem
Silently

or LOUD

More than addressing itself to a specifically black audience, this poem makes a point of driving away a number of potential audiences: whites, women, Jews, gays, liberals, and even blacks—those blacks deemed, by Baraka, the wrong sort. While I can applaud the broadness of mind that chooses to offend many parties equally, and while I think Baraka makes an important point when he says, "Let there be no love poems written/until love can exist freely and/cleanly", the poem is finally an example of how identity can narrow a poem's scope, and can obscure the talents of the writer that Baraka can also be.

The virtue of poems like Baraka's is that they seek to effect social awareness and, by extension, social change. Political poetry of this sort acts as witness to particularities—usually, social wrongs; this doesn't necessarily make for bad poetry, but it does make for a poetry that's more limited. It dilutes poetry, by adding to poetry the role of social documentary. Why call this dilution, rather than enrichment? Because the best poems will sustain scrutiny through several lenses, and won't rely entirely or mostly on identity external to the poem or on ideology exclusive to the poet. We *can*, if we wish to, make persuasive, credible arguments for Hughes's poem as a commentary on the African American condition or the alienation that accompanies sexuality. But when we *remove* those lenses, we don't find ourselves unable to see any other possibilities for meaning; Hughes offers his own poetry of witness to the shared, human condition of longing, of hoping against hope.

Lest I seem to be confining my argument to African American poetry, I should say that there are parallels to be found in what has come to be considered the poetry of AIDS. AIDS poetry—like Black Arts poetry—has and will continue to have its value (all poetry has value, even when its value is only one of reminding us of what good poetry is not). I suspect that AIDS poetry will be valuable as documentation of, and witness to, the effects of a particular plague on a particular time in human history. Those poems that have greater value than that are going to be the ones that see AIDS as mere context within which to see something more timelessly true about the human condition, namely, that we all come to know death in at least two ways eventually: by losing others to it, and by succumbing, in time, ourselves to the fact of death; reckoning with that fact is a crucial part of what it means to be alive.

Does this mean we can't write *as* blacks, *as* gays? Not at all. In fact, it is questionable that we can write as anything other than whatever we are—to some degree, every poem is necessarily autobiographical. But when we choose to favor a particularity of ourselves as human beings, rather than focusing on our more generally human selves, that's when—if ever—a poem can legitimately be called a "black" poem, a "gay" poem. The challenge then becomes one of determining how the poem can resonate both at and beyond the level of identity.

Robert Hayden is a good example of a poet who sometimes chooses to write with race identifiably part of the poem, and sometimes not—in either instance, he managed to produce poetry that never compromised resonance; the result is a lasting body of work. Here is his "The Tattooed Man."

I gaze at you,
longing longing,
as from a gilt
and scarlet cage;

silent, speak
your name, cry—
Love me.
To touch you, once
to hold you close—
My jungle arms,
their prized chimeras,
appall. You fear
the birds-of-paradise
perched on my thighs.

Oh to break through,
to free myself—
lifer in the Hole—
from servitude
I willed. Or was
it evil circumstance
that drove me to seek
in strangeness strange
abiding-place?
Born alien,
homeless everywhere,
did I, then choose
bizarrity,
having no other choice?

Hundreds have paid
to gawk at me—
grotesque outsider whose
unnaturalness
assures them they
are natural, they indeed
belong.
But you but you,
for whom I would
endure caustic acids,

keenest knives—
you look at me with pain,
avert your face,
love's own,
ineffable and pure
and not for gargoyle
kisses such as mine.

Da Vinci's Last Supper—
a masterpiece
in jewel colors
on my breast
(I clenched my teeth in pain;
all art is pain
suffered and outlived);
gryphons, naked Adam
embracing naked Eve,
a gaiety of imps
in cinnabar;
the Black Widow
peering from the web
she spun, belly to groin—
These that were my pride
repel the union of
your flesh with mine.

I yearn I yearn.
And if I dared
the agonies
of metamorphosis,
would I not find
you altered then?
I do not want
you other than you are.
And I—I cannot
(will not?) change.

It is too late
for any change
but death.
I am I.

Hayden may in this poem be addressing the issue of what it means to be African American and to feel alien in the United States. But finally there is nothing in the poem to definitively say that this is the poem's message. Instead, we are told the speaker was "born alien, / homeless everywhere," that he imposed on himself the myriad tattoos, but as hiding place, most likely, and not as cage from which to view the world gawking at him, to the point where people have forgotten that he has yearnings and pride, just as they do. The brilliance of the last line—"I am I"—is in its being as much a statement of the tattooed man himself as it is also truth for the reader the moment that he or she says it aloud. Truth, irrespective of gender, race, and other markers of identity. In this sense, "The Tattooed Man" fits that category of poems that speak to the broader human condition, even as the speaker of the poem intends only to speak about a condition to which few of us—even the tattooed among us—can relate.

But Hayden also chooses at times to write with the particulars of race in mind. In "Middle Passage," one of the most important and successful poems in American poetry of the twentieth century, he shows how this can be done without making the poem's scope more narrow in the process. It is a long poem, and its strategies are many, but some of the ways in which the poem maintains resonance can be seen just by examining the first section:

Jesús, Estrella, Esperanza, Mercy:

> Sails flashing to the wind like weapons,
> sharks following the moans the fever and the dying;
> horror the corposant and compass rose.

Middle Passage:
>   voyage through death
>   to life upon these shores.

"10 April 1800—
Blacks rebellious. Crew uneasy. Our linguist says
their moaning is a prayer for death,
ours and their own. Some try to starve themselves.
Lost three this morning leaped with crazy laughter
to the waiting sharks, sang as they went under."

Desire, Adventure, Tartar, Ann:

Standing to America, bringing home
black gold, black ivory, black seed.

*Deep in the festering hold thy father lies,
of his bones New England pews are made,
those are altar lights that were his eyes.*

Jesus   Saviour   Pilot   Me
Over   Life's   Tempestuous   Sea

We pray that Thou wilt grant, O Lord,
safe passage to our vessels bringing
heathen souls unto Thy chastening.

Jesus   Saviour

"8 bells. I cannot sleep, for I am sick
with fear, but writing eases fear a little
since still my eyes can see these words take shape
upon the page & so I write, as one
would turn to exorcism. 4 days scudding,
but now the sea is calm again. Misfortune
follows in our wake like sharks (our grinning
tutelary gods). Which one of us
has killed an albatross? A plague among
our blacks—Ophthalmia: blindness—& we

have jettisoned the blind to no avail.
It spreads, the terrifying sickness spreads.
Its claws have scratched sight from the Capt.'s eyes
& there is blindness in the fo'c'sle
& we must sail 3 weeks before we come
to port."

> *What port awaits us, Davy Jones'*
> *or home? I've heard of slavers drifting, drifting,*
> *playthings of wind and storm and chance, their crews*
> *gone blind, the jungle hatred*
> *crawling up on deck.*

Thou   Who   Walked   On   Galilee

"Deponent further sayeth *The Bella J*
left the Guinea Coast
with cargo of five hundred blacks and odd
for the barracoons of Florida:

"That there was hardly room 'tween-decks for half
the sweltering cattle stowed spoon-fashion there;
that some went mad of thirst and tore their flesh
and sucked the blood:

"That Crew and Captain lusted with the comeliest
of the savage girls kept naked in the cabins;
that there was one they called The Guinea Rose
and they cast lots and fought to lie with her:

"That when the Bo's'n piped all hands, the flames
spreading from starboard already were beyond
control, the negroes howling and their chains
entangled with the flames:

"That the burning blacks could not be reached,
that the Crew abandoned ship,
leaving their shrieking negresses behind,
that the Captain perished drunken with the wenches:

"Further Deponent sayeth not."

Pilot   Oh   Pilot   Me

As I mentioned earlier, the Middle Passage is the term for the seaway used by slave ships to this country from Africa. The subject of the poem is not, however, just that part of African American history, but of American history, which includes the history of white America. To make this clear, Hayden mixes the fact of American slavery—particular to blacks—with allusions to particulars of white, English literature: the references to Shakespeare's *The Tempest* in lines 17–19, for example, and to Coleridge's "The Rime of the Ancient Mariner" at line 34; the lines from a Protestant hymn (20–21), which will recur, though in increasingly more fragmented form, throughout the poem; the casting of the excerpt from the ship's log (lines 26 ff.) and of the witness's deposition ("Deponent further sayeth,") in the blank-verse tradition of English poetry. The result is a poem that addresses a particular of history, and of race, and at the same time suggests that a larger audience is to be addressed because also implicated—inextricably so. In the poem's first section alone, we can see this inextricable binding of the two races and of their traditions not only on the level of content, but at the level, as well, of prosody: note the mosaic arrangement of lines and stanzas on the page, suggestive of the strategies of montage in jazz and in the art of painters like the black Romare Bearden, like the white Matisse, and reminiscent of the designs that figure largely in African textile art. The result is that Hayden, in writing to the particular, establishes the particular as an essential part of the more general whole.

In her collection *Thomas and Beulah,* Rita Dove shows how identity can inform rather than define the dimensions of a poem, and how the poet—in so doing—needn't compromise the very important aspects of identity particular to him or her. *Thomas and Beulah* would by now be of limited interest if it spoke only to the chronicling of the lives of two African Americans from 1900 to 1969. What Dove achieves, instead, is a collection that is equally about marriage, about the different psychologies not just between a particular man and a particular woman, but between men and women generally, and about the necessarily—because each of us is an individual—differing psychologies between any two people (of whatever gender) who seek to make a shared life between them. In the course of the book, topical issues—the Civil Rights Movement, for example—occur; but again, this is put into the perspective that current events hold always, that is, they inform a part of our lives only. Here is the poem "Dusting" as an example of what happens throughout the book:

Every day a wilderness—no
shade in sight. Beulah
patient among knickknacks,
the solarium a rage
of light, a grainstorm
as her gray cloth brings
dark wood to life.

Under her hand scrolls
and crests gleam
darker still. What
was his name, that
silly boy at the fair with
the rifle booth? And his kiss and
the clear bowl with one bright
fish, rippling
wound!

Not Michael—
something finer. Each dust
stroke a deep breath and
the canary in bloom.
Wavery memory: home
from a dance, the front door

blown open and the parlor
in snow, she rushed
the bowl to the stove, watched
as the locket of ice
dissolved and he
swam free.

That was years before
Father gave her up
with her name, years before
her name grew to mean
Promise, then
Desert-in-Peace.
Long before the shadow and
sun's accomplice, the tree.

Maurice.

Here, Dove accurately captures the reverie that can accompany as simple a task as dusting furniture, and she suggests that dusting can be the devotional act that Gaston Bachelard (in his *The Poetics of Space*) says it is, not only unlocking the intimacy of furniture but unlocking the memory of the one who dusts it. She also captures the very human moment when we all but remember what, for all its importance once, has now grown blurred by the distances of time, experience, and disillusionment. The sense of epiphany and real victory when the name blooms suddenly into Beulah's head is exciting because recognizable, known to us, even as her struggle to remember is a thing we've known, too. Granted, this poem by itself doesn't address particulars of race. One of Dove's strategies is to scatter those particulars throughout the collection of poems—in the course of reading which, we get to see Beulah sometimes as an African American, sometimes as a woman, sometimes as mother, wife, daughter. The final effect is that we see her as a composite of all of those things—she becomes as multifaceted as any human being is, as the I of Hayden's "The Tattooed Man" is. Identity here is not the specific that is spoken to, nor is it the restraint by which the poems are held back.

In part, the difficulty of negotiating this balance—both addressing identity and not compromising a resonance that can at once include and transcend identity—may lie behind the gesture (sometimes deliberate, sometimes inadvertent) among African American poets to write from behind a mask upon which race does not overtly figure. It is a gesture I find hardly new, but increasingly prevalent, and it takes many forms, one of which is to write from behind a mythological persona. Consider Patricia Smith's "Medusa."

Poseidon was easier than most.
He calls himself a god,
but he fell beneath my fingers
with more shaking than any mortal.
He wept when my robe fell from my shoulders.

I made him bend his back for me,
listened to his screams break like waves.
We defiled that temple the way it should be defiled,
screaming and bucking our way from corner to corner.
The bitch goddess probably got a real kick out of that.
I'm sure I'll be hearing from her.

She'll give me nightmares for a week or so;
that I can handle.
Or she'll turn the water in my well into blood;
I'll scream when I see it,
and that will be that.
Maybe my first child
will be born with the head of a fish.
I'm not even sure it was worth it,
Poseidon pounding away at me, a madman,
losing his immortal mind
because of the way my copper skin swells in moonlight.

Now my arms smoke and itch.
Hard scales cover my wrists like armor.

C'mon Athena, he was only another lay,
and not a particularly good one at that,
even though he can spit steam from his fingers.
Won't touch him again. Promise.
And we didn't mean to drop to our knees
in your temple,
but our bodies were so hot and misaligned.
It's not every day a gal gets to sample a god,
you know that. Why are you being so rough on me?

I feel my eyes twisting,
the lids crusting over and boiling,
the pupils glowing red with heat.
Athena, woman to woman,
could you have resisted him?
Would you have been able to wait
for the proper place, the right moment,
to jump those immortal bones?

Now my feet are tangled with hair,
my ears are gone. My back is curving
and my lips have grown numb.
My garden boy just shattered at my feet.

Dammit, Athena,
take away my father's gold.
Send me away to live with lepers.
Give me a pimple or two.
But my face. To have men never again
be able to gaze at my face,
growing stupid in anticipation
of that first touch,
how can any woman live like that?
How will I be able
to watch their warm bodies turn to rock
when their only sin was desiring me?

All they want is to see me sweat.
They only want to touch my face
and run their fingers through my . . .

my hair

is it moving?

It is possible to construct an argument for this poem as a poem about race. The two races are that of mortals and that of immortals, there's an uneven structure between the two, and Smith gives voice to the disenfranchised party. Is this her veiled way of addressing issues between blacks and whites? Maybe. But nothing *in this poem* allows for such an interpretation, and it doesn't occur to us to impose such an interpretation until we know the poet's racial identity. More to the point is the fact that the poem can stand without this interpretation. Without it, this is a poem about that oldest of concerns—again, our relationship to divinity—even if that relationship is one of indifference. Because the question can't be entirely resolved, it's an ongoing one, part of our existence as human beings of whatever race.

The poet Ai has long worked almost entirely from behind masks, and—at least until quite recently—the persona adopted has usually been white and, more often than not, male. She avoids much of the gendering and race-labeling by shifting masks so frequently—her subject becomes, necessarily, the broken and outcast who nevertheless find a way to speak out from and through their condition. As well, Ai often takes on the personae of celebrities—the range is wide, from Elvis Presley and James Dean to Mary Jo Kopechne and Rodney King, and the range itself speaks to Ai's project as being grounded in identity, yes, but less in the specifics of identity than in the relationship between who we are, what we present of ourselves to the public, and how much of what and who we are has to do with an identity not self-chosen but imposed on us by others. The result, I believe, is a poetry of greater resilience and possibly greater shelf life.

But if part of writing from less specifically identity-tagged personae has to do with an attempt on the part of these writers to avoid limiting the poem's resonance, some part, too, surely stems from the belief among many writers that color, gender, sexual orientation are increasingly more incidental than galvanizing and solely definitive. Some of this thinking may have to do with how perspective shifts as pivotal issues become less so. Or to put it another way, an acceptance of difference has the effect of making that difference less a point around which to rally than might once have been the case: it is why the psychology and aesthetic behind the Black Arts Movement were necessary, and still are, but differently so, even as racism still exists but there is at the same time a palpable difference in the climate since the Civil Rights Movement.

Meanwhile, the self seems increasingly to be understood as a construction of many identities, even as race becomes more and more impossible to pin down. It is what the African American poet Cyrus Cassells is getting at, I think, in the notes that accompany his book *The Mud Actor*. There he speaks to the notion of going beyond persona, and explains how he came to understand that he had been able to know himself as many others in other lifetimes. Terming it regression rather than reincarnation, Cassells writes in that book as, variously, a fin de siècle Frenchman, a victim of the Hiroshima bombing, a fifteenth-century Japanese feudal lord, to name but a few. Cassells insists that these are not personae, but true selves from among his many selves. The effect in that book is one of putting the subjects of suffering and otherness into the foreground of the poetry and—by not focusing on a single identity but including instead as many as possible—Cassells conveys something of the universal, human fact of suffering and alienation.

The best poets bear in mind the need to make their poetry as all-embracing, as widely relevant as possible. I certainly don't think we can write all of the time toward that goal, but we can use that goal as a means of determining the degree to which we have produced a poem that transcends the individual who wrote it—which is to say, the poem may have reason to hope for an audience. And we may opt deliberately for a very specific audience—again, the Black Arts Movement serves as example—but we then will have to accept that we not only limit audience, but risk limiting the life and relevance of the poem itself. Fair enough—it's a proverbially free world. What I want in my own work is neither to compromise my individuality nor to be restricted by the particulars of it—and I look for this same calibration in the work of writers whose work I admire. A perfect example, and my final one here, is Yusef Komunyakaa's "Facing It," from his book *Dien Cai Dau:*

My black face fades,
hiding inside the black granite.
I said I wouldn't,
dammit: No tears.
I'm stone. I'm flesh.
My clouded reflection eyes me
like a bird of prey, the profile of night
slanted against morning. I turn
this way—the stone lets me go.
I turn that way—I'm inside
the Vietnam Veterans Memorial
again, depending on the light
to make a difference.
I go down the 58,022 names,
half-expecting to find
my own in letters like smoke.
I touch the name Andrew Johnson;
I see the booby trap's white flash.
Names shimmer on a woman's blouse
but when she walks away
the names stay on the wall.
Brushstrokes flash, a red bird's
wings cutting across my stare.
The sky. A plane in the sky.
A white vet's image floats
closer to me, then his pale eyes
look through mine. I'm a window.
He's lost his right arm
inside the stone. In the black mirror
a woman's trying to erase names:
No, she's brushing a boy's hair.

"Facing It" is the poem with which the collection ends, and it seems fitting
that it should open with the line "My black face fades." Is Komunyakaa
suggesting that he no longer is black, or that the face literally disappears
in the blackness of the Vietnam Veterans Memorial's black granite, or that

blackness—race—is the least of the issues he wants us to consider? I think it's all of the above. But more important, I think Komunyakaa wants us to understand that we cannot look at war without also having to confront the ways in which we—as human beings—are distorted by it, hence the emphasis throughout the poem on optical illusion, disappearance and re-appearance, nothing reliably being what it seems. Notice how, by the end, not only is race transcended, but so is gender, and so is the specificity of the war itself—the points made here are no more confined to the Vietnam War than is the *Iliad* a poem about a single war in a place called Troy.

Ultimately—necessarily—we speak and write from who we are (and when, and how), and what we produce is, if we allow for the many-sidedness of self, bound to be not just reflective of ourselves but of the rest of human civiliza-tion, of which we are finally only the latest part, not the newest. The best writers produce work that resists easy limitation. And the best readers read accordingly: they impose no limits.

Another and Another Before That: Some Thoughts on Reading

One way to look at reading: as the lifelong construction of a map by which to trace and plumb what it has ever meant to be in the world, and by which to gain perspective on that other, ongoing map—the one that marks our own passage through the world as we both find and make it.

If all we can ever know comes filtered through the lens of our own experience, and if we are readers, some part of our very selves will be the result of what we have read—this is obvious enough. Good writers not only have read widely and deeply, but they continue to do so—not in order to be better writers, but because for them the act of reading is as inseparable from living as writing is.

As for the fear that by reading the great work that has come before one's original voice will either be influenced away from itself or overwhelmed into utter silence: an original voice can perhaps half willingly be seduced; it is rarely mastered.

At the moment, I'm writing from a public library at one end of Cape Cod, very much like the library where I worked for three years of high school at the Cape's other end. It was there that, in the course of shelving books, I saw a book called *The Joy of Sex;* no sooner did I open the book than I dropped it, half in shock at a picture I'd seen, and half terrified I'd be seen by the head librarian and fired immediately, on the grounds of—what? Then I picked the book back up—

It was also in that library that I came across the selected poems of a man named Auden. I took the book from the shelf for how the name sounded—or I imagined it should—like "autumn." What brought me to check out the book were these lines to which it instantly fell open: "Lay your sleeping head, my love / Human on my faithless arm; . . ."

I knew nothing about Auden's sexuality—and it would be almost twenty years before I entirely understood my own. But in "Lullaby" I first encountered what, for me, was then just as radical a notion: that love and faithlessness were not necessarily exclusive of each other, and that flaw did not always equal ruin. This can't have been the first time it occurred to me that "normal" was a vexed and relative term, and that there might be the possibility of another way to see almost anything; but this is one time I've not forgotten.

If it is true that what we read helps shape us, just as true is that our choices in reading are the result of our sensibility—teachers aside, who we are is a major force in shaping a personal canon. Back to *The Joy of Sex* and my encounter with Auden's poems: another person would never have picked up the former, simply because of the book's title; and Auden's poem might have bored a different teenage reader.

Until I was in high school, my family moved almost every year—and always in the middle of the school year, always therefore the awkwardness of trying to fit in, in the midst of things, both socially and academically. Whenever we moved, my books came with me, and I know that part of the role of reading became one of finding comfort: my world might have changed, but to re-read *Tom Sawyer* or *The Call of the Wild* was to know the pleasures of stability, of being able to step back into a world that had given pleasure, and have my bearings—to know everyone already, as it were, in the room. A portable world to keep with me in the midst of traveling always—which is exactly what writing would become.

Writing has always been for me an entirely private act—I don't share poems with other writers, I've no particular interest in having my work workshopped. Writing is one of the few spaces where I can be alone and not be questioned as to why or how I choose to be myself. Reading has also been that, from the start. I think it's true to say that, through childhood, the one thing I most looked forward to was being permitted to go upstairs to my room and read. Partly it was the privacy itself, but also the chance to see—in books—that it was okay not to love baseball, a boy could lose his dog and cry about it, and often enough there was fantasy, to show that nothing could be called impossible. It turns out, of course, that there are some limits to possibility; but childhood seems the right time not to know this. Books confirm at the least anyone's right to dream.

In the course of reading, a taste gets shaped—for what appeals or doesn't. And a writer's aesthetic gets not so much shaped as informed. I've learned as much about writing from what I don't enjoy as from what I do. Even as joy is understandable finally only after its opposite, too, is known. Moreover, it is by extended acquaintance with both pleasure and pain that we begin to grasp the notion of degrees. And so it is with reading, whereby the self and the writing that comes from that self acquire both dimension and resonance, by the steady increase of which we win the right to exercise that lately suspect thing, authority. We *do* have the right to an opinion because it comes from more than ourselves, from a self that understands its own context within the history of being human, and within that of the literature by which we express being human.

To have read Homer's *Iliad* is not the same as having seen combat. That is, it would not be enough, only to read—that would be experiencing everything via another's experience. Equally, it would be inadequate to know the world only through one's own actual encounters with it. So, balance is important. It is hard to believe that Dickinson never came across the subject of death in her reading; and certainly she had seen more than her share of dying by the time she could say—and mean—"I like a look of agony."

Range is important. Often, young poets want most to know which poets they should be reading—and yet, any poet worth reading probably read everything that came to hand, out of that insatiable desire to know, that curiosity that makes us want to grapple with the irresolvable and/or memorable and transcribe it in lines.

What I most remember of deep winter 1983 is that I read all of Milton's prose and poetry (in English, anyway) and—yes, from cover to cover—*The*

Joy of Cooking. Some small part of a self is surely changed for having learned the best method for skinning a squirrel and having read the *Areopagitica* in roughly the same space of time.

Everything counts. I've no intention of canceling my subscription to *People* magazine any more than I'd stop getting the *New York Times* each morning.

I don't think there are any "shoulds" in the case of reading—that would lead to the usual thorniness of literary canons. Sure, I find it difficult to imagine writing—or indeed reading in an informed manner—without knowledge of classical mythology, say, or some grounding in the Old Testament; but another might say as much about the *Bhagavad-Gita,* which I have yet to read.

There is nothing wrong with asking for reading suggestions, so long as that request doesn't really mask a desire to have a sort of blueprint provided—an instinct that I fear writing programs tend to encourage, perhaps unintentionally: this notion that there is a "way," a structured means by which to become a writer, as if officially. As I say to my students, craft is teachable, vision is not. To read is to get a sense of the many ways in which vision has manifested itself in the past and continues to do so. We are wasting our time, though, if we believe that we shall thereby gain access to our own vision.

Also, asking what to read in order to be a good writer is rather like asking someone, "What should I do, in order to know life well?" The answer is obvious, to me at least: do all that you can do and care to do. Thankfully, there's no one model for any of this—it leaves the possibilities refreshingly, thrillingly wide open.

As far as I've been able to figure out, the truest—the most genuine, *authentic*—poem is the result of a consciousness articulating itself *as only that particular consciousness can.* Afterward, in the wake of that first making, there are the countless and usual "rules" to account for. That's where craft enters the picture. But the applications of craft must ultimately be governed by consciousness itself; each consciousness, over time (experience, again) incorporates those rules of craft—speaks to and away from the rules—in such a way as to produce on paper the authentic, the poem that is unique to that consciousness alone.

Those rules of which I speak are written down, but each time differently, in everything we read. The task of the writer, then, is hardly easy, but very clear.

Asked what I consider required reading for a writer, I can only say it depends, and is different for every writer. What I offer here is less a list of what to read than an idiosyncratic gathering of those writers who have had an influence on me as a writer and human being in general. This doesn't always have entirely to do with quality, but with timing and need on the reader's part. James L. White's *The Salt Ecstasies* is a lovely but uneven book—but, of contemporary poems, these were the first I read that spoke with disarming honesty about gay desire, desire generally, sex specifically. I myself had not come out yet, and had barely begun writing poems. White's was a crucial voice to encounter, for what it confirmed as possible—longing, homosexual longing, the expression of that longing in a poem. I think it's arguable that Dante's *Inferno* is better literature, but Dante couldn't have given me what White did.

As interesting, to me, as the writers we read is how we come to know of those writers in the first place. James White's book was in the bargain barn in back of a favorite bookstore in Falmouth, Massachusetts. White's book was a dollar, and poetry, and a strangely ordinary blue—and the title poem stirring.

The poet Alan Dugan, after reading an early poem of mine, said: "If you haven't read Cavafy yet, you should." I did. And then read everything of Dugan's.

But when it comes to classical literature, I think I have to credit a book (yes, reading again!) that I bought through the Scholastic Book Club, with which most elementary schools were affiliated when I was growing up—the chance for every student in the class to order a book a month at a discounted rate. My parents agreed I could have the book on codes and code-breaking, which led to my spending a year inventing codes of my own. The following year, we were stationed in Germany; to me, German was a code, so it became the first foreign language I ever studied. A few years later, back in the States, I enrolled in a school where German wasn't offered—but there was room, still, for one more student in the beginning Latin course. Thus began an interest in classical literature that would lead to my getting a degree in Classics and teaching Latin for almost ten years.

And thus, while I wasn't thinking about it, began the development of a sensibility and aesthetic that would end up marking as uniquely mine the poems I would, years away, start writing.

Greek lyric—Mimnermus, Alcman, Alcaeus, Anacreon, and particularly Sappho and Archilochus—I continue to admire the ability of those poets to waste no time in locating the precise point of human vulnerability, and to sing that vulnerability into a great openness. Although many of their poems are short because of manuscript damage and loss over time—that is, not because of a deliberately fragmented style—a single surviving line in many instances can resonate more than do many entire poems; and I think it is from these chance fragments that I learned about the effects of a purposeful fragmentation, as well as about brevity and the crucial element of the actual placement of words in a line or in a series of lines. For the same reasons, the choruses of Greek tragedy have also been significant for me—choruses whose relentless winging toward a truth that is unbearable and yet—borne upon flawless meter and rhythm—is unable to be turned away from, is all prefigured in Greek lyric. The choruses are usually complete, so there's less of the brevity of Greek lyric, but there is a similar exactness and a fuller, more measured music.

I am also drawn to and no doubt influenced by the hieratic and vatic qualities of poetry in ancient times, the way in which poetry and the petition and vow of prayer become one. At the same time, there's a mix of familiarity and awe when it comes to the poet's relationship to divinity. Sappho, in addressing Aphrodite, can essentially wonder why the goddess won't give her an even break when it comes to loss and heartache—and yet the poet never loses sight of the superiority of the goddess; she knows that, without the gods, poets would be nothing.

Mary Barnard's translation of Sappho has its inaccuracies—it also has its charms. For Greek lyric more widely, an exciting translation is Guy Davenport's *Seven Greeks*.

From Pindar's Odes (the Lattimore translation captures the right muscularity) I learned much about the possibilities of syntax. But more from the prose of Cicero, Tacitus, and Sallust. In the case of Cicero, not only are individual sentences models for how syntax can be manipulated to snare and win permanently one's listener, but it's a great pleasure to read an entire speech for its overall structure—and this is a level on which Cicero can be easily enjoyed in translation: the syntax isn't always easily translated, but the structure is. It was with Cicero that I came to understand how stylized and regimented rhetoric once was—I admire the way in which words evinced an athleticism then that seems less in evidence today.

Between the verblessness of many of their sentences, and the asyndeton out of the blue, after some lengthily unfolding sentence has been eloquently, precisely laid before us—these effects in the Roman prose stylists convince me that I learned most from them about the possibilities for surprise in syntax and, by extension, a great deal about the psychology of line break as well.

Frequently, more lessons from prose than from poetry. In many ways, the sentence—the poetic line, as well—is for me a bow astrain; the poem is the arrow whose flight depends so heavily on the bow—and on the fletcher's hand behind it. Essential fletchers: Henry James, especially of *The Golden Bowl;* Proust; Virginia Woolf, especially *The Waves,* especially *To the Lighthouse;* George Eliot, who shows how syntax can be made to bear a great weight of intellect without becoming less fluid; Marguerite Yourcenar's *Memoirs of Hadrian,* for how the graces of syntax and sentence structure seem to graph or mirror the grace of memory itself.

The Old Testament (especially Isaiah, Proverbs, and Psalms).

Oh—and the Apocrypha.

Everything by M. F. K. Fisher, but especially the four or five early books published together as *The Art of Eating.* Not for nothing did Auden—who wasn't bad himself, though I'd easily prefer Fisher—consider her the best prose stylist writing in English.

More poetry, less ancient: Hopkins is near if not at the top of the list—but not just the poems, the sermons and other prose as well. Everything is there in his work—the concern with syntax and rhythm, the classical training, the nexus of sacred and profane, in the later sonnets especially. The conviction wrought of a vision wrung from agony.

The seventeenth-century English poets in general, but Herbert and Donne in particular. Of the former, all of *The Temple,* but also the prose work *The Country Parson.* Of Donne, the *Holy Sonnets,* but also *Sermons on the Psalms and Gospels* and *Devotions upon Emergent Occasions.*

Two essential volumes to which I continue to turn are John Williams's *English Renaissance Poetry* and *The Poetry of Meditation* by Louis Martz.

Berryman's "Eleven Addresses to Our Lord" in *Love and Fame.*

Yes, I traveled everywhere, for a time, with Plath's *Ariel* in my backpack.

O'Hara—for the dialogue-influenced delivery, the unabashedness of emotion, the sudden poignancy. "Meditations in an Emergency." "To the Harbormaster." "Music." "Having a Coke with You." "You are Gorgeous and I'm Coming."

Everything by Li Po and Tu Fu, but especially those poems in a collection called *Bright Moon, Perching Bird,* translated by Seaton and Cryer. Also persuasive is Young's *Five T'ang Poets.* The old translations of Arthur Waley may or may not be the most accurate—I can't claim to know the poems in the original—but as with Barnard's Sappho, they are charming, and I believe the spirit of the original remains intact.

The wonderful, eerie verbal landscapes of Reverdy—whom I discovered via Frank O'Hara, who mentions buying the poems of Reverdy in his own poem "A Step Away from Them."

A story about my copy of a book I mentioned earlier—Williams's *English Renaissance Poetry.* It was given to me by one of my teachers, Robert Pinsky, who urged me to read the poems included by Fulke Greville. Once I opened the book, I found it had been the copy of Frank Bidart when *he* was a student. Something seems to be getting said here about reading, writing, and how the communion between the two makes possible the continuation of a literary tradition.

Five favorite contemporary books that seem to me oddly neglected but from which I continue to learn: Pamela Alexander's *Navigable Waterways,* Linda Gregg's *Too Bright to See,* Peter Klappert's *Lugging Vegetables to Nantucket,* Laura Jensen's *Bad Boats,* and Martha Collins's *The Arrangement of Space.* Pushed to say what I've learned from each, I'd say—respectively: how experiment becomes invention; that sacrifice is most persuasively enacted on the page when brief and with the swiftness of mercy; that play and comedy need not compromise depth of feeling; how to go on sheer nerve because there is no other; about sequencing, that the arrangement of the words is as important as the words themselves.

From Robert Hayden's poetry, I learned that the only obligation of the poet is to write honestly from that part of identity that is the essence of self past race, sexuality, gender. Which is to say that I see such aspects of identity as simultaneously crucial to and incidental to our individual versions of being human. In Hayden's work, I find everywhere the particular and what transcends it intertwined. Hence, a poem like "Middle Passage" is as much an examination of a moment in racial history as of national history and of the kind of brutality that marks human history more generally. The father in "Those Winter Sundays" is any father, and he is the particular, African American father who seeks to offer all he can to his sometimes less-than-appreciative son: love, hard generosity, an example both of endurance and of responsibility. What is the color of any of these?

Everything by Randall Jarrell, but especially *The Woman at the Washington Zoo* and *The Lost World;* I've learned so much from him about how syntax and structure can variously enact, mirror, and prefigure psychic crisis.

Also a book he wrote for children—which I still read—called *The Bat Poet.* It says as much about being a bat as about being a poet—there are similarities.

And his prose, reminiscent of a time when reviews were written with unflinching honesty and unabashed intelligence. Integrity, crossed with taste.

H. D. Again, the vatic, the hieratic. A conviction that victory comes in many forms, and that the vision that is poetry is one of them—as she says in *Hermetic Definition,* "where there is Olympia, Delphi is not far." She also understood that all literature is influence, that tradition means a handing down: "the torch was lit from another before you/and another and another before that . . ."

The emperor Marcus Aurelius wrote his *Meditations* in the midst of watching his empire get steadily eroded by barbarians. He turns away to the interior of the self not as escapism but as a means of understanding how a self is made: via experience, community (in which friends and foes are equally instructive), and—yes—reading. A kind of guide for the shaping of character, and for the ways in which—to be shaped—we must take advantage of even the least inviting lessons—for instance, those afforded by the example of an empire in shambles. He intended what he wrote to serve as guidance for one of his heirs. His writings have proven to be worthwhile guidance for many heirs since—myself among them.

At one point in the *Meditations,* Marcus Aurelius writes about the body as a corpse, and its life a back-and-forth one of being carried, and the soul its doomed and small courier. He is more or less quoting, though he doesn't say so, someone else with whom he assumes his reader will be familiar. It was the second century AD, when to be a reader at all, let alone a writer, was to have read as much as was available. Why should this be any different now? Time, as they always said it would, has passed, and there's considerably more to read now than there was back in the second century. But my point is not that we should have read everything. Maybe folly figures somewhere in all of this. If we are genuine readers and writers, we should see squarely the impossibility of reading everything there is to read—and yet, impossibly, we should want to *try.*

The Book as Bridge?

I may cross a bridge in order to reach you, or someone else whose distance from me I'd like to lessen, but more often, I find, I cross a bridge in order to go from one place to another place—that is, what matters to me is more the shift in location than in the proximity to another human being. Or maybe what's more accurate to say is that I cannot reach you *until* I've left one place and reached the next space in which, eventually, I might find you.

Step outside the metaphor, and all I'm saying is that the audience, if it enters the mind of this writer, enters later. My first concern is to reach myself, to fashion a bridge by which what I want to say, how I want to say it, and whatever tools I may have with which to say it can be brought together into, at the least, articulate speech and, at best, what I call poetry.

I have written elsewhere of poems seeming to me to be advance bulletins from the interior of the self. In the time that precedes the making of a poem, it's as if my mind is casting around in familiar terrain, when suddenly a half-light gets thrown onto something I'd either not suspected, or had preferred not to, in myself. And because to be human is, if nothing else, to desire to know, I begin asking, pushing further. The poem is the visible evidence of my having struggled with and temporarily mastered—by knowing—another part of myself, or of the world I live in, or of those who also live there. For another person, this struggle might manifest itself as a lush garden, a perfectly risen soufflé—or a fallen one—or the carpenter's precision where each post meets its beam. For me, the proof of the gesture of inquiry is the poem itself. The poem is evidence that I have moved from the self I was to the different self I am now—different, because my knowledge has been made different; the poem is a bridge between those two selves. And if the poem has meaningful resonance with a reader, it is more a matter of good fortune than of any intention on my own part.

⁓

Not every poet, of course, works this way. I'd say the majority of poetry—and fiction—means from the start to get the reader's attention and tell variously an instructive and/or entertaining story. Maybe that means that poetry is many things but, since I'm fond of distinctions, I'll simply say there's a difference I find between poetry and story, as between fiction and story. Coleridge's "Frost at Midnight" is poetry; his poem "The Rime of the Ancient Mariner" is story.

⁓

But a poem is not, of course, a book of poems—and the assembly of a book of poems is presumably more than self-inquiry—or the evidence of same. The fact of the book, if assembled for publication and distribution, means a consciousness, no matter how intuitive the writer, of audience. We *mean* to say something; and whether the book has a narrative arc or is more the record of a particular mind in motion, whether that motion is linear and hence sequential or simultaneous and many-directioned, in the manner of symphony or collage—whatever the method, we intend at some level for what we mean to be listened to, considered, and finally understood.

Falling back on my own experience, I would still maintain that the first task at hand is not to convey meaning to an audience, but to the self. I am not one of those poets who can write toward a theme—rather, a period of time will pass, poems will be written, and eventually it seems a door has shut, a project has announced its closure, or the closure of a phase of it; then begins the questioning: what is—was—the project? In the course of reading over the last forty or so poems I've written, I'll begin to see commonality, as well as points of shift in terms of how the same subject has been considered over time, and how and where progression and/or deepening has occurred. I wait for the project to announce itself—and once it has done so, my task becomes one of arranging the poems in such a way that will most mean-ingfully record the project's theme in all of its shiftings forward and back.

That's where the audience comes in. I am presuming a reader who will read the book from the beginning to end, or one who is willing to do so—that's part of the contract that I'm offering, in full knowledge that not every reader will wish to participate in such a contract. But if, as is the case for most poets anyway, I don't write in order to be able to eat, then I have a freedom to be interested only in those who *do* wish to participate in the contract I'm offering, and to ignore the others.

Maybe, as the philosopher Santayana once said, art *can* be compared to heraldry—both, he said, can be defined as "self-exhibition on a shield of self-defense" (in his prologue to *The Last Puritan*). A poem is—should be—more than self-exhibition; but it's fair, I think, to say that self-inquiry always contains an element of exhibitionism. If a poem is the evidence of self-inquiry, then the assembly of a book of poems is the socialization of self-inquiry: and what is socialization but a bridge by which two parties might begin to meaningfully interact?

⁀❧

One way to socialize is to seduce. To persuade. Given the book as a bridge, why should the reader wish to cross it, or why this one, as opposed to the many others? General seduction—the kind that will secure almost anyone— requires only two components: ease of access, and a conformity to convention, so that recognition will be immediate. These guarantee a fearlessness on the part of the to-be-seduced—in this case, the reader—the particular fearlessness that thrives in an *absence* of risk. Many books—the majority—fall within this category of seduction, and some for perfectly good reasons. A children's primer, a cookbook, a handbook on first aid: in each instance, the point is to instruct, which requires attracting an audience, and the making it easy—pleasurable, even—for the audience, once attracted, to stay awhile.

Imagine a bridge fitted with one of those conveyor belts designed to move travelers through airports: we have only to step onto it, and we are carried. . . . There is a kind of writing whose purpose is purely an entertainment of the kind that does not wish to provoke any further intellectual or emotional inquiry past what is immediately on the page. The difference is like the one between when I have just read an article on Elizabeth Taylor's latest husband and when I have finished a story by Chekhov. The former is, to my mind, not less than literature, but it is different from literature, whose form of entertainment *always* provokes further thought—that is, it has resonance.

The original is in a bind, decidedly, when it comes to seduction. On one hand, what is original is initially strange; and, at best, the strange may draw us closer to itself, but it isn't likely to hold us. A second complication: the original is never strange without also being disturbing—and the disturbing triggers in most of us an instinct to put a distance between ourselves and what disturbs us.

Within the metaphor of seduction, we might say that there are those writers for whom seduction is more ambitious: Gerard Manley Hopkins, Emily Dickinson—they are surely less interested in attracting the attention of readers than in attracting the attention of God—just as Walt Whitman, for all his democratic expansiveness (and for all of his ability to prefigure what now gets called the marketing of books) is after the God inside himself.

Or, to turn to something more contemporary, consider these lines with which the poet Frank Bidart opens his first book of poems, *Golden State*. The poem is "Herbert White," which begins:

"When I hit her on the head, it was good,

and then I did it to her a couple of times,—
but it was funny,—afterwards,
it was as if somebody else did it . . .

Everything flat, without sharpness, richness or line."

Bidart knows these lines can't be anything *but* disturbing to a reader—how daring to write them at all, let alone announce with them one's entrance into the writing and reading community. But Bidart is on a quest for, among other things, a way of defining morality in terms of those individuals who would seem to live outside it, and for showing that, incongruously, morality somehow *includes* these individuals. That's a lot to expect a reader to commit to, and the methodology doesn't necessarily help. But what Bidart, Hopkins, Dickinson, and Whitman all have in common is a commitment to his or her own vision *first*, a belief in the quest, an honesty or earnestness that, finally, they could not change even if they wanted to. It's a combination of integrity and of being possessed, I want to say. And it has nothing at all to do with shifts of fashion, or with anything like marketability or publication.

If the book is a bridge, then I am interested in those who, of their own free will, would cross it. I want even more than that. I want what I have elsewhere called the athletic thinker, the one who sees difficulty as an irresistible challenge and who finds a decided pleasure both in the mastering and in the mastery of difficulty. The athletic reader *requires* risk, *requires* mystery, and comes with an openness to both.

But in writing, as everywhere else, it is rarely enough to want a thing. Once we get past the self-inquiry stage, and find ourselves assembling a book, we have our own share of responsibility in getting what we mean across to our readers. There's a considerable amount of ground available between pandering to an audience and daring an audience to try to understand what we have written. The arrangement or ordering of poems—or chapters—can say as much as can the content of individual poems and chapters—can reinforce that content, serve as complement to it, or serve as foil. We can experiment with language without having to compromise certain conventions: if the word "shovel," for example, is going to be a synonym in this poem for "carrot," then we have a responsibility to make that somehow clear—and if we don't do so, we have no right to any understanding from an audience. As I say to my students, in art we are free to do anything except expect agreement with anything we may choose to do.

The poet Ellen Bryant Voigt has spoken of "retrievable" knowledge. A sentence in a given passage may be unwieldy, for example, but it can be parsed—it is for the reader, in that case, to do so. The myth of Daphne and Apollo may be a new one to us, but it is easily enough found out.

It is, as they say, a two-way street or—as they don't say—a two-way bridge. I wrote a book in which a stag appeared at several isolated points—the risk was that I might seem redundant. But as I was assembling the book, it seemed to me that the stag was many things—art, God, perfection and the elusiveness of it, and perhaps most of all just a stag, despite the artist's impulse to hang the greater valence of symbol around the animal's neck. In arranging the book, I scattered and ordered the "stag" poems across the manuscript so as to assist the reader in seeing how the stag could be seen each time as different from its earlier appearance. But there my work ends. It is up to the reader to notice how the book opens with a speaker pursuing a stag and closes with a speaker being pursued *by* a stag—already, with that shift, we have the possibility that part of the book's narrative might concern reversal, and that's before we look at the actual content of the two poems or of the poems that come between.

But if a reader simply observes a large presence of stags in a book, and goes no further than that initial observation—that is, never bothers to ask *why?*—then we have nevertheless done what we can, and we shall have to hope for better readers, the sort who will say, as Helen Vendler did upon first reading the then little-known poet Louise Glück: "The most profound source of elation in reading a new species of poet is the surprise in every line as a new voice and a new sensibility declares itself."

Part of the bridge that the book represents is one that teaches or otherwise challenges us to build our *own* bridges. For me, authentic reading is not a matter of watching the writer erect his structure, but of becoming an apprentice myself to the venture at hand. At some point, we give over our trust to the writer, to the writer's project, we commit some part of ourselves to what we don't entirely understand yet, but have faith in; call it the writer's vision; and call that readerly commitment another version of what's meant by a leap of faith. And in the leaping, we have traced in the air a kind of bridge, have we not?

❧

For me, to write is a form of prayer, however secular the subject of the writing at hand. Writing is as private as prayer—it contains, as prayer does, an implicit faith in there being somewhere a listener and at the same time a sober realization that prayer is finally one-directional. Somewhere in my deciding to try to turn what I feel and what I think into something sayable must be a belief that what I have to say matters, and that this mattering will be, more than apparent, *relevant* to someone else—but who is that? Not the reader, I want to say; or, if a reader, then first the reader inside myself. If, by chance, the poem is later published, then of course there are other readers. But that has nothing to do with me. Nor does prayer, anymore, figure. The shift from writing to being read—if the first is prayer, the second more approximates communion.

❧

There are bridges we cross in order to save time, or because how else shall we cross this river, this gorge, this stretch beneath which nothing? But there are also bridges we cross in order to learn what lies at the other end, what worlds begin there. Part of this, as I've said, is faith—we believe there *is* another end, and that something *in fact* starts there. And part is the intellectual athleticism I mentioned earlier. But no small part is patience, the particular patience that discernment requires. Consider the following paragraph, which is the opening to a short story:

> The small locomotive engine, Number 4, came clanking, stumbling down from Selston with seven full wagons. It appeared round the corner with loud threats of speed, but the colt that it startled from among the gorse, which still flickered indistinctly in the raw afternoon, out-distanced it at a canter. A woman, walking up the railway line to Underwood, held her basket aside, and watched the foot-plate of the engine advancing.

Reading only that paragraph, would we have been able to pronounce its author a genius? As he discusses in his book *Portraits from Life,* Ford Maddox Ford could, and did, and he was right; thus began the career of D. H. Lawrence, on the strength of a paragraph of his story "Odour of Chrysanthemums." In discussing the basis for his confidence, Ford points to a number of details in the paragraph: the fact that the locomotive is a specific one—Number 4— shows an author with "the power of observation, [who] is going to write . . . from the inside . . . the sort . . . who knows that for the sort of people who work about engines, engines have a sort of individuality. He had to give the engine the personality of a number"; and rather than stating that the train is slow, or assigning it a specific speed, Lawrence makes it clear that (again Ford) "an engine that . . . cannot overtake a colt at a canter must be a ludicrously ineffective machine"; isolating the detail of "gorse flicker[ing] indistinctly in the raw afternoon," Ford notes its economy, how in a single phrase we learn the landscape, time of day, weather, and season. In short, Ford was able to discern, through care and patience, this much about the paragraph's author: "He knows how to open a story with a sentence of the right cadence for holding the attention. He knows how to construct a paragraph. He knows the life he is writing about in a landscape just sufficiently constructed with a casual word here and there. You can trust him for the rest."

And Lawrence's good fortune was in having his work come before a reader whom *he* could trust. A sensibility declares itself, and someone listens: and a bridge is born.

⌖

It is one thing to be discovered, quite another to have *been* discovered some time ago, and to find that something like a career has come into being. At that point, it is possible for a writer, if not to assume, then to be able to say with some accuracy that there is more of a chance than not that his or her next book will be noticed—for better or, of course, for worse. Which is to say that it becomes impossible not to be aware of audience, once we have been made aware of it that first time. To this, I can only say that while I do ask myself, at some point between having finished a book and having turned it over to the publisher, "Will people like this book, will they think it better or worse than the last one, will I have met or failed to meet whatever expectations of promise might be out there?"—while I ask those questions, I know already that I have written what I *had* to write, for *me*. Were that not the case, I'd have held onto the manuscript.

I think of a career not in terms of individual books that get published, but in terms of the career of my concerns, obsessions, and ideas as that career shapes and reshapes itself across the vicissitudes of a life. And thinking this way helps me to see the value of each installment, as it were, of the larger project. I would no more stake more in one book over another than I would say my twenties were better or more necessary than my thirties—as it turns out, both decades have been essential for getting to my forties, even as I know that what I write now is necessarily written in the wake and under the inevitable influence of all that I've written before.

That helps put the audience in perspective. As for the audience's views on the subject—well, if reviewing trends are indicative, then it seems not everyone shares my view. More often than not—or so it has seemed to me—reviewers tend to consider a writer's latest work as if it had appeared from within a vacuum, and this can lead to a great deal of misunderstanding, as it would if we were to judge someone to be a good cook on the basis of the perfect meal he just served us: how do we know this isn't the only meal he knows *how* to make? Do we know he himself made it, or did he get it catered in? More than a good or bad cook, is he an honest man?

Back, then, to the particular bridge I'm calling faith. The reader I'm hoping for, once the books are out there, is the one who will commit not just to a poem, but to a book of them; not just to the one book, but to each as it follows. I want the reader who will consider the book both on its own and in the context of what's come earlier—the one who, if he sees differences in style or content, will not wish that I'd written as once I did, but will be eager to know how I'm writing now and will give careful thought to the possible answers as to why the writing is as it is. It's a tall order, sure. It's asking for commitment to and a trust in a writer's vision, and not just for a small moment. I'm not *expecting* this from a reader—that would be arrogance on my part. But I *am* saying that I am willing to have no readers rather than readers who cannot offer the sort of commitment that I believe—I have to believe—the work deserves. And that isn't arrogance at all, but integrity.

Publication—is the Auction
of the Mind of Man—
Poverty—be justifying
For so foul a thing

Possibly—but We—would rather
From Our Garret go
White—Unto the White Creator
Than invest—Our Snow

(*from # 709*)

So says Emily Dickinson—and, at the level of writing a poem, I agree entirely It's a private act, one exclusive to the garret of the mind itself. To decide to try publishing our work means—or should mean—that we think what we have to say is worth being heard *outside* our own heads, and that we have reason for thinking this way. It also should mean that we are not willing to compromise the integrity of the work, the individuality of style and of voice, for the sake of publication or for being represented in a particularly marketable way. Once those compromises have occurred, publication is indeed an auction of the mind, as opposed to how I prefer to see it, namely, as the *extending* of a mind, as a hand is extended; and now another hand moves closer, as if to take it. . . . They remind me of the separate parts that make a drawbridge. In raised position.

Abstraction on Parnassus:
American Poetry of the 1950s

꽃

We see a picture of a tree standing beside a lake. We agree that there is a lake, that a tree stands beside it. But what we experience inside us when visually confronting a lake and tree necessarily will differ from viewer to viewer: one has perhaps lost a friend who drowned in a lake; or trees may be, variously nostalgic—we recall enjoying the cherries we won by climbing a tree in childhood—or sinister, in that they bring slowly to the surface an otherwise repressed memory of having been raped in a tree house. Whatever the individual response, when that uniquely experiential detail is given physical form, as arrived at via the individual artist's consciousness, or what we have come to call vision, the physical form will in turn be unique to individual experience. We have abstraction, a psychologically experiential detail from the representational or narrative world that we experience, in terms of the senses, more or less in the same way, but a detail made unique because of its being the particular translation of a particular psyche and sensibility that are in turn, for each of us, uniquely ours.

꽃

Neon Signs

WONDER BAR
.
. .
.

WISHING WELL
.
. .
.

MONTEREY

.
.   .
.

MINTON'S
(ancient altar of Thelonious)

.
.   .
.

MANDALAY
Spots where the booted
and unbooted play

.
.   .
.

SMALL'S

.
.   .
.

CASBAH

.
.   .
.

SHALIMAR

.
.   .
.

Mirror-go-round
where a broken glass
in the early bright
smears re-bop
sound

.
.   .
.

—LANGSTON HUGHES

That poetry is organic has been believed as far back as Aristotle, and pretty much in the same way, namely, as a plant is organic—can grow, is generative. But the prevailing corollary to this belief has been that the artist is the one who controls, tempers, and trains the plant to reach a form previously established as appropriate—as the "correct" form of beauty. If one wanted to write an epic in the ancient Greco-Roman period, for example, one would write it in dactylic hexameter, the meter established for epic verse. In Greek tragedy, there is one meter for heated conversation, another for lament. This has been no less the case for poetry in English—hence, the literary clout/dominance, for so long, of such formal structures as the sonnet, blank verse, the ballad stanza, etc., all of which implement pattern in terms of at least one of three things: rhyme, line length, and stanza length. Given this fixity of form, the distinguishing mark of any individual poet's gift had long rested in the degree of success with which he or she managed to uniquely inhabit the form and to seemingly shape the form around his or her content and aesthetics without actually *changing* the form in any extreme way. By the 1950s, however, there is a twist—on the American front—in the understanding of a poem's organic qualities. Yes, a poem is a living, generative thing, but the content of each poem (as filtered through the psychological lenses of individual experience) is now believed to *generate* the form the poem will come to assume. And the success of a poem comes to rest in the degree to which the poet has allowed the poem to announce, as if spontaneously, its shape on the page. Predictably enough, given the idea that traditionally established forms were confining, the new forms are referred to as "open."

⤖

[from] Howl

I

I saw the best minds of my generation destroyed by madness,
    starving hysterical naked,
dragging themselves through the negro streets at dawn looking for
    an angry fix,

angelheaded hipsters burning for the ancient heavenly connection
   to the starry dynamo in the machinery of night,
who poverty and tatters and hollow-eyed and high sat up smoking
   in the supernatural darkness of cold-water flats floating across
   the tops of cities contemplating jazz,
who bared their brains to Heaven under the El and saw
   Mohammedan angels staggering on tenement roofs
   illuminated,
who passed through universities with radiant cool eyes
   hallucinating Arkansas and Blake-light tragedy among the
   scholars of war,
who were expelled from the academies for crazy & publishing
   obscene odes on the windows of the skull,
who cowered in unshaven rooms in underwear, burning their
   money in wastebaskets and listening to the Terror through the
   wall,
who got busted in their pubic beards returning through Laredo
   with a belt of marijuana for New York,
who ate fire in paint hotels or drank turpentine in Paradise Alley,
   death, or purgatoried their torsos night after night
with dreams, with drugs, with waking nightmares, alcohol and
   cock and endless balls, . . .

(1–11)

⌐ALLEN GINSBERG

⌐⊸

The idea that content generates form is the natural response to a conviction
that one's content is not adaptable to accepted forms—what has changed,
then, in terms of content, so as to demand a new aesthetic handling of it?

A collision of sorts seems to have occurred in the 1950s, between a public assumption of moral stability and an increasing conviction, privately,
that morality itself needs to be reexamined. The result of this collision
was a sense of moral claustrophobia; and—even as actual experience of
the world seems increasingly to differ from what is being told to us of the

world by those in charge—in poetry, as in the visual arts, content begins to exert a pressure on form that the established forms are unable to incorporate, or support, refusing instead to accept certain types of content as appropriate for poetry. It is the eventual inability of both sides to coexist that forces the break that, in poetry, takes the shape of opening up the form, and of thinking of poetry less as a record of individual experience in the context of universal experience, and more as a record of individual experience in the context purely of the individual; and ultimately, there arises the notion of poetry as not a record of experience at all, but as an experience in and of itself.

Everything that Acts Is Actual

From the tawny light
from the rainy nights
from the imagination finding
itself and more than itself
alone and more than alone
at the bottom of the well where the moon lives,
can you pull me

into December? a lowland
of space, perception of space
towering of shadows of clouds blown upon
clouds over
              new ground, new made
under heavy December footsteps? *the only
way to live?*

The flawed moon
acts on the truth, and makes
an autumn of tentative
silences.
You lived, but somewhere else,

your presence touched others, ring upon ring,
and changed. Did you think
I would not change?

          The black moon
turns away, its work done. A tenderness,
unspoken autumn.
We are faithful
only to the imagination. *What the
imagination*
      seizes
as beauty must be truth. What holds you
to what you see of me is
that grasp alone.

     ━DENISE LEVERTOV

What sorts of content might not be appropriate for poetry, in the opinion of the literary establishment of the 1950s? Racial unrest is one example. In 1951, Langston Hughes published his book-length poem, *Montage of a Dream Deferred*, a book that looks closely, exhaustively, at the joys and losses and increasingly restless anger and frustration of African Americans who have yet to win their civil rights. The book's epigraph (the words are Hughes's own) points directly to the relationship between that content and the forms which that content will take on the page: "In terms of current Afro-American popular music and the sources from which it has progressed—jazz, ragtime, swing, blues, boogie-woogie, and be-bop—this poem on contemporary Harlem, like be-bop, is marked by conflicting changes, sudden nuances, sharp and impudent interjections, broken rhythms, and passages sometimes in the manner of the jam session, sometimes the popular song, punctuated by the riffs, runs, breaks, and distortions of the music of a community in transition." Even as jazz is believed to have evolved as the unique means of expression for an alienated community, Hughes sees the poem's form as evolving similarly *out of* the needs of that community, and *toward* the accurate expression of those needs. In this, Hughes differed from the earlier, more popular trend among African American poets, namely, that of choosing to employ the traditions of form—traditions established by a white, male, and originally English elite—while writing about issues of race. The poems that resulted from these writers often seem static, precisely because the conformity to authority—in terms of prosody and form—is at odds with content that calls authority to task. The two forces cancel each other out, and with them goes any genuine sense of urgency. Hughes, however, suggests that form should reflect the culture it is grounded in from the start, and that an honest respect for content means trusting content to be able to find its own way into expression. Although the connection doesn't often get made, it is easy to see how this idea about language and its deployment on the page prefigures and leads to the more radical forms—from prosody to spelling—that will emerge in the poems of the Black Arts Movement of the 1960s.

Another supposedly inappropriate subject for poetry at the time: a frankness—about sexuality, drugs, deception of society on the part of a government we are told to trust—a frankness that challenges authority in general, and in particular suggests that morality is finally more fluid and individually determined than we had been led to believe. When I read Ginsberg, I see the obvious Whitmanian influence, yes (Whitman, who found the long line the only one possible for suggesting an openness, a release from the social restrictions of the mid- to late-nineteenth century). But it also seems to be as much pure anger as a desire to widen the embrace of a poem to include what is deemed unincludable that generates the wild and seemingly unruly lines of his poem "Howl."

A third type of content that challenged the notions of appropriateness in poetry was that of psychological breakdown or trauma. John Berryman is a good example from the 1950s, since he is at that time producing the poems that will become *The Dream Songs*—a collection that has three epigraphs, including this one from Olive Schreiner: "But there is another method." Indeed, Berryman—who, it should be borne in mind, began as a master of traditional English prosody (as did Ginsberg)—arrives at a form that, once discovered, governs the entire collection, as if to suggest this were the inevitable form generated by the particular of Henry, the poem's persona/ protagonist. Here is "Dream Song 29":

> There sat down, once, a thing on Henry's heart
> só heavy, if he had a hundred years
> & more, & weeping, sleepless, in all them time
> Henry could not make good.
> Starts again always in Henry's ears
> the little cough somewhere, an odour, a chime.
>
> And there is another thing he has in mind
> like a grave Sienese face a thousand years
> would fail to blur the still profiled reproach of. Ghastly,
> with open eyes, he attends, blind.
> All the bells say: too late. This is not for tears;
> thinking.
>
> But never did Henry, as he thought he did,
> end anyone and hacks her body up
> and hide the pieces, where they may be found.
> He knows: he went over everyone, & nobody's missing.
> Often he reckons, in the dawn, them up.
> Nobody is ever missing.

What's odd is that the form of each of the dream songs *has* its regularity—one can find rhymes or slant rhymes, there is stanzaic pattern; but the syntax is handled in a way that is not the generally received one. The result is a sensation of a mind at war with itself, wanting to yield to slippage of order, yet yearning for the solidity that a regularity of rhyme and stanza pattern might represent. This will turn out to be characteristic of all the poets—at one point or another—who will be labeled Confessional in the 1960s: Sylvia Plath, Robert Lowell, Anne Sexton—their poems, formally, suggestive of a structural warpedness, reflective, I believe, of content that is as drawn to as it is on guard against its own crisis.

[from] **For Love**

> *for Bobbie*

Yesterday I wanted to
speak of it, that sense above
the others to me
important because all

that I know derives
from what it teaches me.
Today, what is it that
is finally so helpless,

different, despairs of its own
statement, wants to
turn away, endlessly
to turn away.

If the moon did not . . .
no, if you did not
I wouldn't either, but
what would I not

do, what prevention, what
thing so quickly stopped.
That is love yesterday
or tomorrow, not

now. Can I eat
what you give me. I
have not earned it. Must
I think of everything

as earned. Now love also
becomes a reward so

remote from me I have
only made it with my mind.

Here is tedium,
despair, a painful
sense of isolation and
whimsical if pompous

self-regard. But that image
is only of the mind's
vague structure, vague to me
because it is my own.

(1–36)

— ROBERT CREELEY

❧

The cases of the precursors to the Black Arts Movement, and of the Beat
poets, and of the soon-to-be-dubbed Confessional poets all seem to confirm as truth the dicta of one of the most significant literary schools of
the 1950s—the Black Mountain School, which included, among others,
Charles Olson, Robert Creeley, and Denise Levertov. The latter two are
among the most vocal on the relationship between form and content, and
on the need for that relationship, as traditionally defined, to be revised.

Creeley: "Form is an extension of content."

Levertov: "Form is the *revelation* of content."

❧

[from] I, Maximus of Gloucester, to You

> Off-shore, by islands hidden in the blood
> jewels & miracles, I, Maximus
> a metal hot from boiling water, tell you
> what is a lance, who obeys the figures of
> the present dance

1

the thing you're after
may lie around the bend
of the nest (second, time slain, the bird! the bird!
And there! (strong) thrust, the mast! flight

> (of the bird
> o kylix, o
> Antony of Padua
> sweep low, o bless

the roofs, the old ones, the gentle steep ones
on whose ridge-poles the gulls sit, from which they depart,

> And the flake-racks

of my city!

2

love is form, and cannot be without
important substance (the weight
say, 58 carats each one of us, perforce
our goldsmith's scale

> feather to feather added
> (and what is mineral, what
> is curling hair, the string
> you carry in your nervous beak, these
>
> make bulk, these, in the end, are
> the sum
>
> (o my lady of good voyage
> in whose arm, whose left arm rests

no boy but a carefully carved wood, a painted face, a schooner!
a delicate mast, as bow-sprit for

forwarding

(1–32)

⌐CHARLES OLSON

⌐◦

In 1950, Charles Olson published his essay *Projective Verse,* which is verse
composed by field; more specifically, from the entry in the *Princeton
Encyclopedia of Poetry and Poetics,* it is a process of composing verse "in open
forms resulting from the poet's taking the stance of an object among other
objects, rather than imposing himself upon content or materials." Hence,
all form is open, in that it is subject to shifts according to shifts in the field
(of observation, of psychology, of *angle* of observation, of response on the
part of mind *and* body). In particular, Olson attaches form to the breath's
natural pace according to exertion and to shifts in emotional register. His
poems often look strophic, without the regularity of strophe (as we would
expect in the choruses of Greek tragedy)—as if to suggest rhythm, but the
rhythm of breathing, whose overall regularity is punctuated with moments
of wild irregularity, even as consciousness itself is.

⌐◦

Music

    If I rest for a moment near The Equestrian
pausing for a liver sausage sandwich in the Mayflower Shoppe,
that angel seems to be leading the horse into Bergdorf's
and I am naked as a table cloth, my nerves humming.
Close to the fear of war and the stars which have disappeared.
I have in my hands only 35c, it's so meaningless to eat!
and gusts of water spray over the basins of leaves
like the hammers of a glass pianoforte. If I seem to you
to have lavender lips under the leaves of the world,

I must tighten my belt.
It's like a locomotive on the march, the season
        of distress and clarity
and my door is open to the evenings of midwinter's
lightly falling snow over the newspapers.
Clasp me in your handkerchief like a tear, trumpet
of early afternoon! in the foggy autumn.
As they're putting up the Christmas trees on Park Avenue
I shall see my daydreams walking by with dogs in blankets,
put to some use before all those coloured lights come on!
        But no more fountains and no more rain,
        and the stores stay open terribly late.

— FRANK O'HARA

O'Hara's poems are examples of form generated by a content that is sheer character, charisma; the poems in general are peripatetic, in terms of context, and quotidian in terms of subject, or at least initially so—the speaker is always clearly the poet himself, letting us watch him walk and think through a city while doing the most ordinary things. In short, the content is grounded in the person of the poet, for which reason, presumably, O'Hara referred to his own poetics as Personism. O'Hara's poems, in terms of form, often recall the form of Ginsberg (I am thinking especially of lineation), but the form seems generated out of less overtly sociopolitical concerns; rather, O'Hara's content is so much of the individual, so unabashedly documentary of the self in its seeming ordinariness, that—necessarily, O'Hara would say—the formal needs of a poem will have to emerge from the character of the person whom it is the poem's "business" to describe (by speaking for). The surprise—and consequent staying power of the poems—is in their ability so often to transcend any particularity of speaker, suggesting that if we examine ourselves long enough, we will stumble upon all of the truths of what it is to be human, ordinary and extraordinary at once.

What the movements in American poetry of the 1950s tell us is that there are alternative methods for attaining and conveying the truth—and that, just as the truth is fluid and various according to each individual, so must be the forms by which any truth gets articulated. We needn't be bound to tradition, though we ought not dismiss it entirely either. In the process of opening form up, Levertov points out that certain tools become all the more crucial—line break, for instance, and control of rhythm, given a renunciation of all the standard controls. This holds true even for Concrete poetry—a term which came into the language in 1958—a form of poetry that relinquishes even the standard arrangement of words and/or the connotations of words; words—letters, even—find themselves arranged across an object that could be anything from a page of paper to a stone to the side of a collapsed barn; and, given that the word may be in isolation, or may be a non-word, a free arrangement of letters, the words themselves become ideograms whose meaning is entirely itself, free of connotation. Even this form of poetry, though—or so I believe—must arrive at a trackable pattern eventually, in the course of the particular artist's work; otherwise, an openness of form becomes merely a means of justifying rampant and self-indulgent incoherence.

That is, to open form is not entirely to relinquish control—but what control is at work is to come from the individual, rather than from an authority that has managed to establish itself as the *sole* authority. In the turning away from conventions of form, content, and the relationship between the two, we end up having to reach *some* sort of system that itself becomes analagous to tradition, only on a more individual basis. Another way to put this is that each artist ends up having a distinctive symbology or iconography, and a distinctive vision—which means that the work may not be immediately recognizable as art, because it isn't art as understood; that is, it has drawn away from the "norm," even as it reflects what an individual has drawn *personally* away from a *communally* experienced scene or event. Etymologically, abstraction means "a drawing away from." In poetry, this drawing away resulted in the free verse that Frost referred to as playing tennis without a net.

But what if we change the definition of "net?"

What about the particular joys—and challenges—of playing netless?

On George Oppen's "Psalm"

Veritas sequitur . . .

In the small beauty of the forest
The wild deer bedding down—
That they are there!

          Their eyes
Effortless, the soft lips
Nuzzle and the alien small teeth
Tear at the grass

          The roots of it
Dangle from their mouths
Scattering earth in the strange woods.
They who are there.

          Their paths
Nibbled thru the fields, the leaves that shade them
Hang in the distances
Of sun

          The small nouns
Crying faith
In this in which the wild deer
Startle, and stare out.

A psalm? How so? When I first discovered it, I held George Oppen's poem "Psalm" suspect as one of those poems about very little at all—one whose title, implying substance, in fact hopes to "cover" the poem's absence of it. The modes of psalm being two—praise and lament—I was willing to take the poem, at best, as simply an act of witnessing some deer, witness as a form of recognition, recognition as a form of deeming a thing worth recognizing: perhaps a stretch, but a kind of praise, anyway, for one of God's creatures—given the cues of the title and epigraph, that we should read this poem through the lens of theology. As for lament—well, I found none.

But, the epigraph's reference to Aquinas notwithstanding, it was via Gerard Manley Hopkins that I came to read the poem differently, and to appreciate more fully the relationship between syntax and narrative. Hopkins discusses (in "The Principle or Foundation") the praising of God, and the different options for praise available to humans as opposed to the rest of creation. A key difference is that the latter

> glorify God, *but they do not know it.* The birds sing to him,
> the thunder speaks of his terror . . . the honey [is] like his
> sweetness . . . they give him glory, but they do not know
> they do . . . they never can . . . But man can know God, *can*
> *mean to give him glory.* This then was why he was made, to
> give God glory and to mean to give it . . .
>
> (italics his)

By this reasoning, then, it is enough for the deer, "That they are there," their praise is manifest in their deer-ness itself, be it in the form of tearing at the grass or "merely" startling, and staring out. But in the shift in phrasing that occurs from "That they are there!" (3) to "They who are there." (13)—from the ecstasy of exclamation, whose punctuation makes the fragment seem somehow complete and/or expected, to the stranded relative clause whose punctuation, in suggesting the end of a finished sentence, throws the fragmentedness into greater relief—in this shift, a stall seems at work, at the level of syntax, a moment of reassessing more soberly what had earlier been surprised outburst; and I believe that this is where Oppen faces squarely the notion that humans have a greater responsibility when it comes to praise. Humans have the ability to *articulate* praise, via language, and therefore a duty to do so.

Syntax is the chief tool that language has for conveying meaning. And it is at the level of syntax that Oppen puts forward his concerns about praise, our obligation to give praise, and the limits to our ability to do so. Throughout the poem, there are what I'll call dislocations in the syntax, places where the syntax—as if inevitably—gets derailed. Technically, for example, the subordinate clause "Their eyes / Effortless" (4–5) must modify "the soft lips" (5), but that makes no sense. "They who are there" (11) takes us back to the deer only because the phrase so closely resembles line 3, which described the deer; but by conventional syntax, the phrase must refer back to the "strange woods" of line 10. Again, sense is strained. Another dangling modifier occurs at stanza 4, whose "Their paths / Nibbled thru the fields" seems to modify "the leaves that shade them." When we get to "the small nouns" of the final stanza, they seem to refer to the deer again, until we realize that the deer won't appear for another couple of lines; are the small nouns, then, the "distances / Of sun," or the leaves, or the fields, or the paths through them?

The syntax both embodies and enacts a constant feinting, a casting outward—only to fall short, each time, of "complete" meaning. The tension between the attempt to mean and the routine failure to *entirely* mean becomes emblematic of a parallel tension: between the duty we have to try to praise God to the best of our capacities, and the limitations to those capacities, finally, insofar as we are human—small nouns—and therefore necessarily flawed.

In its immediate content, Oppen's poem is an act of praise in the form of granting witness. At the level of syntax, the poem articulates the gesture itself of praise, of attempting to give it; and it articulates the inadequacy inherent to that attempt and subtly laments that inadequacy. Praise and lament. And a persuasive example of how syntax can generate and sustain the psychological narrative of a poem. And Oppen's "Psalm"? A psalm, indeed.

Twist, Tact, and Metaphysics:
Gwendolyn Brooks's
"A light and diplomatic bird"

A light and diplomatic bird
Is lenient in my window tree.
A quick dilemma of the leaves
Discloses twist and tact to me.

Who strangles his extremest need
For pity of my imminence
On utmost ache and lacquered cold
Is prosperous in proper sense:

He can abash his barmecides;
The fantoccini of his range
Pass over. Vast and secular
And apt and admirably strange.

Augmented by incorrigible
Conviction of his symmetry,
He can afford his sine die.
He can afford to pity me

Whose hours at best are wheats or beiges
Lashed with riot-red and black.
Tabasco at the lapping wave.
Search-light in the secret crack.

Oh open, apostolic height!
And tell my humbug how to start
Bird balance, bleach: make miniature
Valhalla of my heart.

Perhaps a conviction that one is oppressed—or indeed, a very real oppression—is not necessary for original art to be produced. There are many examples, however, of how the artist's desire to speak against the powers that be and at the same time not invite a silencing retribution from those powers has meant devising a means of bringing into a workable balance honesty, ambition, and pragmatism—and, in the case of the best poets, this has usually pushed the writing toward an originality in terms of how language will be used. After all, language cannot in such instances be used in conventional ways, in part because to participate *conventionally* in existing conventions (as opposed, say, to the appropriating and refining of English forms by Claude McKay and Countee Cullen) would amount to a condoning of those conventions; and in part, a use of language in conventional ways risks making the message too patently clear to those against whom the message is directed. The trick is to make the message accessible to those *to whom* the work is directed, so as to make possible a dialogue concerning those whom the work is *about* and/or *against*. The first-century AD historian Tacitus managed to speak candidly about Roman tyranny, hypocrisy, and moral decline while living under tyranny and censorship (a censorship often effected by killing the author) through a drastically fragmented and compressed syntax and a vigilantly skewed irony of psychological eye. Much of Emily Dickinson's force lies in a combination of her famously slanted vision, and her subtle manipulations of the hymn form's conventions of rhyme and meter, all of this cast in a syntax that generates meaning on more than an immediate level—this, her strategy for speaking out against the dominant structures of religion, and as a woman at that, whose voice ought more rightly (so would society then have dictated) remain silent. A third example is the African American tradition known as "signifying," in which a combination of rhyme, meter, and carefully coded imagery allowed the singer to speak openly either against the powers that be, or to speak about subjects deemed inappropriate by those powers—sexual bawdiness, for example. It seems no accident that this tradition first comes into prominence during the early slavery period in this country, appearing in field songs, blues lyrics, genres where African Americans could speak candidly about their condition and about those responsible for it. Finally—though hardly the end of the list one could produce—Hopkins's inability to comfortably reconcile faith and physical desire, his need to question faith sometimes and sometimes desire (each a pressure quite different from slavery or censorship, but each a very real pressure indeed) is surely behind the syntax that can make his poems on first listen seem written in another language than English altogether.

The poetry of Gwendolyn Brooks is rarely without its complexities, even those poems that are cast in the voice of a child, or those that can sound childlike because of their simplicity of rhyme and meter and their apparent wordplay for wordplay's sake alone; in almost all instances, though, the seeming simplicity is itself a form of masking, is an artistic strategy. "A light and diplomatic bird," however—which appears in the long section "The Womanhood" in *Annie Allen*—has always stood out for me because of its lack of simplicity, seeming or otherwise; rather, it presents particular difficulties initially that have everything to do with the artist's concern as to how best to convey a message that certain elements in society would rather not see conveyed. Those elements vary, according to the capacity in which we can determine Brooks to be speaking: as an African American in pre–Civil Rights America? as a woman in pre-feminist, male-dominated America? For much of *Annie Allen*, both are possible and likely. The book, overall, depicts the passage from girlhood to womanhood, treating that passage as a version of epic (hence, the central section, "The Anniad," a not-so-subtle argument, via punning, that Annie's is no less of an epic journey than was that of Aeneas, as told in Virgil's *Aeneid*). The book also contains poems that focus on the particular "condition" of being not just a woman but a black one, as well as what it means to be black, regardless of gender. But the poem under discussion offers no evidence to *restrict* its applicability to race and/or gender, any more than Dickinson's are especially about or from a speaker who is white, a woman, and from Amherst. As with Dickinson's work, this particular poem by Brooks suggests a speaker who is human first of all, and who questions the ways of God toward humankind. Brooks does not compromise her blackness or her gender in *Annie Allen;* rather, by including such poems as "A light and diplomatic bird"—poems that are more widely existential in their focus—Brooks reminds us that race and gender are but particulars within the general dilemma of what it is to be human, mortal, flawed.

Dilemma is very much the point from this poem's start, in which the speaker is counseled by the natural world (nature being the place, according to the Transcendentalists, wherein to read God's necessary lessons). The bird is exemplary, in being "diplomatic," even its physical gesture (of leaning) cloaked by or subordinate to the psychological/emotional gesture of leniency ("lenient"); the "dilemma of the leaves" resolves quickly into the seeming answers to the dilemma, namely, "twist and tact," the former of which I read as a form of accommodating and incorporating change (as opposed to remaining rigid, unbending—to be unable to twist is as bad as to be unable to be made straight, which is of course the meaning of stanza three's "incorrigible" at its Latin root). The problem is that tact and diplomacy are being advised by those who cannot know what it is to be in a situation in which tact and diplomacy are irrelevant and useless (or in which they no longer counter but have been overridden by a growing impatience with suffering). With the introduction of the "Who" in stanza two, we are no longer speaking of a bird or of the leaves but of an unnamed "he" as the subject of critical scrutiny. Whoever "he" is, stanza four makes it clear that he is one whose power is superior to that of the speaker, hence the emphasis on his ability to afford pity. His position doesn't require tact and leniency. His is the conviction that is permitted to be "incorrigible," not the speaker's.

Many elements convince me that the subject here is not so much a man, or a white one in particular, but God. Stanza two is possibly the one whose meaning is the most difficult to parse, but lines 5–7, in their suggestion that somebody has sacrificed what he needed most, out of pity for somebody else's possible plight—

Who strangles his extremest need
For pity of my imminence
On utmost ache and lacquered cold

—recall the dual idea of God sacrificing his son for the sake of humankind, and of that son (Christ), first through the Incarnation and finally through the Passion, allowing himself to suffer and die for human sin and as a means of generating the grace by which that sin might be absolved. As humans, we should presumably be grateful. But Brooks's potentially blasphemous argument is that gratitude is less the point than is just desert. After all, can't God afford a little pity, given that everything is his to control anyway? His luxuries are the real thing, in contrast with illusory ones or those that offer illusory ones (barmecides); his subjects are puppets (here, it is notable that Brooks uses, for "puppets," "fantoccini," a word that emphasizes the inability of the puppet to speak—the word is related to *infans*, the Latin for *that which cannot speak* or is *without power*). His plan, divine or otherwise, is rigid, symmetrical, and unbounded by time ("sine die"), a secret that can only be partly penetrated by the "search-light" of human inquiry. So vain is this inquiry that the speaker is forced from the scientific type of investigation (mechanical light into natural, primeval darkness) to the hope of prayer—hence, the vatic opening to the final stanza, as heaven itself seems to be addressed ("Oh open, apostolic height!"). And, as is commonly the case with prayer, no immediate and apparent answers are forthcoming; the poem ends with the triplet of imperatives ("open," "tell," "make") to which the poem leaves no room for response—or, more likely, cannot find any adequate response.

Job's complaint to and about God was hardly subtle—then again, neither were his sufferings, plague and the death of his family among them. Brooks opts, as an artist, for strategies that are perhaps less direct but no less forceful, and an examination of the strategies that she employs makes clear that—consciously, or not—she is aware of the lessons of Dickinson, Hopkins, the Roman rhetoricians, and the African American literary tradition. Stanza one of her poem, as we have seen, shows the speaker being presented with advice as to how to conduct herself. It would also seem to be the artist's prelude to her poem, a prelude in which she states (or the bird and leaves reveal to her—the bird and leaves in this case familiars, or forms of conscience) her awareness that her argument is one that will itself require a certain tact, an ability to twist her argument in such a way as to be traceable by the reader, and uncompromising both in its meaning and in its honesty. But how to speak honestly in open view of a power whose force is as potentially destructive as it is reliably unpredictable? An examination of the various strategies employed reveals Brooks's poem as a kind of study of the artist working out for herself the most effective way in which to deploy her argument on the page, with this very question in mind.

Following the prelude stanza, a variety of distinct and increasingly more complex strategies is evident. Stanza two puts particular pressure on syntax; it is the most complex of the stanzas in this regard—and strikingly so, following stanza one's very direct pair of declarative sentences—in that it omits the expected pronoun that would ordinarily precede "Who," thereby leaving it in doubt, until line 8, as to whether we are in the midst of a question or a statement. As well, the sentence is interrupted—its meaning deliberately stalled—by the two prepositional phrases of line 6 ("For pity of my imminence") and 7 ("On utmost ache and lacquered cold"). Finally, the stanza ends on a note of ambiguity: "Is prosperous in proper sense." Does Brooks mean that her subject is prosperous in the proper sense of the word "prosperous"? Or does she mean that he prospers when it comes to proper sense—that is, has his fair share of good sense, and then some?

Stanza three suggests—mostly, but not unequivocally—the former: that he is prosperous, and can afford, therefore, the diplomacy (or complacency regarding the *status quo*) of stanza one. His luxuries are real, as opposed to those of the barmecides who, in the *Arabian Nights*, offer luxuries and gifts that are finally all illusion; the fantoccini, as mentioned earlier, are puppets to this superior power. These two words—"barmecides" and "fantoccini"—are part of the new strategy this stanza employs as a means of cloaking meaning, namely, a vocabulary that, given the rarity of both these words in English, is surely deliberate in its obscurity. As well, assonance is heavily employed here, the short *a* appearing no fewer than nine times in eight lines, most forcefully in line 12 ("And apt and admirably strange"). Assonance is not especially a strategy for cloaking meaning, though I would argue that one way to distract attention from the negative force of a line's meaning is to heighten the line's melody (a lightness of music vs. a gravity of meaning), or to pitch the sound somewhere between lullaby and drone (a sameness or repetition of sound distracting us from the details of meaning). Finally, the ambiguity that we saw in line 8 of stanza two is also present in stanza three. In the phrase "The fantoccini of his range / Pass over," does Brooks intend the fantoccini as the subject of her sentence? Or is the sentence inflected, so that the verb phrase "pass over" is to be understood as dependent on the main verb "can," whose subject is the "he" of the previous line, in which case the fuller meaning would be: he [can] pass over the fantoccini of his range—which?

Again, the ambiguity is not resolved. Instead, by stanza four—having used syntax, high diction, and assonance—Brooks turns to a heavily Latinate vocabulary. Latinate words have occurred earlier in the poem (five times in the first stanza, four in the second, six in the third), but stanza four is the one which has its first two lines bracketed with what I want to call strongly Latinate words—"Augmented," "incorrigible," "Conviction," and, from Latin via the Greek, "symmetry" (13–14)—words which we tend more readily to associate with the technical, scientific, or highly rhetorical, than we would "apt," for example, or "lenient." Stanza four is also the one in which we have *actual* Latin—sine die (literally, "without day")—a phrase that is immediately followed by the rhetorical device of anaphora:

> *He can afford* his sine die.
> *He can afford* to pity me
>
> (italics mine)

a device common to the Greco-Roman rhetorical tradition, to western European liturgical tradition, and to the African American religious tradition that continues, almost solely, to keep Greco-Roman rhetorical tradition a part of American public speaking.

As stanza four moves into stanza five, Brooks discards (we expect as much, by now) the former stanza's strategies of conveying meaning for a new and even more surprising one: a synesthesia of imagery. First, the temporal is considered in terms of the visual ("hours at best are wheats or beiges"); then the sense of taste is pitched against the sense of touch, all as a means of discussing heat and the lack of it ("Tabasco at the lapping wave"). In both instances, Brooks conveys a sense of futility, as the speaker describes her own predicament—to be able to know time only as color is hardly to know time at all. As well, Brooks here juxtaposes the state of God—one of power, genuine luxury—with that of the speaker, which at best is a kind of neutrality ("wheats or beiges") punctuated on occasion by the red of riot and by a black that is left undefined (18). Futility is further suggested when we realize, at line 19, that there is no reconciling the heat that the tongue knows with the cool of a "lapping wave"—again, one is taste, one is touch. At line 20, however, the synesthesia is broken away from, as we reach a consistently visual image: "Search-light in the secret crack." The move from unreconcilable senses to a harmony or consistency of sense would seem to indicate that the former futility might now be escaped from, that we are moving closer to resolution or solution. But the visual image of line 20 is one of searching, of investigating what is secret—and after being led by the pattern of imagery to hope that the secret (of God's ways?) will now be brought to light, the poem's final stanza opens with a line that shows we have finally come no further: why else pray for the heights to open, unless our attempts—by other, more practicable means—to enter them, to see into them, have failed already?

Which is to say that Brooks's poem has come only one step further from where it began. If the opening stanza suggested to the speaker an appropriate way to engage with the world (through tact and diplomacy and twist), the poem's conclusion asks how—how to achieve "bird-balance," how to "bleach," make colorless the very real (because present) "riot-red and black" that characterize the "wheats or beiges" of a life? How to reduce to miniature the human wants and ambitions that Brooks calls (using Norse epic tradition as her reference point) the "Valhalla of [the] heart"?

These are the questions that, for me, make "A light and diplomatic bird" a distinctly metaphysical poem. It has in common with, say, George Herbert and Henry Vaughan—and yes, Emily Dickinson—a certain trajectory of interrogation that itself springs from the need to respond to pressures not easily reconciled by those living beneath those pressures: given the *what*, nevertheless *how* and *why?* As with those other poets, Brooks would seem to understand that the truest answer is *not* to answer, except by the poem itself, less an answer than a record of the artist's continued attempt to articulate and resolve dilemma in a new fashion, given that the old ones have not served. On one level, each of the stanzas in Brooks's poem can be seen as one in a succession of attempts to approach answer, as the poem's argument unfolds; each stanza's strategy a kind of casting at a target that is finally withheld from human knowing. A second level of interpretation is that each of the stanzas' strategies is one in a series of careful attempts to put at least a veil's distance between her audience (God, I believe) and her refusal to accept unquestioningly the disparities she finds in her relationship to that audience—this relationship, it turns out, is nothing less than the human condition. In her poems—be they race-specific, gender-specific, or neither—Brooks reminds us that the best, the most lasting poets do not so much resolve the human condition; they persuasively *enact* it, singing—writing—against. Within. Toward.

Vision in Control:
Sylvia Plath's "Winter Trees"

I am not sure that many readers of Sylvia Plath—poets, scholars, or "civilians"—think of control when considering her work. This has everything to do with 1) a willful resistance to reading Plath as a writer of control, because to view the work as the product of an unfocused, troubled mind makes it easier to turn away from the difficult truths she would have us see clearly; and 2) it has become impossible *not* to consider the life when considering the work, and the easier task (because increasingly more natural in a tabloid culture that makes the so-called Confessional poets look downright demure) is to voyeuristically dwell on the already-exposed life rather than apply to the poems the critical scrutiny they deserve and—like all art that is lasting—will sustain. Much of the problem lies in the ambiguous position—a kind of junior membership—of women in the academy, in Plath's time and, sadly, undeniably, in ours. We can see this, for example, in the reaction to Ted Hughes's *The Birthday Letters,* which only purports to be another version of the Plath-Hughes story, but which was quickly brandished by reviewers (male, mostly) as the *correct* version of the story, confirming an image (that at last had begun to erode somewhat) of Plath as a hysteric, a reactionary, a man-hater who too greedily craved the successes reserved for men.

The work that is lasting (in any poet) is that which not only survives the writer but survives the cultural memory of the writer's life—it is significant, the time required for literature to reach a distance that renders the writer of the literature more historical, and less referential to our own era. Aeschylus, Dante, Shakespeare have attained this; Dickinson and Whitman have not—no American writer has, the literary culture is still too new. If we have yet to be able to read Dickinson without (somewhere in our minds) remembering white dresses, recipes for bread, refusals to descend the stairs for a gentleman caller, then we are not likely to be able to avoid, in Plath, the memory of a disturbed psychology, a disturbed life (from childhood, to—and through—marriage) that ended in suicide. This need not prevent us, though, from reading the work fairly—which means assuming that it exhibits control, and giving it the opportunity to prove this. It is my sense that in any artist, including those who are suicidal, it is never the *artist* who wishes to die. If anything, art becomes one of the few safe spaces for the artist, and will often prove to exhibit a control that is nowhere apparent or findable in the life. Another word for this control is vision, and it is evident in all genuinely great writing. Plath is no exception.

Vision is not *merely* in control, however. We see this in many of the poems of *The Colossus*, where an overly exacting attention to meter and rhyme often either hamstrings the poems or makes them reminiscent of school figures in skating or of musical scales, the point of which is less artistry than dexterity. Consider, for example, "Man in Black." Not a bad poem, but a poem whose success, for me, rests primarily on its ability to "pull off" the feat of being a single, coherent sentence stretched across seven stanzas, all of which are cast in pure syllabics and in *terza rima*. (If "Mushrooms" is an exception, this is largely due to its subject matter, which concerns the building urgency of controlling what, unchecked, threatens to overwhelm; shackles, rhetorically speaking, are in this instance very much called for.) It is the common predicament: how to write formally without seeming to, and yet seeming to enough, so that one's mastery of craft is evident to the reader/listener?

Plath never lost interest in formal issues, even in her freest work. What appears to happen in the later poems is a relaxation of formal control. In fact, though, this isn't relaxation so much as it is the confidence of a writer for whom formal issues have at last become reflex; and with this fluency comes the ability to work more sophisticatedly—which is to say, with greater subtlety (this need not—and does not—compromise the content of the poem, which is rarely subtle). The other area of control is that of imagery. This isn't always in evidence; too often, there is too much that seems gratuitous, self-indulgent: "Cut" comes to mind, as does "Fever 103." To understand the difference, we have only to compare these with a poem like "Morning Song," in which a smaller set of images is adhered to, each image being given the space—one tercet each, precisely—in which to develop fully; or like "You're," whose context of mingled play and celebration actually requires an overdensity of images, reflecting the giddy indecisiveness of a speaker who would name her never-quite-nameable joy. When this figurative control works in tandem with formal control in Plath, the poems are indeed wondrous. "Winter Trees" is only one of many available examples:

> The wet dawn inks are doing their blue dissolve.
> On their blotter of fog the trees
> Seem a botanical drawing—
> Memories growing, ring on ring,
> A series of weddings.
>
> Knowing neither abortions nor bitchery,
> Truer than women,
> They seed so effortlessly!
> Tasting the winds, that are footless,
> Waist-deep in history—
>
> Full of wings, otherworldliness.
> In this, they are Ledas.
> O mother of leaves and sweetness
> Who are these pietàs?
> The shadows of ringdoves chanting, but easing nothing.

Suggestive of a kind of daydreaming or randomness of thought—perhaps that of a waking speaker?—the poem proceeds associatively but never loosely or unfollowably: having started at the reasonable equation of the dawn's darkness and damp with the damp and dark of ink, it quite naturally follows that fog be the equivalent of the blotter on which, in ink, some hand has drawn a stand of trees—and a drawing of trees is indeed a botanical drawing, of sorts. Here, the dash cues us; it's here that Plath then thinks of a *particular* sort of botanical drawing, the sort that shows the tree cross-sectionally—making visible, inside the trunk, the concentric rings by which the tree's age can be determined. The first rhyme of the poem begins at this point, and is maintained for three consecutive lines ("drawing," "ring," "weddings"—and, internally, "growing"), on purpose; for this is the point at which the speaker moves from seeming randomness of subject toward a focus on what will become the one subject. The rings of trees speak to the trees' age, age implies memories—no, that's not quite it; the concentricity of the rings, "ring on ring"—a ring on a finger, which equals a wedding—"ring on ring," a *series* of weddings (even as the rhyme makes these three lines of the stanza a series, separate from the rest of the stanza). The stanza seems to *find its way* into structure, toward a rhyme that is then lingered on, as the poem and speaker of it find their way toward their subject, linger as the focus is narrowed and, having found the subject—no less, it turns out, than the place of women as they have been viewed throughout civilization—they are launched into the next stanza.

Not coincidentally, as stanza two brings the subject into greater clarity, there is an increase of regularity in terms of rhyme: the somewhat stuttering, halting rhyme of stanza one (*a-b-c-c-c*) shifts to what the first three lines of stanza two lead us to think will be *a-b-a-b*, with various possibilities for the final line. Instead, we get *a-b-a*, then two lines that do and don't rhyme as we might expect. "Footless" doesn't rhyme with "women," but it isn't quite the rhyme of "effortlessly," either—which, however, *contains*, but finally withholds the rhyme for "footless." And while "history" is a rhyme for "bitchery," it also bears the same half-relationship to "effortlessly" that "footless" does. Rhyme, then, is in effect here, but it is unstable or, at best, fluid. As with stanza one, this is deliberate, an example of Plath's ability to control the poem, carefully calibrating the relationship between form and content. For it is in this stanza that, in turning to the subject of women, she would like to destabilize what would seem to be the unacceptably fixed roles of women, to be exposed in the next stanza.

What triggers this desire for destabilization is the contrasting freedom of the trees, making them "truer than women"—in the arboreal world, Plath suggests, fertility is effortless, the transient (those footless winds) can be tasted without being binding (the sensual has no punishable or otherwise limiting consequences). Granted, there is some compromising of freedom: the trees are grounded at the waist. Here, a dash; and here, the imagery becomes more complicated, but never uncontrolled. One way to read "waist-deep in history" is that history begins, for the trees and, by extension, for women in our culture, at the waist and below—at the sexual. This reading seems justified by the image we encounter upon entering the poem's final stanza: the image of Leda, whose place in mythology is guaranteed by the facts of her rape and of her being, as a result, the mother of another problematic archetypal woman, Helen of Troy—herself also associated with rape and, for many of the Trojans, with a certain bitchery, as the *Iliad* makes clear. If we wonder how we got to the subject of Leda, by the way, we have only to return to the line "waist-deep in history," which also implies a life from the waist up—whereupon the poet's eye is directed to the upper portion of the trees, the leaves, resembling many small wings, by which the poet is then reminded of the many small feathers to the wings of a swan—the guise in which Zeus descended upon Leda.

From here, the associations proceed smoothly: Leda is a famous mother; "O mother [of God]" is a common means of invoking another culturally prominent mother, the Virgin Mary. And, like Leda, Mary too gives birth to the child of a divinity, though the circumstances, we are told, are very different; Mary is not in any way associated with rape—hence, Virgin—but with having the good fortune to have been chosen as a vessel of God; Leda's situation might more accurately be called bad luck. But in juxtaposing the two women, Plath suggests that there is reason to consider them together, that together these two archetypal women tell a truth about women more generally throughout history and civilization—that they are alternately the victims of dominant male figures or are meant to show gratitude for the patronage of such figures; and that the ability to give birth is a dubious gift—it is in the giving of birth, after all, that Mary guarantees her transformation into the suffering, grieving pietà, suggested in Plath's question at line 14: "Who are these pietàs?" She means, I think, the trees; but she also means Mary, and perhaps Leda also; perhaps all women, ultimately.

The last line of the stanza seems, at first, to be the intended answer to the question—but it is in fact only a return to the context within which the poem has ostensibly taken place. If it seems a bit jarring, this is deliberate. It's the line in which the speaker, in a sense, jerks herself back into reality—as if, after dilating from an ordinary dawn into a meditation on women, she were reminding herself: "only dawn, remember, only trees." But something else is jarring about this line, and the answer again lies in the poem's form.

From the irregularity of stanza one to the increased (but deliberately flawed) regularity of stanza two, we come to the first four lines of stanza three, and encounter complete regularity—an *a-b-a-b* rhyming quatrain that also shows a syllabic regularity nowhere evident earlier in the poem: 8-6-8-6. The poem becomes most stable, most regular in terms of rhyme and meter, precisely when it is discussing two of the most culturally fixed and archetypal women in literature, in history, both. Plath's response is to reject all of it; the steady movement toward formal regularity parallels the steady narrowing of focus whose point, once understood, is unacceptable. Hence, the final line of the stanza (of the poem), which has no rhyme, which has no metrical affinity with any other line in the poem—in effect, the line shatters all the regularity that's been worked toward, even as the poet attains new vision and rejects all previously received notions of what, as a woman (and perhaps as a woman who is also a poet?), she is expected to be.

Patiently, meticulously won, this is hardly the erratic and rage-powered gesture of a woman out of control. Nor is the poem an irresponsibly random collection of images; rather, the images become the reliable map they should be. The form and its absence, meanwhile, are the means by which the poet skillfully constructs and modulates her argument. "Winter Trees" is, like all of Plath's best poems, proof that associative technique is a far different thing from what it has increasingly become confused with, namely, permission to write irresponsibly and self-indulgently in the name of late twentieth-century, early twenty-first-century chaos; and that formal elements need not be confining—nor, however, are they immune to being abused. The mark of the great poet (of whatever school) is control—again, vision. Plath continues to be misunderstood by so many of her readers, and what gets lost is what so distinguishes her finest work: a clarity of vision by which the world is re-envisioned; and an intelligence and hard courage of eye, which does not flinch.

Coin of the Realm

The last thing that most human beings seem capable of trusting naturally—instinctively—is themselves, their own judgment. It is the result, I think, of an early training away from imagination, imagination being the means by which we think of a thing unconventionally—outside the norm. Those who raise us want the best for us—they hope to protect us from exclusion. But exclusion, at some level, is required in the making of the artist—art begins in the particular privacy of exile. What is required to be an authentically original artist is an inability to think conventionally—this, coupled with a for-the-most-part unconscious unawareness that one is thinking differently in the first place. It helps to have a sense of nothing left to lose, nothing therefore in the way of our speaking honestly; what's to fear, if no one is listening anyway, or if we believe that no one is listening? Or if we believe that the listeners can't hear, ever, what it is that we hear?

Hence to the cinema, generally, and most poetry, hence to the color choices available in the new cars, a governing mediocrity that promises to do no harm by standing out, by making what was once correctly called "a statement." Not to fit in would mean being held accountable, having to argue at some level for an individuality we believe in and trust—having to believe in ourselves, that is, rather than having our worth be determined for us according to how much others are willing to invest in us. It's related, I believe, to the irresolvable bind that attaches to democracy: how on one hand individuality is desirable, but on the other hand there's a need to work in unison, and that can't happen if there isn't a large swath of agreement where the majority conduct their daily lives. But the result can be—and mostly is—a blurring of signature, until everything looks the same. An X we hide behind. *X is everything I keep meaning to cross out.*

While the performance of art and the enjoyment of art may be democratic, art itself is not. Nor is the making of it, finally. More than having its own signature, art *is* its own signature—irreplicable, strange, never seen before, not seeable again elsewhere in the future. Time and space, at best, contextualize art—they do not confine it.

—⁊⌐

I have never been one to show my work to others while I'm still in the process of making it. Partly, I don't trust them to be able to be objective, free of any notions of how they themselves would make a given poem. And partly, I don't trust myself not to be swayed by how they might think of the poem. Or to put it another way, the poem hasn't yet earned from me the trust with which, eventually, I will be able to pronounce the poem finished, and as good as it can possibly be, and impervious to change, no matter how strongly suggested. Resistance—which, finally, is a form of belief, isn't it, a belief in the self over that which threatens to engulf it?—resistance is crucial to the making of art, an essential tool and one of the most dangerous, as well, for it can lead to a resistance to the fact of flaw. It's as if the making of art occurred in a crucible, where power and vulnerability find meaningful calibration. Or they should. It's a tall order. Of course it is.

But how not to care about others' opinions? How not to want to be accepted? And how to get past the need for acceptance, and take the risk of "unlock[ing] the heart, and let[ting] it speak," to paraphrase Matthew Arnold, who goes on to say—in his poem "The Buried Life"—that

> I knew the mass of men conceal'd
> Their thoughts, for fear that if reveal'd
> They would by other men be met
> With blank indifference, or with blame reproved:
> I knew they lived and moved
> Trick'd in disguises, alien to the rest
> Of men, and alien to themselves . . .

(16–22)

How to trust ourselves, without compromising that gregariousness that is also a very real part of what it is to be human?

Trust your gut. In God we trust. Trust me.

Am I trustworthy, on moral grounds? If the ground shifts—is shiftable?

⸎

About conformity, I also understand that it is inevitable—necessary, in fact, in terms of survival of the species. We're still animals and if we don't so much live by instinct anymore as fumble forward by means of it—technology having assisted the gradual devolution of instinct by making it in so many cases expendable—then it makes sense to think of conformity as protective camouflage, a way in which to pass undetected among the crowd. When I look for the exceptions—those who are most likely to dress, style, and con-duct themselves in ways that seem to demand our attention—I find myself returning to two groups: the young in general, and artists in particular. I note, too, that these are two groups whose sense of freedom (or recklessness, perhaps) in large part comes from an indifference to the fact of mortality, or a seeming ignorance of it, or a fearlessness in the face of it. Again, a version of nothing-to-lose, or a belief in that. And—whether on the skateboarding ramp, or across the blankness of a page or canvas—risk becomes, in turn, effortless: instinctive, we might say.

Risk; resistance. Exile.

By not fitting the norm, we become, at best, noticeable, and at worst we become easily discernible targets—of suspicion, fear, ridicule, or at least the possibility of these is always present. The original is always problematic because no one knows at first quite what to do with it, how to incorporate it into the norm from which it so stands out. In a sense, what that norm provides is an archetype, a myth that most of us can enter easily. That is all that advertising is, finally, and it is at the root of the notion of genre. We know what art is by defining it and then accepting as art only what fits the definition. More disturbing, we tend less and less to define ourselves than to wait for the definition to be provided—whether by advertisers or critics—and then we shape ourselves to fit the definition.

Specific to the artist is the danger of falling victim to a myth of the self, shaped by the self. What seems to happen is that, as a result of not fitting into the world at large, the artist turns to a world whose primary coordinates are the art and the maker of it. Fair enough. But it can become increasingly difficult to distinguish the art from the life, or so I have found. How much of a given poem is a record of what actually happened? And how much of what happens next happens in response to what began as "mere" imagination, in the form of a poem? How much of who I am now is the response to a projected self I've styled on paper? If (as I once suggested in a poem) art can become eventually all we have of what was true, what if we can no longer distinguish between truth and art? Does the distinction have to matter?

⤙⤚

I think trust is mostly all that I have written about, all these books later. An inability to trust what and who I believed myself to be, in terms of sexuality, equaled a form of self-betrayal, and, eventually, the betrayal of someone who long had trusted me. And yet it was because of the trust invested in me that I had the freedom, the opportunity, to meet and fall in love with the man who's been my partner ever since. Trust leads to betrayal leads to love leads to trust. How much of what has kept us together has to do with an understanding about the murkiness of trust, and an unspoken agreement not to ask about it, or not too much?

The whole of Sophocles' play, *Philoctetes,* spins around the notion of trust. The betrayed Philoctetes, abandoned by his shipmates because of the smell of his open wound, trusts no one. He also possesses the bow and arrows without which the Greeks will never win the Trojan War. On the premise that allegiance to the state outweighs allegiance to an individual, the young Neoptolemos is assigned to win the trust of Philoctetes, and then take the bow and arrows from him—he manages both things, and all would be well if it weren't for a moral conscience that causes Neoptolemos to wince at having betrayed another's trust. When is betrayal acceptable? Necessary, even? And if betrayal must exist in the world, when is it ever safe to trust? And yet how to live without putting one's trust somewhere? In the end, the intervention of Herakles is required, the implication being that only the gods, finally, can be absolutely trusted. Or, to put it another way, the play presents us with both the problem and the uneasy-making lure of trust—as it is with duty: the irresolvability of it, the apparent lack of earthly answer.

Strangeness attracts, initially. But what keeps us there? What is it that enables us to trust a stranger (assuming, that is, that we are not children, but adults of some experience with the world and with how to negotiate its complexities)? At first, I think we look for signs with which to associate the strange with the familiar: if the man at the door is a stranger, but is wearing a mailman's uniform, we are probably right in thinking this *is* the mailman, though there are movies and real-life incidents enough to remind us that even this kind of reasoning isn't guaranteed. If the stranger wears no uniform, we might look at what he is wearing—are the clothes clean? Do they seem to fit? Are they, in fact, his? After which, we might look at the man himself, and determine the degree to which what we see in the eyes or in the gesture of hand or mouth resembles what is our notion of good intention or at least lacks what resembles our notion of harmful intent. Even then, having decided that all is well, we may be making a mistake in opening the door to this stranger—but we stand persuaded enough. And we open the door . . .

In the case of the stranger, we seek familiarity of context. In the case of original art—that particular, initial stranger—authenticity engenders trust. An authenticity to the strangeness itself is what I mean here; I need to know—or believe—that what I'm looking at or reading or hearing is not artifice, no act, but instead what I've come to call a matter of *I-can't-help-it*. Dickinson, Hopkins—they write the way they do in part because they want to, but mostly because they have to: there is no choosing, any more than there can be when it comes to sensibility. Each poet writes, necessarily, from the sensibility that is unique to him or her—or perhaps I should say that this is the case once the poet has surrendered entirely to that sensibility. When we look at very early efforts by most poets, we may see the glimmers of the poet he or she would eventually become, but we mostly see the influences that prevent the work from attaining the authenticity, the true originality that will eventually make the work both unforgettable and impossible to confuse with any other voice.

Part of how a voice declares its authenticity has to do with consistency over time. The strange voice shows no sign of changing, or at least not significantly, and we begin to suspect that we are in the presence of the genuine—this doesn't have to mean that it's art; but whatever it is, it's authentic. This consistency by which authenticity begins to be recognizable has its downside for the artist because it looks at first very much like stubbornness, especially in the environment of the classroom. It is the one way in which I believe the teacher can be useful when it comes to art: not in creating or shaping the original, but in recognizing it and then getting it to recognize itself and thereby begin learning how to find and determine its own shape. To believe that one's success as a teacher can be measured by how many of one's students bear the teacher's mark is a mistaken notion; also, a very common one. And it explains—to stay within the context of poetry—the disparity between the ever-growing number of first books being published each year and the very low number of voices that we can truly call new, strange, unheard before.

But if consistency over time can persuade us of a voice's authenticity, how to explain the experience of recognizing something authentic from the very first moment of hearing, reading, or seeing it? Here, I have to return to my earlier mention of the artist surrendering entirely to his or her own sensibility. What this amounts to, I think, is trusting the stranger in ourselves. When we see the original, it is recognizable as such because everything in the piece of art suggests a maker behind it who, for better or worse, had no doubts, or had no time for doubting, or for whom other circumstances—internal, external—had rendered doubt a luxury no longer affordable. When as artists we trust, finally, the stranger in ourselves, it isn't a matter of rightness. It is how it is, and must be. And, in trusting that stranger, we may—as in the case of any stranger—be led astray, may even have to pay with our lives for having trusted. This is where the artist is tested, and where risk, again, figures—if risk is even the right word for it. I once wrote of the fish that, in the legend of St. Guignolé, would give themselves over to the saint at his ringing of a bell—a gesture that continues both to trouble me, and fascinate:

> that immediate and last gesture
>
> of the fish leaving water
> for flesh, for guarantee
> they will die, and I cannot
>
> rest on what to call it.
> Not generosity, or
> a blindness, trust, brute
>
> stupidity. Not the soul
> distracted from its natural
> prayer, which is attention,
>
> for in the story they are
> paying attention. They
> lose themselves eyes open.

For the artist, the gesture of trusting the stranger in the self is a form of losing the more familiar and conscious self "eyes open." It is parallel to the leap of faith that genuine faith requires. Much of what is called art resembles that gesture. But authentic art *is* this gesture, and is no less sacred. If it looks like madness, so be it. Since when is the sacred not comprised, in part, of madness, if by madness is meant a taking leave of our senses, a departure from the more easily recognizable part of the self? Departure, dislocation: these are two possible translations for the Greek *ekstasis*—from which our own word, ecstasy, is derived.

There's an experience many poets have spoken of, when they believe that some ear other than their own hears what some hand other than theirs puts down on paper. In those moments, when they come, I trust that ear, that hand. Absolutely.

⟿

Human beings are gregarious by nature, and artists are not exceptions, and most artist retreats are in fact communities by whatever name: colony, conference, institute. But the pull of opinion is strong—so much so, that finally art itself can only be made in private because only in the space of privacy, where we are accountable to no one else, is it possible to invest absolute trust in ourselves as makers, and in the thing being made. And the odd sense of misgiving that we tend to have once our work has been made public has nothing to do with our doubting the wisdom of our having trusted our abilities; rather, it is at the moment of presentation that we remember what we had forgotten, that there are opinions other than our own. Call it arrogance, but it seems to me essential that the artist forget all opinions *but* his or her own in the period of creation. And afterward, what difference can opinion make? We've made what we had to, and now we're past it. When an original artist loses originality, it more often than not has to do with his or her having turned the distant abstraction of audience into something all-but-concrete and ever-hovering in the studio itself. Opinion—in the form, variously, of reviews, prizes, and acceptances (or rejections) for publication/recitals/showings—opinion will understandably have its effects on each of us; don't we want to be loved? But outside opinion must have no bearing, finally, on the art itself and on how we make it. A workshop, for instance, can be useful for providing a sense of how our work is being received by a random group of others. But even then, that tells us nothing about the essential "value," the success or failure, of the work itself; and ultimately the notion of value is always too late, irrelevant to the completed work.

Can we trust no one, then, but ourselves, and even then are we still at risk of having trusted wrongly? I think it's a matter, again, of calibration. To trust the opinion of a particular teacher or other respondent to the work doesn't mean we have to alter the work (or not) in accordance with the response; instead, that kind of opinion can be useful in providing us with a means of thinking more consciously—in a sense, more objectively—about the work that arose initially from instinct and intuition; and it's this ability to be objective that allows us to revise our own work—which is the craft part, the part that is learnable. The rest is vision.

Maybe, when it comes to art—the making of our own, as much as the recognition and appreciation of the art of others—trust, instinct, and a good dose of ambivalence (with regard to ourselves, others, and others' opinions about ourselves) all figure, or probably should. On one hand, we need to test for authenticity in art, as we do in friendship, to which art has its parallels. Hence, in his treatise on friendship, Cicero says that we should withhold some of our affection until we've tested the character of our friends—even as (he goes on to say) we would try out the horses before we hitched them to a chariot and let go of the reins. But what about those scenarios spoken of earlier, when we find ourselves trusting a voice instantly, utterly, or when we surrender without question to the stranger inside ourselves? That is where risk figures, and is necessary for the artist. Risk wasn't Cicero's subject, it was Caesar's, and—in the context less of art, perhaps, than of the very particular art of politics—the difference shows.

⇀ᴧᴄ

The original is strange, at first. But in the course of being tested for authenticity over time, passing those tests, and winning eventually our trust, the original becomes familiar to us. The good part of this is that we turn with confidence to those voices or visions whose strangeness first attracted us *because* of an originality that, itself, doesn't change significantly, though the way in which it deploys itself will and should change over time. The voice of Henry James is unmistakable; but early James is not late James, any more than the body at thirty is the body at fifty—we still know ourselves in the mirror. We turn to a particular artist for a sensibility we believe we can count on, as we can count on a certain level of satisfaction with what that sensibility will produce. And, if we truly trust that sensibility, we will trust it through its own necessary evolution. This evolution is another mark of the authentic artist, it seems to me—the result of, in part, an impatience with stasis, and in part a desire always to be taking new risks, for the sake both of the art and of the pleasure in risk itself. It is rather—back to friendship, again—like the comfort of being able to turn to a longtime friend, on whose charms and flaws we have come to rely; we want that reliability, and yet we wouldn't want the conversation to remain unchanged over thirty years. We wouldn't want to stop learning—which is to say, there should remain room for strangeness, between friends, as between lovers, as between the artist and the inner stranger with whom the artist is constantly negotiating and renegotiating that relationship of which the only evidence, finally, is the art itself.

Although the development of intellect and of imagination isn't a requirement for being human, it certainly can make for a more interesting human being, a person of meaningfully resonant character and spirit. And this development comes, I think, as much from outside stimulation as from an openness to—and even an enthusiasm *for*—such stimulation, in the form of travel to new places, or meeting new people, or exploring a new interest, or facing an old fear. But if not required for being human, this kind of development is crucial for an artist, if he or she is to avoid becoming first static, then stagnant. The familiar has its necessary pleasures; nevertheless, *"[n]ovitates . . . non sunt illae quidem repudiandae"*—Cicero, again: new things are not to be rejected. He is speaking of the adding of new friendships to those that exist already. And I think he means, too, that within an existing friendship there must be room always for further deepening. The implication is that intimacy is finally Protean in its nature, or it should be, if intimacy is to avoid becoming "only another form of separation," as Howard Moss so cleanly, so correctly puts it. If I seem, once more, to be speaking of art, well, intimacy is also an art, is it not? And of course, danger is always possible, where pushing past what is known is concerned. But the artist doesn't play safe; and the artist, in the face of risk, prefers *Yes* to *No*—

> language should be—and
> is—flexible,
> it recalls, in
>
> this way, morality,
> how there's nothing, it
> seems, not to be given
>
> in to.

I still believe that, yes, even knowing the dangers such a belief can lead to. As I understand it, I don't get to choose.

Coin of the Realm

Wrecked tiaras; plundered tombs ago—Beauty

was form, and form was discipline when, at last,
it forgets itself. Glamour and scandal weren't yet
the same. Devotion was what it mostly still is:

a force. A willed exception. Some wore armor—
and to those who wore it others knelt, making of
the body and its gestures a complicated,

though very efficient braid of courtesy and
debasement—against all of which, no voice
from either party is said to have cried out, ever:

in fact, they worked together, so well, it made
labor seem a music, almost, in the way
the fluttering of a tattered flag—the sound

of that—and that of a whole one also fluttering
make a kind of music, though a music born
of accident, which they had long since stopped

trying to distinguish from fixed circumstance,
which is to say fate—their version of it—
which they did believe in. They believed in the gods,

and it is true the gods lived, for a time,
among them. Less credible: that the gods,
when they retreated, did so because convinced

no one prayed anymore, or not enough.
Or not to them. They simply left. In the wake
of which, the citizens continued turning wilderness

into settlement. Inscribing, as had been the custom,
each new building with that motto in which,
if anywhere, they seem clearly to have intended

to announce a sensibility they either thought
most defined them, or they hoped it would seem to:
Trust Me, As I Trust You—Meaning what, though?

That they were naïve? unexacting? shrewd?
Each possibility is a real one,
as the difference it makes is real, when it comes

to determining not what manner of end they came to—
that part is legend—but to what degree, having found
you must, you must call it something, you will call it

inevitable. Deserved, even. Maybe worth what it cost.

Acknowledgments

Thanks to the editors of the following journals and anthologies, in which the essays herein first appeared:

"Anomaly, Conundrum, *Thy-Will-Be-Done:* On the Poetry of George Herbert" in *Green Thoughts, Green Shades: Essays by Contemporary Poets on the Early Modern Lyric,* Jonathan Post (ed.), University of California Press, 2002

"*Another and Another Before That:* Some Thoughts on Reading" in *Planet on the Table: Poets on the Reading Life,* Sharon Bryan and William Olsen (eds.), Sarabande Books, 2003

"The Case for Beauty" in *Crossroads: Journal of the Poetry Society of America,* Spring 2001

"Coin of the Realm" in *New England Review,* Spring 2004; the poem "Coin of the Realm" first appeared separately in *Pleiades,* Winter 2004.

"Myth and Fable: Their Place in Poetry" as part of the Online Classroom of The Academy of American Poets

"On George Oppen's 'Psalm'" in *Dark Horses,* Joy Katz and Kevin Prufer (eds.), University of Illinois Press, 2004

"Poetry, Consciousness, Gift: The Model of T. S. Eliot" was first delivered as the 2000 T. S. Eliot Memorial Lecture for the T. S. Eliot Society, and later published in that society's annual newsletter.

"Sea Level" in *Boys Like Us: Gay Writers Tell Their Coming Out Stories,* Patrick Merla (ed.), Avon Books, 1996

"Twist, Tact, and Metaphysics: Gwendolyn Brooks's 'A light and diplomatic bird'" as part of a symposium on Gwendolyn Brooks, *Field,* Fall 1999

"Vision in Control: Sylvia Plath's 'Winter Trees'" as part of a symposium on Sylvia Plath, *Field,* Fall 1998

The following essays were first delivered, in different versions, at the following venues:

"Abstraction on Parnassus: American Poetry of the 1950s," as part of a symposium entitled "The Aesthetics of Abstraction: Beyond the Canvas," at Washington University's Gallery of Art, January 1999

"Association in Poetry," as a talk on craft at the Napa Valley Summer Writers Conference, July 1998

"The Book as Bridge?" as part of "Making a Place for Literature: A Conference on Literary Publishing and Communities of Print," University of Michigan, March 2002

"Boon and Burden: Identity in Contemporary American Poetry," as a craft talk at the Warren Wilson MFA Program for Writers, January 1997

"A Brief Stop of the Trail of the Prose Poem," as a craft talk at the Warren Wilson MFA Program for Writers, January 1998

Poems and prose from "Anomaly, Conundrum, *Thy-Will-Be-Done:* On the Poetry of George Herbert" are cited from *George Herbert and Henry Vaughan,* Louis L. Martz (editor), Oxford University Press, Oxford, 1986.

The interview with Nick Flynn appeared in the Summer 2001 issue of *BOMB* magazine.

The poem "Anthem" (in "No Rapture: The Psalms and Restiveness") also appears in my book *The Rest of Love,* Farrar, Straus & Giroux, 2004.

CARL PHILLIPS is the author of seven books of poetry, most recently *The Rest of Love* and *Rock Harbor*, and has translated Sophocles' *Philoctetes* for Oxford's The Greek Tragedies in New Translation Series. He has received numerous awards, including the Kingsley Tufts Award, an Award in Literature from the American Academy of Arts and Letters, the Lambda Literary Award, and fellowships from the Guggenheim Foundation and the Library of Congress. He teaches at Washington University in Saint Louis.

The text of *Coin of the Realm* has been set in Adobe Garamond, a typeface drawn by Robert Slimbach and based on the type cut by Claude Garamond in the sixteenth century. Book design by Wendy Holdman. Typesetting by Stanton Publication Services, Inc., St. Paul, Minnesota. Manufactured by Friesens on acid-free paper.